The Disability Pendulum

CRITICAL AMERICA
General Editors: Richard Delgado and Jean Stefancic

The Disability Pendulum

The First Decade of the
Americans with Disabilities Act

Ruth Colker

NEW YORK UNIVERSITY PRESS
New York and London

NEW YORK UNIVERSITY PRESS
New York and London
www.nyupress.org

© 2005 by New York University
All rights reserved

Library of Congress Cataloging-in-Publication Data
Colker, Ruth.
The disability pendulum : the first decade of the
Americans with Disabilities Act / Ruth Colker.
p. cm. — (Critical America)
Includes bibliographical references and index.
ISBN 0–8147–1645–8 (cloth : alk. paper)
1. United States. Americans with Disabilities Act of 1990—His-
tory—20th century.   2. People with disabilities—Legal status, laws,
etc.—United States—History—20th century.   I. Title.   II. Series.
KF480.C648   2005
342.7308'7—dc22   2004025443

New York University Press books are printed on acid-free paper,
and their binding materials are chosen for strength and durability.

Manufactured in the United States of America

10 9 8 7 6 5 4 3 2 1

to S. C-E

may you be treated with compassion and respect

and in loving memory of M. W-N

Contents

Acknowledgments

I have been very fortunate to write this book in a highly supportive atmosphere at the Michael E. Moritz College of Law at the Ohio State University. The assistance of a generous grant from the USX Foundation helped support much of the empirical research found in this book. I also benefitted from grants from the Center of Law, Policy and Social Science at the College of Law.

Many research assistants assisted with the empirical and case law research found in this book and helped with earlier versions of much of this scholarship that was published elsewhere. Earlier versions of chapter 3 were published at 34 *Harvard Civil Rights–Civil Liberties Law Review* 99 (1999) and 62 *Ohio State Law Journal* 239 (2001). My research assistants who contributed to that work included Kristen Carnahan, Catherine Cetrangolo, Michelle Evans, Leslie Kerns, Kristin Martinez, and Theodore Wern. Political science graduate students Wendy Watson and Kevin Scott also assisted me in designing the coding sheet for the database and in data analysis. (Kevin Scott is now a political science professor at Texas Tech and has joined me as a coauthor in other work.) The Equal Employment Opportunity Commission and the American Bar Foundation were also very helpful in sharing data and information with me as I engaged in this research. Professors Deborah Merritt and James Brudney gave me useful guidance as I delved into empirical research. I thank them for their unwavering support.

Earlier versions of chapter 4 were published at 39 *Wake Forest Law Review* 1 (2004) and 8 *Journal of Gender, Race, and Justice* 33 (2004). This work benefitted from the research assistance of Christopher Geidner and Matthew Kear.

An earlier version of chapter 5 was coauthored with Professor Adam Milani and appeared at 53 *Alabama Law Review* 1075 (2002). Research assistants John Deeds and Rachel Rubey were extremely helpful in providing the fifty-state research that underlies this work.

An earlier version of chapter 6 was published at 21 *Berkeley Journal of Employment and Labor Law* 377 (2000). Amanda Dine-Gamble, Leslie Kerns, Beth Paxton, and Theodore Wern provided valuable assistance for this work.

Chapter 7 reflects some work that I coauthored with James Brudney that appeared at 100 *Michigan Law Review* 80 (2001). This work benefitted from the research assistance of John Deeds, Michelle Evans, Brian Ray, Stephanie Smith, and Paul Wilkins.

All of my work benefitted from assistance from the College of Law Library research staff, as well as the assistance of Michele Whetzel-Newton, Nancy Darling, and Carol Peirano. Tragically, Michele passed away before this book could go to print, but her enormous secretarial talents are reflected in this manuscript. It was my privilege to have an opportunity to work with her. This book is dedicated to her memory. This book is also dedicated to my son, Samuel Colker-Eybel, who is a daily reminder of the arbitrariness of the category "disability."

Preface

I began writing this book after reading Ruth Shalit's 1997 article in the *New Republic* on the Americans with Disabilities Act. That article reported that the ADA and other disability statutes have created a "lifelong buffet of perks, special breaks and procedural protections" for individuals with questionable disabilities. Soon thereafter, *Reader's Digest* and the *Wall Street Journal* printed articles with similar assertions. Those assertions were contrary to my sense of the development of the ADA, but before long I found that there was little or no empirical research available to assess that claim.

I soon devoted myself to trying to collect empirical data on judicial decisions under the ADA. Although it was difficult to collect accurate trial court data, I was able to conclude that appellate judicial decisions were overwhelmingly prodefendant. Although the national media had been reporting that decisions under the ADA were proplaintiff, I was happy to see a receptivity to my findings in the national media. National Public Radio and other media outlets were kind enough to share my research with the general public. In this book, I seek to make research on all three major titles of the ADA available to the public. I hope this work will be useful to the growing disability studies field as well as to individuals who simply want to become more educated on the success and failures of the first decade of judicial enforcement of the ADA.

The story of the first decade of enforcement of the ADA has been one of massive disappointment for the disability rights community. The courts have interpreted the definition of disability narrowly, making it difficult for individuals to be both "disabled" and "qualified" to bring successful ADA lawsuits. The courts have also interpreted the constitutional scope of the ADA so narrowly that it is very difficult for private individuals to bring suits against state actors unless they can allege a constitutional deprivation of due process. The accommodation title, which requires private facilities to be accessible, has been a source of successful litigation for individuals with disabilities, but the limited set of remedies has made it difficult for lawyers to be able to afford to take these cases on a pro bono basis.

Despite these disappointments, there have been some positive developments under the ADA. The Supreme Court has concluded that individuals with HIV infection are covered by the ADA, that individuals such as Casey Martin have the right to play golf under conditions of accommodation, and that the ADA may require states to make courthouses accessible.

This book tells the story of a swinging pendulum. After the Supreme Court renders a narrow interpretation of the ADA, it is usually followed by a more proplaintiff ruling. The story is not one of consistent prodefendant or proplaintiff victories. The prodefendant victories tend to be broad; the proplaintiff victories tend to be narrow. This book seeks to capture a snapshot of that swinging pendulum. After the first decade of judicial enforcement of the ADA, the pendulum is swinging in a prodefendant direction. It will be interesting to see if the pendulum swings back to the center in the next decade.

The Disability Pendulum

1

Introduction
High Hope Followed by Public Backlash

Look, I'm not going to pick on an invalid.[1]
—President Ronald Reagan, August 1988
(Response to a reporter's question about
presidential candidate Michael Dukakis)

The Americans with Disabilities Act presents us all with an historic
opportunity. It signals the end to the unjustified segregation and exclusion of persons with disabilities from the mainstream of American
life. As the Declaration of Independence has been a beacon for people all over the world seeking freedom, it is my hope that the Americans with Disabilities Act will likewise come to be a model for the
choices and opportunities of future generations around the world.
—President George Herbert Walker Bush,
July 26, 1990 (ADA Signing Statement)

In 1988, the enactment of the Americans with Disabilities Act
was virtually unthinkable. The president of the United States considered
it appropriate to describe a presidential candidate as an "invalid." Yet, in
1990, the president considered it important to support and sign the Americans with Disabilities Act. No longer could public figures appear to be
against the rights of individuals with disabilities. As the *New York Times*
aptly commented a year before the ADA's passage: "No politician can vote
against this bill and survive."[2] How did the idea of supporting disability
rights move from a joking matter to a serious one that nearly all public figures supported? This book will critically examine the effectiveness of the
ADA and ask why it may have fallen short of its high hopes and aspirations. This chapter will provide a general introduction to the ADA.

Chapter 2 will provide a basic overview of the history underlying the enactment of the ADA. We will see that Congress understood itself to be passing a broad-based disability statute. To the extent that there were compromises, they did not modify the basic commitment to broad civil rights protection. Businesses were given some extra time to comply and the restaurant industry received some of the protection it requested to permit it not to employ individuals with contagious diseases. Otherwise, as we shall see, the ADA reflected a boldly proplaintiff piece of legislation that Congress understood to protect unpopular groups such as individuals with HIV infection and former drug users.

Chapter 3 will use empirical tools to assess the effectiveness of ADA Title I. ADA Title I prohibits discrimination in the employment sector. Empirical data suggest that the courts have overwhelmingly interpreted Title I in favor of defendants. Chapter 3 will ask whether the data reflect a judicial backlash against the ADA or whether other factors might also explain these negative results.

Chapter 4 will explore two explanations for the strongly proplaintiff results under the ADA: (1) an inappropriately narrow definition of the term "disability," and (2) misuse of the summary judgment standard to the disservice of plaintiffs. Case law concerning the definition of disability has had a profound impact on the effectiveness of the statute because plaintiffs cannot bring suit under the ADA unless they meet the definition of disability.[3] Although Congress indicated in the findings section that it expected the statute to protect more than 43 million disabled Americans, the effect of these prodefendant rulings has been to limit statutory coverage to a relatively narrow band of plaintiffs. In particular, the "mitigating measures" rule has required plaintiffs to demonstrate that they are disabled *after* a court takes into account the ameliorative effects of mitigating measures. That rule has made it nearly impossible for plaintiffs to demonstrate that they are both "qualified" and "disabled" because the mitigating measure that they use to help them be qualified then renders them nondisabled.

Abuse of the summary judgment process has harmed those plaintiffs who may have managed to survive the courts' stringent definition of disability. Despite Congress's instructions that terms like "reasonable accommodation" and "direct threat" were to be determined in a fact-intensive setting, most amenable to a jury, trial court judges have routinely decided those issues adversely to plaintiffs without sending them to the jury. This abuse of the jury process is inconsistent with the legal standard that is supposed to govern this area of the law.

Chapter 5 will examine ADA Title II. ADA Title II prohibits discrimination by state or local government. The constitutionality of the entirety of ADA Title II with respect to suits by private individuals against state actors remains in doubt following a recent but narrow Supreme Court decision that upheld the constitutionality of some of ADA Title II. This chapter will demonstrate how the Court's decisions under ADA Title II have followed a pendulum—the Court interprets the statute broadly, then restrictively, and then more broadly. Further, the lower courts have put pressure on the Court to relax its narrow interpretations of ADA Title II. Because of various narrow interpretations of ADA Title II, state law is an important backup protection for many individuals with disabilities. Chapter 5 will argue, however, that state law typically provides very inadequate legal recourse for individuals with disabilities when they face discrimination by the state.

Chapter 6 will examine ADA Title III. ADA Title III prohibits discrimination at private entities such as restaurants, motels, and places of amusement. Although ADA Title III provides for a broad scope of coverage, it has a very limited enforcement mechanism. Typically, aggrieved individuals can sue only for injunctive relief and may not seek monetary damages. That limited enforcement scheme has provided few incentives for private entities to comply with the law.

To be a more effective enforcement mechanism for individuals with disabilities, the ADA would benefit from some modest statutory amendments. The definition of disability should be amended to clarify that individuals should be considered disabled even if mitigating measures can ameliorate some of their disabilities. Further, the enforcement scheme under ADA Title III should be amended to include monetary relief. Nonetheless, seeking to amend the ADA would be a poor political strategy because it would open up the statute to amendments that might further limit its effectiveness. Amending the ADA also might not markedly improve its effectiveness. If the problem with the ADA is judicial hostility, rather than poor drafting, then the amendment process is unlikely to solve the problems discussed in this book.

Chapter 7 examines the Supreme Court's treatment of the ADA in the larger context of its treatment of Congress in the past decade. It concludes that the Supreme Court has "dissed" Congress in interpreting the ADA and other pieces of major legislation. The problem with the ADA's failed promises, therefore, largely lies with the Supreme Court rather than Congress's basic framework in enacting the ADA.

Before we can explore those assertions in depth, it is helpful to have a broad overview of the ADA. That overview follows.

I. From Insensitivity to Endorsement to Backlash

Congress first enacted modest disability rights legislation in the early 1970s, although active enforcement of those laws did not begin until at least 1978, when groups of individuals with disabilities began to stage sit-ins at federal buildings. Beginning in the 1980s, disability rights advocates sought to enact broad-based legislation that would accord civil rights to individuals with disabilities that would be comparable to those available to African Americans and women. For more than a decade, those efforts stalled because the disability rights community did not have sufficient support among the civil rights community or the political branches of government to attain such legislation. Many of its efforts were geared toward preventing the Reagan administration from dismantling the gains from the 1970s rather than moving forward with new legislation.

One jump-start for passage of broad-based disability rights legislation came from the insensitive remark by President Ronald Reagan, quoted at the beginning of this chapter. During the Bush-Dukakis presidential campaign in August 1988, rumors began to circulate from supporters of political extremist Lyndon H. LaRouche, Jr. that Governor Michael Dukakis had undergone psychiatric treatment during two stressful times in his life—when his brother died in 1973 after being hit by an automobile and when he lost the Democratic gubernatorial primary in 1978. In light of the negative public reaction to Senator Thomas Eagleton's (D-Mo.) disclosure that he had received treatment for mental illness soon after he was chosen as Senator George McGovern's (D-S.D.) running mate in the 1972 presidential campaign, these rumors were thought to be hurting the Dukakis presidential campaign. A reporter for a LaRouche-controlled publication, the *Executive Intelligence Review*, asked Reagan at a press conference what he thought about Dukakis's refusal up to that point to give the public access to his medical records concerning his alleged treatment for mental illness. Reagan responded: "Look, I'm not going to pick on an invalid."[4] Reagan later said he had "attempted a joke" but "it didn't work."[5] He never offered a full apology. Vice President (and presidential nominee) George H. W. Bush, at a visit to a defense plant in Annapolis, Maryland, said he was "not going to get drawn into this mini-controversy."[6] The media soon predicted that Reagan could hurt the presidential election campaign of Vice President Bush through such offhand and insensitive remarks.

After initially refusing to be drawn into the controversy, Vice President Bush responded on August 11, 1988, by urging Congress to enact the Americans with Disabilities Act.[7] Although it is difficult to imagine that candidate Bush was aware of the fine details of the sweeping disability rights legislation then pending in Congress, he did make this campaign pledge. (Some people trace his support of disabilities rights legislation to the fact that his son Neil is dyslexic and his son Marvin had had a colostomy.)[8] Following his inauguration as president, Bush instructed Attorney General Richard Thornburgh to work with Congress to pass major disability discrimination legislation. Reagan's insensitive "invalid" comment, therefore, may have helped lead to George H. W. Bush's support of the ADA.

For many reasons—both personal and political—Thornburgh took seriously his instructions from President Bush. Thornburgh's son Peter had suffered a serious brain injury in a 1960 car accident, and Thornburgh and his wife, Ginny, thereafter became leading advocates for individuals with disabilities. As the parent of a child with a disability and the spouse of a partner who was very active in working on disability rights issues, Thornburgh was supportive of the president's request. Moreover, the request permitted Thornburgh to increase his power base in the executive branch as he performed an important task at the request of the president.

Thornburgh worked with Congress and a group of dedicated disability activists to draft legislation that would be acceptable to both the disability and business communities. A year and a half later, Bush signed the Americans with Disabilities Act (ADA) into law on July 26, 1990.

The story of the passage of the ADA is a story of unprecedented bipartisan support for civil rights legislation, as well as one of very close scrutiny by Congress. On May 9, 1989, Senator Tom Harkin (D-Iowa),[9] along with 33 of his colleagues, introduced the ADA in the Senate as S. 933. The House version of the ADA—H.R. 2273—was introduced on the same day. The Senate Committee on Labor and Human Resources held four hearings on the bill. It reported the bill out on August 2, 1989, by a vote of 16 to 0. After two full days of debate, the Senate passed a version of the ADA on September 8, 1989, by a vote of 76 to 8.

More than twenty hearings were held on the ADA in the House. The Education and Labor Committee reported the bill out on November 14, 1989, by a vote of 35 to 0. The Energy and Commerce Committee reported the bill out on May 13, 1990, by a vote of 40 to 3. The Public Works Committee reported the bill out on April 3, 1990, by a vote of 45 to 5. The Judiciary Committee reported the bill out on May 2, 1990, by a vote of 32 to 3. The House passed this version of the ADA on May 22, 1990, by a vote of 403 to 20.

After two conferences convened to resolve differences between the Senate and House versions, the ADA passed Congress with overwhelming bipartisan support. The final vote in the House of Representatives was 377 to 28; in the Senate, 91 to 6. Unlike the Civil Rights Act of 1964, it faced neither serious opposition nor a threat of filibuster. Democratic Senator Edward M. Kennedy (Mass.)[10] heralded the ADA as an "emancipation proclamation" for people with disabilities;[11] Republican Senator Orrin Hatch (Utah) called the act "the most sweeping piece of civil rights legislation possibly in the history of our country."[12] As the chapter's first epigraph suggests, President Bush signed the ADA into law with the hope that it would be a model for the world. The political climate within the executive branch had changed markedly concerning disability issues within a several-year period.

The United States has been a worldwide leader in enacting a broad bill of rights for individuals with disabilities. Other countries, such as Great Britain, Australia, and Canada, have also enacted nondiscrimination statutes but none of these protections are as comprehensive as those found in the ADA.[13] The U.S. Congress applied the disability nondiscrimination standards that had existed for the public sector under Section 504 of the Rehabilitation Act to the private sector when it enacted the ADA. It also used the racial nondiscrimination standards found in Titles II and VII of the Civil Rights Act of 1964 as models in drafting many of the nondiscrimination provisions found in the ADA. The ADA benefitted from our experience in enforcing prior disability nondiscrimination statutes, as well as racial nondiscrimination statutes.

Despite the high hopes that surrounded the enactment of the ADA, its passage soon produced a public backlash. Following a few years of enforcement activity, columnist Ruth Shalit reported in the *New Republic* that the ADA has created a "lifelong buffet of perks, special breaks and procedural protections" for people with questionable disabilities.[14] A senior editor at *Reader's Digest* asserted that plaintiffs "have used the ADA to trigger an avalanche of frivolous suits clogging federal courts."[15] Similarly, author Walter Olson complained that the ADA has the potential "to force the rethinking and watering down of every imaginable standard of competence, whether of mind, body, or character."[16]

The media barrage against the ADA caused some people to think that the ADA was producing an inappropriate windfall for disability plaintiffs and their lawyers. As we will see in chapter 3, there is, in fact, no empirical support for such a conclusion. Hence, the U.S. Commission on Civil Rights has blamed "misleading and sometimes inaccurate news coverage" for the public's negative perception and "gross misunderstanding" of the ADA.

The Supreme Court has interpreted the ADA narrowly, often disappointing the disability rights community. Narrow judicial interpretations of the term "individual with disability" have limited the applicability of the act. Decisions protecting states' rights have exempted the public sector from coverage. These decisions have been contrary to Congress's intentions in passing the ADA.

Rather than take responsibility for narrowing the reach of the statute beyond what was envisioned by Congress, Justice Sandra Day O'Connor has criticized the drafters of the ADA for writing an ambiguous statute. She said that the ADA is an example of what happens when a bill's "sponsors are so eager to get something passed that what passes hasn't been as carefully written as a group of law professors might put together."[17] Justice O'Connor made those remarks at Georgetown Law School. Georgetown's Professor Chai Feldblum, who clerked for Supreme Court Justice Harry Blackmun during O'Connor's tenure on the Court and who is often credited with being a leading architect of the ADA, disagreed with O'Connor's assessment. Feldblum observed that "this law was the product of two years of careful research, drafting and negotiation between disability-rights lawyers and business community lawyers." Feldblum is correct. The ADA was considered by four committees of the House of Representatives, with each committee authoring a lengthy report.[18] It was then reported out by the House Rules Committee.[19] After different versions of the ADA passed in the House and Senate, it was also the subject of two conference reports.[20] This voluminous record speaks for itself. The ADA received much more detailed consideration by Congress than any other prior civil rights legislation.

Justice O'Connor's comments reflect the ahistorical lens that a majority of the Court insists on using in interpreting the ADA. As Professor Cynthia Estlund has observed: "[T]he commitment to textualism among at least a majority of the current Court tends to preclude both a resort to the ADA's rich legislative history and deference to the administrative agency, and to foster an almost obsessive focus on the complicated and open-textured text itself."[21] The ahistorical approach requires the words of the ADA to resolve all conceivable disputes under the statute. Members of Congress, however, throughout the debate over passage of the ADA, made reference to the extensive committee reports that accompanied passage of the bill. They expected that the judiciary and the various agencies charged with enforcing the ADA would rely on these reports to resolve the fine details of the bill.

Although the agencies have followed this history closely in drafting regulations, the Supreme Court has not. When the ADA's statutory language has necessarily embodied some ambiguity, a majority of the Court has refused to fill the gaps by inquiring into evidence of Congress's intentions as expressed in these reports and the congressional legislative record. Instead, the Court has used the latitude created by that ambiguity to interpret the statute as narrowly as possible. Chapter 2 will recount the story of the ADA's journey through Congress so that the reader can see the scope and clarity of Congress's vision when it enacted the ADA. It may be true that the literal language of the ADA "did leave uncertainties as to what Congress had in mind," as suggested by Justice O'Connor, but it is also true that an inquiry into the history and context of the statute can easily resolve many of these uncertainties. It is disappointing that the Court has taken such an ahistorical approach in interpreting this landmark legislation. "The Court is narrowing the scope of the ADA one provision at a time and constructing a statute that does less for disabled individuals and puts less of a burden on employers than the ADA's congressional proponents appear to have envisioned."[22]

Despite the backlash against the ADA, the ADA has helped transform many aspects of American life. Cities have installed thousands of curb ramps, buses have routinely become equipped with lifts, and hotels often provide accessible rooms for their guests. Although many of these changes may have been required by state law that preceded enactment of the ADA, it took national attention to a new civil rights statute to provide the impetus for these important changes.

Before assessing the effectiveness of the ADA, one must have a good working knowledge of the act's basic structure, as well as a basic understanding of the statute's history. The next section of this chapter will provide some background information about the historical antecedants to the ADA, as well as a general description of the ADA itself. Chapter 2 will provide a detailed discussion of the passage of the ADA.

II. Statutory Background

A. The ADA's Legislative Models

The modern story of the protection of disability rights began in 1970 when Congress passed its first landmark disability legislation in the education area.[23] It would take two more decades before that model could be broadly extended to most aspects of civic life through passage of the ADA. These historical precedents set the ultimate framework for the ADA while also providing evidence of the judicial hostility and ambivalence that accompanied passage of these laws. We will see these same strains of judicial hostility in reaction to passage of the ADA in subsequent chapters.

1. EDUCATION FOR THE HANDICAPPED ACT

The first landmark disability statute enacted by Congress was the Education for the Handicapped Act, in 1970.[24] It mandated, for the first time, that children with disabilities receive a free and appropriate public education. (Today's version of this law is entitled Individuals with Disabilities Education Act and goes by the acronym IDEA. I will use that acronym to describe the statute even before its name formally changed.) Gone were the days when children could be absolutely excluded from school because of their disability. Over the next thirty years, Congress has amended the statute many times to give content to what is considered a "free and appropriate public education" for children with disabilities and to mandate that they receive this education in the most integrated setting possible. It has also extended the statute's reach, often covering children from ages 3 to 21. (At the same time, Congress has also increased the latitude of the states to discipline children with disabilities who are disruptive in the classroom.) This law, however, typically affects only children educated in the public school system.

The theory underlying the IDEA is that children with disabilities face unique problems in the educational context and therefore need a specialized statutory response to those problems. The IDEA affects only a subset of children with disabilities—those whose disabilities mean that they require "special education" services. The IDEA is not applicable to many situations that might involve children with disabilities who face discrimination in the educational context. For example, if a school district tried to exclude a child from a school program because he was HIV-positive, that would not be an IDEA problem. Assuming the child was healthy enough to attend school during the regular school day, that child would not have had need of special education services and therefore would not have qualified for an "individualized education plan" under the IDEA. Similarly, the parent of a child who attends public school might use a wheelchair and find the building inaccessible. Hence, the parent may not be able to attend parent-teacher conferences or school programs. That would also not be an IDEA problem because the child is not in need of special education services due to the parent's disability.

2. Moving Beyond the IDEA: Section 504 of the Rehabilitation Act

Beginning in the 1970s, Congress was also interested in creating a legislative response to problems not addressed by the IDEA. It wanted to extend the reach of federal antidiscrimination law beyond the area of education and to provide more comprehensive protection in the education area for individuals with disabilities. Two approaches were available to Congress. It could follow the IDEA model and create additional, special legislation that addressed only disability discrimination issues. Alternatively, it could amend existing race-based civil rights laws to prohibit disability-based discrimination.

Each model had advantages and disadvantages. The creation of "special" legislation for the disability community might send the signal that individuals with disabilities are somehow inferior to other groups qualifying for antidiscrimination protection. Moreover, it would take a great deal of work to draft and enact freestanding legislation for individuals with disabilities. Amending existing laws might be simpler and faster. Amending existing laws, however, posed its own set of problems. Those laws were typically written from a race-discrimination perspective and might not work effectively in the disability context. Concepts like reasonable accommodation and accessibility do not have good analogs in the law of race discrimination but are crucial to the law of disability discrimination. Moreover, the civil rights community might be reluctant to open up existing law to amendment out of fear that additional amendments might be offered that would undermine those laws. Because of the need to work in coalition to get laws passed in Congress, it was important for the disability rights community to be sensitive to the needs and interests of other civil rights communities if it were to attain successful passage of disability discrimination measures.

Congress attempted to strengthen the rights for the disability community through both models. In the 1970s, Senators Hubert Humphrey (D-Minn.) and Charles Percy (R-Ill.), along with Representative Charles Vanik (D-Ohio), made unsuccessful efforts to amend Title VI of the Civil Rights Act of 1964 to include "handicapped" as a protected category. Title VI prohibits discrimination on the basis of race at entities that receive federal financial assistance. Such an amendment would have had a broad-ranging impact on state government, hospitals, and public schools (including higher education) because they receive federal financial assistance.

Instead of amending Title VI, Congress agreed to pass a provision devoted entirely to the problem of disability discrimination by entities that receive federal financial assistance. The language of this new provision within the Rehabilitation Act of 1973 was modeled closely on Title VI. This new provision contained the following, relatively simple paragraph:

No otherwise qualified handicapped individual in the United States, as defined in section 7 (6), shall, solely by reason of his handicap, be excluded from the participation in, be denied the benefits of, or be subjected to discrimination under any program or activity receiving Federal financial assistance.

Section 7(6) defined the term "handicapped individual" to mean

any individual who (a) has a physical or mental disability which for such individual constitutes or results in a substantial handicap to employment and (b) can reasonably be expected to benefit in terms of employability from vocational rehabilitation services provided pursuant to title I and III of this act.[25]

The scope of this Rehabilitation Act provision was fairly narrow. It applied only to entities that were providing vocational rehabilitation services and covered only individuals whose disability affected their employability. A year later, the definition of "handicapped" was expanded to include the three-prong definition that has been the foundation of disability discrimination law for the past three decades. The 1974 statute defined "handicapped" as meaning

> any person who (a) has a physical or mental impairment which substantially limits one or more of such person's major life activities, (b) has a record of such an impairment, or (c) is regarded as having such an impairment. (Rehabilitation Act of 1974, Pub. L. No. 93-516 § 11(11), 88 Stat. 1617, 1619 (1974))

When the bill passed Congress, Senator Humphrey and Representative Vanik stated that this provision—often called "Section 504"—carried over the intent of their prior bills to make Title VI applicable to individuals with disabilities.

There was little public discussion or debate of the provision. It was part of a large funding statute that received considerable attention and, in fact, was vetoed twice by President Richard Nixon for reasons unrelated to the nondiscrimination provision. It was signed into law on September 26, 1973.[26] The president's objections to the two previous versions of this bill were monetary. At no time was there any dispute between the administration and Congress over the wisdom of the nondiscrimination provision that was eventually codified as Section 504. Although it was not part of the first House resolution for the Rehabilitation Act, the Senate version, which contained the nondiscrimination provision, was accepted in conference with no more than the notation "The House recedes."[27]

For the first decade following the act's passage, Section 504 was the basis of little litigation. Beginning in the 1980s, however, the disability community began to take advantage of the law so that the courts had to begin to define what it meant for an individual to be a victim of disability-based discrimination. Meanwhile, the Education for the Handicapped Act continued to evolve to become the modern IDEA, with Congress amending the statute repeatedly to enhance educational opportunities for children with disabilities.

As these statutory standards evolved, one can see early signs of judicial ambivalence or even resistance. In 1979, the Supreme Court held in *Southeastern Community College v. Davis*, 442 U.S. 397 (1979) that it was lawful under Section 504 for a nursing program to deny admission to Frances B. Davis because of her hearing impairment. Although Davis had been previously trained and certified as a licensed practical nurse, the nursing school was entitled to fail to admit her because of her purported inability to perform certain functions in which she would not be able to read lips. In a unanimous opinion, the Court held that it was inappropriate to interpret Section 504 to impose "an affirmative-action obligation on all recipients of federal funds." Because the Court found that the nursing school would have to make "major adjustments" to its curriculum in order for Davis to be able to complete the program successfully, it could lawfully deny her admission. While recognizing that the "line between a lawful refusal to extend affirmative action and illegal discrimination against handicapped persons" will not always be clear, the Court held that the conduct in this case was lawful. This tension between affirmative action and reasonable accommodation continues today under the ADA. (For example, Judge Richard Posner has characterized a reasonable accommodation that he concluded was not required under the ADA as "affirmative action with a vengeance.")[28]

Similarly, a few years later, in *Board of Education v. Rowley*, 458 U.S. 176 (1982), the Supreme Court held that the Education of the Handicapped Act did not require a school district to pay for a sign language interpreter for Amy Rowley, a deaf student, who was attending first grade at the time of the lawsuit. An interpreter was not needed, according to the Court because Rowley was an "excellent lipreader" and an above-average student. Hence, the Court concluded that she was receiving an appropriate public education without the provision of a sign language interpreter. Although the Court recognized that she was not receiving as much education as a child who can hear, the education she was receiving was adequate for the purpose of federal law. The dissenting justices (Justices White, Brennan, and Marshall) focused on the statute's intent to provide children with disabilities an *equal* education. The majority, however, was satisfied with the provision of an *adequate*, rather than *equal* education.

The *Rowley* case foreshadows a tension that later emerges under the ADA. How much equality is really required by federal nondiscrimination legislation in the disability area? Are there monetary limits on equality? Again, one sees hints of the affirmative action quandary. Would the provision of a sign language interpreter to Rowley be considered affirmative action by the other students? Is it special treatment or equal treatment?

The *Rowley* case also reflects the limited perspective that courts bring to disability discrimination cases. The courts saw the problem in the *Rowley* case as one of Rowley's not being able to understand what was being said in the classroom. But the failure to provide a sign language interpreter to her presents other problems as well. Depending on Rowley's oral speaking skills, the failure to provide an interpreter may inhibit her ability to communicate her ideas to others in the classroom. Professor Martha Minow suggests that the Court should have understood that the entire learning community was harmed when Rowley's classmates could not communicate with her.[29] Further, a failure to help Rowley attain her education potential will hurt society as a whole if she is then unable to contribute to society through her vocational skills. Children who are born deaf typically do not advance beyond a fourth- or fifth-grade reading level. As a deaf child, Rowley was at severe risk of facing educational challenges, yet the Court permitted the school district to do little to combat that risk because she apparently entered grade school with above-average reading skills. The Court's decision put the burden of education on her parents rather than the school district. Similarly, the failure to enroll Davis in the nursing program precluded the nursing profession from receiving the skills of another trained nurse, while also limiting the economic earning capacity of Davis.

Despite the setbacks in the *Rowley* and *Davis* litigation, the disability community had some basis to believe that the courts might be receptive to claims of disability discrimination. In 1985, the Supreme Court held in *City of Cleburne v. Cleburne Living Center*, 473 U.S. 432 (1985), that it was a violation of the Constitution's guarantee of equal protection for a city to act on the basis of prejudice to deny a special-use permit for the operation of a group home for the mentally retarded. This holding helped create some momentum to amend the Fair Housing Act to prohibit disability discrimination in housing. Nonetheless, even this positive legal result foreshadowed some judicial resistance to protecting individuals with disabilities. While recognizing that the plaintiffs had a meritorious claim in that case, the Court also declined to conclude that individuals with disabilities are a "suspect class" entitled to "heightened scrutiny" by the courts. As we will see in chapter 5, this failure to conclude that individuals with disabilities are a suspect class laid the foundation for later limiting Congress's power to protect individuals with disabilities. Thus, the seeds of judicial ambivalence can be found even in one of the landmark victories for the disability community.

3. FAIR HOUSING ACT AMENDMENTS

Despite these signs of judicial ambivalence with the existing disability discrimination laws, the disability community began to push more vigorously for new antidiscrimination laws that would extend Section 504's rules to the private sector. As with the passage of Section 504, two approaches were available: Congress could pass freestanding legislation for individuals with disabilities, or it could seek to amend existing race-based civil rights laws to cover individuals with disabilities. The disability community had a trial run at a middle-ground approach in 1988. It drafted an amendment to the Fair Housing Act that would extend that statute's protections to disability discrimination.[30] This approach involved the amendment of an existing civil rights law. But the amendment did not merely add the word "disability" to the list of covered grounds of discrimination. Instead, it created a new rule of nondiscrimination that specifically prohibited disability discrimination in housing. These rules recognized a reasonable accommodation obligation and also mandated that new construction be handicapped accessible under the national, "ANSI" guidelines of the American National Standards Institute.

The disability community's success in working with other civil rights organizations to amend the Fair Housing Act emboldened it to believe that it could work in coalition with others to enact sweeping disability-discrimination legislation. It properly sensed that Congress was willing to take this giant step forward.

III. Enactment of the ADA

A. The ADA's Statutory Models

Chapter 2 will tell the legislative story of how Congress enacted the ADA. The general framework that underlies the ADA, however, can be found in its historical precedents: Section 504 of the Rehabilitation Act and the Civil Rights Act of 1964.

By the late 1990s, when the ADA was being drafted, Section 504 had an extensive array of regulations and nearly three decades of case law interpreting its provisions. Drawing from Section 504 in enacting the ADA made sense to both the disability community and the business community. For both groups, this foundation meant that the ADA would be built on settled precedent so that there would be some legal certainty about the meaning of some of its central terms like "disability," "reasonable accommodation," and "undue hardship." The protections offered by Section 504 were supposed to be the floor, not the ceiling. Hence, Congress specifically provided in the ADA that "nothing in this chapter shall be construed to apply a lesser standard than the standards applied under [Section 504]."[31] This simply interpretive rule, however, has been ignored by the courts as they have construed the definition of disability much more narrowly under the ADA than it had been interpreted under Section 504. For example, lower courts interpreting Section 504 routinely found that individuals with conditions often controllable with medication, such as epilepsy or diabetes, were "disabled."[32] In fact, that proposition was entirely uncontroversial under the Section 504 case law. The original House sponsor of the ADA—Tony Coelho (D-Calif.)—had epilepsy and clearly understood himself to be covered by the ADA's definition of disability. Nonetheless, lower courts have found that individuals with epilepsy are not disabled for the purpose of the ADA, when medication is effective in permitting them to engage in daily activities such as working (despite also recognizing that Congress thought individuals with epilepsy were covered when they enacted the statute).[33]

Similarly, the lower courts interpreting Section 504 unanimously concluded that HIV infection was a covered disability under the act.[34] Yet, courts interpreting the ADA have repeatedly concluded that certain individuals with HIV infection do not meet the statute's definition of disability.[35] When the Supreme Court ruled in *Bragdon v. Abbott*, 524 U.S. 624 (1998), that Abbott, who was infected with HIV, met the definition of "disability" under the ADA, it did not actually go as far in its holding as the history of the ADA would have required. Rather than conclude that individuals with HIV infection are *per se* disabled (as prior courts had concluded under Section 504 and as Congress had in its consideration of the ADA), it concluded that Abbott was disabled pursuant to an individualized inquiry. Although an individualized inquiry was basic to court decisions under Section 504, the Court took that inquiry to new heights under ADA in requiring such an inquiry for serious medical conditions like HIV infection.

Section 504, however, was not the only model for the ADA. Congress also borrowed extensively from Titles II and VII of the Civil Rights Act of 1964. Title II of the Civil Rights Act of 1964 primarily bans discrimination on the basis of race at hotels and restaurants. Congress modeled its public accommodation rules in ADA Title III on this foundation. Title VII of the Civil Rights Act of 1964 bans discrimination on the basis of race or gender at places of employment. Congress modeled its employment discrimination rules in ADA Title I on this foundation.

The ADA therefore had a very firm foundation in Section 504 as well as in Titles II and VII of the Civil Rights Act of 1964. That foundation should have made its meaning readily understandable in the early years of its history. As we will see, especially in chapter 2, the courts have not interpreted the ADA consistently with prior interpretations of Section 504.

B. The ADA's Language

The ADA comprises five main titles. Preceding these titles is a section entitled "General Provisions" that lists findings and definitions that cover the entire act. The finding that has played the largest role in litigation under the ADA has been the first finding, in which the act states that "some 43,000,000 Americans have one or more physical or mental disabilities, and this number is increasing as the population as a whole is growing older." 42 U.S.C. § 12101(a)(1).

Although Congress recited the 43 million figure as a *minimum* figure to suggest that a substantial portion of the American population is disabled and would benefit from the protections of the ADA, the courts have used the figure as a justification to *limit* the scope of statutory coverage. They have ignored that Congress recited that this figure was *growing*, and that a purpose of the ADA is to "provide a clear and *comprehensive* national mandate for the elimination of discrimination against individuals with disabilities." 42 U.S.C. § 12101(b)(1) (emphasis added).

The general provisions section contains the definition of disability that is used throughout the act. Through a three-prong definition, it states that the term "disability" means, with respect to an individual:

(A) a physical or mental impairment that substantially limits one or more of the major life activities of such individual;

(B) a record of such an impairment; or
(C) being regarded as having such an impairment.
42 U.S.C. § 12102(2).

This is an important and broad-ranging definition of disability. The first prong of the definition is not limited to physical impairments; it also covers individuals with cognitive or psychological impairments. Even if one is not actually disabled at the time of discrimination, the statute provides that a suit can be brought if the individual has a record of a disability under the second prong or is falsely being regarded as disabled under the third prong.

The ADA, however, is unlike most other civil rights statutes in that it requires an individual to demonstrate that he or she is a member of a protected class in order for a lawsuit to go forward. Under Title VII of the Civil Rights Act of 1964, an individual can bring a gender-discrimination lawsuit irrespective of whether the individual is a man or a woman. Similarly, one can bring a race-discrimination lawsuit under Title VII irrespective of whether one is black or white. The primary legal question under Title VII is typically whether the employer considered an impermissible factor—race or gender—not whether the individual is the member of a protected class.[36]

By contrast, under the ADA, one can bring suit only if one establishes that he or she is a member of the protected class as an individual with a disability. Although Congress did not intend that requirement to be a substantial hurdle, in fact, it has become one. A plaintiff frequently loses at the summary judgment stage at trial because the employer successfully argues that the employee is not an individual with a disability. In that instance, the court determines that the individual is not disabled and therefore never even sends to the jury the question of whether the plaintiff faced unlawful discrimination on the basis of disability. Chapter 3 will examine those narrow interpretations of the definition of disability and the misuse of the summary judgment standard.

ADA Title I

Assuming a plaintiff can get past the hurdle of demonstrating that he or she is an individual with a disability, then the case may proceed under one of the ADA's main titles. ADA Title I is the employment title. It generally provides:

> No covered entity shall discriminate against a qualified individual with a disability because of the disability of such individual in regard to job application procedures, the hiring, advancement, or discharge of employees, employee compensation, job training, and other terms, conditions and privileges of employment.

ADA Title I is of crucial importance to individuals with disabilities. It requires that employers not discriminate against individuals who, with reasonable accommodations, can perform the essential functions of the employment position that such individual holds or desires. Although the media frequently criticize the reasonable accommodation requirement, the available empirical data suggest that that requirement has not been particularly costly. The literature suggests that more than two-thirds of reasonable accommodations cost less than $500 and that the average cost is probably around $200.[37] Each of these accommodations is estimated to save employers around $5,000, on average, in lower job training costs and insurance claims, increased worked productivity, and reduced rehabilitation costs after injury on the job.

Enactment of ADA Title I caused some people to hope that the unemployment rate for individuals with disabilities would decline as a result of increased statutory protection. It is estimated that only one-third of people with disabilities who are qualified to work can find jobs. The employment rate for persons without disabilities is 80.5 percent, but the rate is 27.6 percent for persons with severe functional limitations and 20.6 percent for persons who require personal assistance to perform a life activity. Those people with disabilities who do find jobs are often kept at low-level jobs and prohibited from advancing at the workplace. The available empirical data suggest that the unemployment rate for individuals with disabilities has remained relatively unchanged (or has worsened) since the enactment of ADA Title I. This fact has caused some researchers to assert that the ADA has been ineffective. The assertions will be discussed in chapter 4. I will argue that it is too early to know if the ADA has been ineffective in changing the unemployment rate for individuals with disabilities. Possibly, it is unrealistic to expect that the enactment of the ADA's civil rights model would improve the employment rate of individuals with disabilities. Other countries, like Australia, have tried more of a social service model to increase employment for individuals with disabilities.[38] Congress's goal of improving the employability of individuals with disabilities through enactment of the ADA may have been naive or misguided.

ADA Title II

Although ADA Title I is certainly important, ADA Titles II and III are equally important because, as noted above, many members of the disability community are unemployed, and possibly unemployable, and therefore cannot take advantage of ADA Title I. ADA Title II provides:

> No qualified individual with a disability shall, by reason of such disability, be excluded from participation in or be denied the benefits of the services, programs, or activities of a public entity, or be subjected to discrimination by any such entity.

ADA Title II covers nearly any program or activity conducted by a public entity ranging from higher education to prisons to public health care. ADA Title II broadens the coverage already existing under Section 504 of the Rehabilitation Act of 1973. Section 504 prohibits entities that receive federal financial assistance from discriminating on the basis of disability. Because most branches of state or local government receive federal financial assistance, ADA Title II and Section 504 are often coextensive. The only activity funded by state or local government that ADA Title II and Section 504 do not extensively regulate are primary and secondary education because that area is primarily regulated by the Individuals with Disabilities Act (IDEA). Discussion of the IDEA is beyond the scope of this book; it deserves its own, full-length attention.

ADA Title III

Title III of the Americans with Disabilities Act protects individuals with disabilities from discrimination at places of public accommodation. It provides:

No individual shall be discriminated against on the basis of disability in the full and equal enjoyment of the goods, services, facilities, privileges, advantages, or accommodations of any place of public accommodation by any person who owns, leases (or leases to), or operates a place of public accommodation.

Unlawful discrimination under ADA Title III takes the form of outright exclusion, discriminatory policies and eligibility criteria, as well as physical barriers that impede accessibility. ADA Title III provides broad coverage, requiring accessibility and nondiscrimination at entities that individuals visit on a frequent basis in order to obtain the basic essentials like food, lodging, and health care, as well as at entities that individuals visit on a frequent basis to enhance the quality of their lives, such as restaurants, hotels, and places of amusement and recreation. ADA Title III plays an enormously important role in the integration of individuals with disabilities into society. The most well known ADA Title III case has been *Casey Martin v. PGA*, 531 U.S. 1049 (2001), in which the Supreme Court held that ADA Title III requires the PGA to permit Martin to use a golf cart while playing professional golf. The *Martin* decision is not reflective of the overall trend of the ADA to favor defendants.

As a package, the ADA contains marvelous language. It provides comprehensive protection from the moment one is born or becomes a person with a disability and might need access to public services to the time when one might enter the workforce or seek to use a forum for public entertainment. Countries such as Canada, Australia, and Great Britain admired the willingness of the United States to enact the ADA and enacted their own disability discrimination statutes modeled after the ADA's extensive array of protections.[39] Although the disability discrimination laws of other countries have been interpreted liberally, the ADA has been interpreted narrowly by the appellate judiciary in the United States, resulting in overwhelmingly prodefendant appellate outcomes, particularly under ADA Title I. This book will explore why and how the ADA has been interpreted so narrowly even while it is also having a transformative effect on American life.

The ADA's Journey
through Congress

The ADA is the last ditch attempt of the remorseless sodomy lobby to achieve its national agenda before the impending decimation of AIDS destroys its political clout. Their Bill simply must be stopped. There will be no second chance for normal America if the ADA is passed.[1]

The ADA is truly landmark legislation for individuals with disabilities because it reflects the first time that the federal government has imposed rules on the private sector that it has generally applied to the publicly financed sector for nearly thirty years. It is the culmination of more than two decades of law-reform efforts by the disability community.

Nonetheless, the story of the passage of the ADA can reveal two conflicting stories. On the one hand, it is a story of Congress demonstrating a very strong commitment to increasing the rights of individuals with disabilities. When attempts were made to cut back on these rights, especially for individuals with HIV infection, Congress refused to compromise. On the other hand, it is a story of blatant homophobia, with some members of Congress feeling comfortable using labels like the "homosexual lobby" to describe the supporters of this legislation. With respect to the homophobia, Congress caved quickly by explicitly excluding from coverage all conceivable sexual minorities.

Despite the fact that Congress demonstrated an unwavering commitment to drafting a statute with a broad definition of disability that clearly covered HIV infection, the courts have reacted with considerable ambivalence. The judiciary has often acted as if some of the *failed* amendments were successful. The ADA is *not* a piece of legislation in which members of Congress tried to sneak in language and hide its true meaning. Instead, it was legislation created as part of a careful and deliberate debate in which nearly everyone generally agreed about the meaning of the statute. (And that agreement included a decision to exclude sexual minorities from potential coverage.) The judiciary should use this clear legislative history to guide its interpretation of the ADA.

Nonetheless, some members of the Supreme Court have insisted that the courts should ignore legislative history.[2] Some justices have often interpreted the ADA more narrowly than could have possibly been contemplated by Congress.[3] It may be true that *some* statutes do not have a clear, genuine underlying purpose, but the ADA is *not* one of them. From its earliest incarnation in 1988, to the ultimately passed version in 1990, Congress considered an unabashedly liberal piece of legislation that broadly protected the disability community. As with any piece of legislation, there were compromises as part of the enactment process, but none of the compromises undercut the basic broad scope of this historic legislation. No one who voted for (or against) this legislation understood it to have anything other than a broad purpose: to assist more than 43 million Americans with disabilities.

The ADA, in that sense, is unlike any other major piece of civil rights legislation enacted by Congress because there was no serious opposition. The Republican administration worked with a Democratic Congress to strengthen the rights of the disability community. The statute was drafted carefully and in much more detail than any other civil rights statute. Historical descriptions of the ADA by Justice O'Connor and others should not cause us to forget the consistent and purposeful history that resulted in the drafting of this historic legislation.

I. From National Council on the Handicapped to 1988 Bill

The legislative history of the ADA actually starts in 1985 and 1986 when Congress reacted to two D.C. District Courts' denials of motions to dismiss Rehabilitation Act claims, finding that transsexuals and transvestites could be covered by the Rehabilitation Act.

The first case, *Doe v. U.S. Postal Services*[4]—was an unpublished decision by Judge John Pratt in a D.C. District court. In what Judge Pratt describes as a "sad case," "Jane Doe" had her job offer rescinded after she informed her new employer, the U.S. Postal Service, that she would be un-

dergoing sex reassignment surgery and would prefer to begin employment dressed as a woman. The employer rescinded the job offer even after
the plaintiff offered to delay her surgery and continue to dress like a man.
She brought a cause of action under both Title VII and the Rehabilitation
Act. Her Title VII claim failed even though the supervisor clearly denied
her employment because of her intention to change her gender from male
to female. The court then considered her Rehabilitation Act claim and denied the defendant's motion to dismiss finding that the Rehabilitation Act
was not intended to cover only "traditionally recognized handicaps." Accordingly, her case was permitted to go forward to trial. There is no
record of whether Doe was ultimately successful in her Rehabilitation Act
claim after trial.

The second case—*Blackwell v. United States Department of Treasury*[5]—received even more attention from Congress, although the plaintiff was not ultimately successful. Plaintiff William A. Blackwell alleged
that he had been denied employment with the Treasury Department because he wore "feminine clothing" to his two job interviews. Rather than
fill the position with Blackwell, who was entitled to priority consideration
under the reduction in force (RIF) program, the second interviewer closed
the position. Blackwell argued that he was not hired because he was a
transvestite. Blackwell's case survived a motion to dismiss, with the court
finding that transvestites can qualify as disabled under the Rehabilitation
Act.[6] At trial, the Treasury Department argued in defense that the interviewer perceived Blackwell to be a homosexual (a status not legally protected from discrimination under federal law), not a transvestite, and that
the interviewer could not have engaged in unlawful discrimination without Blackwell's bringing his "disability" to the interviewer's attention.
The court overlooked the testimony that the first interviewer openly discussed Blackwell's appearance with him, and asked him if "there was ob-
jection to his life-style."[7] The interviewer, however, testified that by "life-
style," she was referring only to his perceived homosexuality, not his
transvestitism. The trial court apparently found this testimony to be credible and entered judgment for the Treasury Department.

On appeal, in an opinion written by Ruth Bader Ginsburg, the D.C.
Circuit affirmed the judgment dismissing the complaint while vacating
the lower court's discussion that required plaintiff to give precise notice
of his handicapping condition.[8] Blackwell had also offered a Title VII theory of discrimination, arguing that he was a victim of sex discrimination
(because his job was apparently conditioned upon a "male" appearance).

Like every other court that has considered this theory of discrimination, the D.C. Circuit rejected this argument, finding that Congress did not intend Title VII to cover such causes of action.

Even though Blackwell was not successful in his claim of discrimination, Congress spent a significant amount of time responding to his case. In May 1988, when Congress was considering overriding President Reagan's veto of the Civil Rights Restoration Act of 1987,[9] Senator Jesse Helms (R-N.C.) spoke at length about court decisions that had found that the Rehabilitation Act covered "transvestism and other compulsions or addictions, which churches or religious schools might once have felt comfortable in regarding as moral problems, not medical handicaps."[10] Senator Edward Kennedy (D-Mass.) responded by stating that the Moral Majority had mounted a massive campaign against the Restoration Act, arguing that it reflected the "intent of Congress with regard to the inclusion of homosexuality as a protected classification under the present law."[11] (Of course, no senator was ever able to cite a case in which a court had found that homosexuals were covered by the Rehabilitation Act.) These arguments against the Restoration Act were not successful. Congress voted 73-24 to override Reagan's veto.[12] The debate about "transvestism" was not successful at overturning the Restoration Act, but it was successful at distracting Congress from the merits of extending the general coverage of various civil rights statutes.

The purpose of the Civil Rights Restoration Act of 1987 was to overturn the Supreme Court's decision in *Grove City College v. Bell*.[13] *Grove City* was a very technical decision about the meaning of the term "program or activity" as found in Title IX, Title VI, and Section 504. The Court in *Grove City* had interpreted the term narrowly, which, in turn, limited the application of those federal statutes. The Civil Rights Restoration Act overturned *Grove City* so that all the activities of an entity receiving federal financial assistance would be subject to these statutes, not simply the unit receiving federal financial assistance.

Despite the fact that neither *Grove City* nor the Civil Rights Restoration Act mentioned disability status, some members of Congress argued that the Civil Rights Restoration Act's expansion of the definition of "program or activity" could have devastating effects on businesses because they might be forced to hire gay, lesbian, or transvestite employees who would be characterized as "disabled" under the Rehabilitation Act. *Grove City* was a sex-discrimination suit brought under Title IX; it did not even directly involve the Rehabilitation Act. But members of Congress argued that its holding would apply to suits brought under Section 504 of the Rehabilitation Act because Section 504 and Title IX contained the same "program or activity" language. Senator Helms used the *Blackwell* case to argue against the Civil Rights Restoration Act by asserting that if the bill were to become law, then schools and day care centers would "be prohibited from refusing to hire a transvestite."[14] He did not ask Congress to amend the definition of disability to exclude transvestites from coverage; instead, he asked Congress to sustain Reagan's veto of the entire Civil Rights Restoration Act. Although, as we will see, Congress eventually caved to his request to exclude transvestites from coverage, it also voted, against Helms's wishes, to sustain the president's veto.

Despite losing in his attempt to sustain Reagan's veto, Helms persisted with his goal to exclude sexual minorities specifically from being afforded federal statutory protection. When Congress considered the Fair Housing Act Amendments in 1988, Helms insisted on an amendment stating that the term "handicap" shall not apply to an individual solely because that individual is a transvestite.[15] The amendment was accepted in the Senate by a vote of 89-2, with the negative votes coming from Senators Alan Cranston (D-Calif.) and Lowell Weicker (R-Conn.).[16] This is virtually the same language that Helms later offered under the ADA.[17] Thus, by the time the transvestite exception was offered under the ADA, the Senate was already on record as having acquiesced to this exception under the Fair Housing Act. There was little point in objecting to this highly popular language when there was no record of a transvestite even prevailing under Section 504.

The transvestite issue, however, was only one example of Congress's exempting sexual minorities from ADA coverage. An examination of the general history underlying the ADA shows that Congress quickly and repeatedly caved on excluding coverage of sexual minorities under the ADA, while maintaining an overwhelming commitment to cover individuals with HIV infection.

The first draft of the ADA was the culmination of work by several important bodies. President Reagan had created the National Council on the Handicapped, an independent federal agency whose fifteen members had been appointed by Reagan and confirmed by the Senate. The council issued two reports: *Toward Independence* (1986) and *On the Threshold of Independence* (1988). Reagan had also created the Commission on the Human Immunodeficiency Virus Epidemic, which had authored a report in 1988. The HIV commission found that omnibus civil rights legislation was needed to prevent disability discrimination, and that such legislation should cover HIV-related discrimination.[18] The importance of protecting people with HIV infection from disability discrimination is found in every major report and speech surrounding the passage of the ADA, beginning in 1988.[19]

Senator Weicker introduced S. 2345 on April 28, 1988. (Like many politicians who became active supporters of the ADA, Weicker had a personal experience with disabilities issues; he had a child with Down syndrome.) This version of the ADA was cosponsored by 13 other senators including Tom Harkin (D-Iowa), Paul Simon (D-Ill.), Robert Stafford (R-Vt.), Kennedy, Christopher Dodd (D-Conn.), Spark Matsunaga (D-Hawaii), Lincoln Chafee (R-R.I.), John Kerry (D-Mass.), Robert Packwood (R-Oregon), Patrick Leahy (D-Vt.), Daniel Inouye (D-Hawaii), Alan Cranston (D-Calif.), and Robert Dole (R-Kans.). The original sponsors included 5 Republicans and 9 Democrats, reflecting the bipartisan nature of this legislation throughout its consideration. Before the end of the legislative session, S. 2345 had 27 cosponsors.[20]

Senator Weicker spoke in favor of the legislation when he introduced it. His opening remarks, unfortunately, were not entirely accurate in describing the proposed bill. He said that the definition of "'physical or mental impairment' in this bill . . . is a verbatim repetition of the definition of the same phrase in section 504 regulations."[21] In fact, the definition of "disability" (which was then termed "on the basis of handicap") was much broader than had existed under any previous federal (or state) law. An individual had only to demonstrate that he or she was treated differently "because of a physical or mental impairment, perceived impairment, or record of impairment."[22] The term "physical or mental impairment" required proof only of a "physiological disorder or condition, cosmetic disfigurement, or anatomical loss affecting one or more systems of the body" or "any mental or psychological disorder, such as mental retardation, organic brain syndrome, emotional or mental illness, and specific learning disabilities."[23] (It also contained "perceived impairment" and "record of impairment" categories.)

Interestingly, the only inaccurate descriptions of the ADA occurred in 1988, when the ADA was not likely to pass. By the time Congress seriously considered the ADA, members appear to have become well informed about the statute.

In the House, Representative Coelho introduced H.R. 4498—the ADA—on April 29, 1988. (Coelho himself was a victim of discrimination because of his epilepsy.)[24] There were 47 cosponsors. The list, however, was less bipartisan than in the Senate. Republican cosponsors included Silvio Conte (R-Mass.), James Jeffords (R-Vt.), Constance Morella (R-Md.), Claudine Schneider (R-R.I.), and Christopher Shays (R-Conn.). Before the end of the legislative session, the number of cosponsors had grown to 125. (When the ADA was reintroduced in 1989, the sponsor list was more bipartisan.)

The chief Republican sponsor in the House was Silvio Conte. He spoke in favor of the legislation on April 29, 1988. Like Senator Weicker, he asserted that the definitions in the bill, including the definition of disability, drew on the definitions already in Section 504, which assured consistency, clarity, and enforceability.[25] His remarks, however, were not offered live on the House floor. No live debate occurred at this time.

The text of the ADA was identical in both the Senate and House. The 1988 bill was not divided into titles as the final bill would be. Instead, it had sections banning different types of discriminatory activities. Section 4 prohibited discrimination in employment, housing, public accommodations, transportation, and telecommunication. Section 5 prohibited discrimination in access to services or programs; prohibited architectural and other barriers; and made it unlawful to (1) refuse to grant reasonable accommodations, (2) impose disqualifying selection criteria, and (3) engage in associational discrimination because of someone's relationship to an individual with a disability. Section 6 prohibited discrimination in housing (which was not retained in the final bill). Section 7 provided limitations on the duties of accommodation and barrier removal. Section 8 required various entities to promulgate regulations to enforce the ADA. Section 9 provided the rules with respect to enforcement.

Each of the sections was stronger than it would be in the enacted bill. The definition of "reasonable accommodation" made no mention of the defense of undue hardship (or any other cost defense).[26] It provided for reasonable accommodations for all categories of individuals with disabilities, including individuals with a perceived or record of impairment.

The section on architectural barriers was very broad. It made no distinction between new, altered, and existing structures. It also specifically mentioned communication and transportation barriers that were not listed in the enacted ADA. The architectural barriers section provided that it "shall be discriminatory (A) to establish or impose; or (B) to fail or refuse to remove any architectural, transportation, or communication barriers that prevent the access or limit the participation of persons on the basis of handicap."[27]

The defenses that were provided in this section were minimal. This early version of the ADA also included considerably stronger language with respect to the removal of communication barriers than did the final bill; it permitted the Federal Communications Commission to require the provision and maintenance of devices such as Telecommunications Devices for the Deaf (TTD's), visual aids such as flashing alarms and indicators, decoders, and augmentative communication devices for nonvocal persons, such as language symbol or alphabet boards.[28] Ultimately, the only communication device that was mandated by the ADA was the provision of telephone relay services for individuals with hearing impairments.

The enforcement section of the 1988 bill was also very strong. It provided that

> [a]ny person who believes that he or she or any specific class of individuals is being or is about to be subjected to discrimination on the basis of handicap in violation of this Act, shall have the right, by himself or herself, or by a representative, to file a civil action for injunctive relief, monetary damages, or both in a district court of the United States.[29]

The exhaustion of administrative enforcement procedures was required only for actions involving employment discrimination. Claims of discrimination involving barriers to access at public accommodations could be brought by private citizens for monetary damages. In contrast, the bill that was finally enacted permitted private parties who had accessibility complaints to obtain only injunctive relief—a weaker remedy.

The only aspects of the 1988 bill that appeared weaker than the enacted bill were twofold. First, the 1988 bill referenced only 36 million Americans as being disabled (S. 2345 sec. 2(a)(1)). Later versions referenced 43 million Americans (although the versions contained a narrower definition of disability!). Second, the 1988 bill used the same definition of "public accommodations" as found in Title II of the Civil Rights Act of 1964.[30] The enacted bill used a broader definition.

There was widespread support for the 1988 bill in the Senate; 27 senators ultimately cosponsored the legislation. Nonetheless, as expressed by Senator Dole (a sponsor), some of the sponsors had reservations about the details of the bill. The major problem with the 1988 version of the

ADA was that it departed from the framework used for nearly thirty years under Section 504 by failing to embody its basic definition of disability and by not using the undue hardship defense that had become basic to interpretations of Section 504. Even on the day when the ADA was first introduced, Dole, a key proponent of the ADA, spoke in favor of the need for such a bill but also stated that compromises were needed that would weaken the bill:

> I have reservations about many aspects of this bill including the elimination of the undue hardship criteria for reasonable accommodation, clarification on what constitutes a public accommodation and what such public accommodations would be required to do under the retrofitting provisions of this bill, what do we mean by transportation services and what is the scope of the provisions of this bill to intrastate transportation systems.[31]

Discussion of the ADA continued on April 29, 1988, with Senator John McCain (R-Ariz.) joining the list of cosponsors.[32] He, too, spoke of reservations:

> While I have some reservations about portions of the bill—among which are the elimination of "undue hardship" for reasonable accommodation, clarification of what constitutes a public accommodation and which public accommodations would be required to retrofit in order to come into compliance with the bill, and how the bill defines transportation services and what is the scope of the bill's provisions with regard to intrastate transportation systems.[33]

The theme of reservations continued on May 16, 1988, when Senator Donald Reigle (D-Mich.) spoke in favor of the bill:

> We need to consider carefully whether we should eliminate the undue hardship criteria for reasonable accommodation, as this bill proposes.
>
> We also need to consider the considerable expenses that businesses, and state and local governments would be required to incur under this bill. These entities may need federal assistance to facilitate compliance, and I believe the Federal Government may have to share the responsibility in this regard.[34]

On June 6, 1988, Senator Weicker tied passage of the ADA to recommendations of the Presidential Commission on HIV.[35] This speech continued a theme struck throughout consideration of the ADA, that it would be a helpful response to the AIDS crisis.

Discussion of the ADA heated up in the House after Reagan's disparaging remark about candidate Michael Dukakis's reported mental illness. On the floor of the House, Coelho commented: "[L]ast week, President Reagan made a wisecrack about 'invalids.' As a person with epilepsy, I resent the callous attitude exhibited by the Reagan-Bush administration toward those with disabilities, of which this remark is symptomatic."[36] Shortly thereafter—on August 11—presidential candidate Bush supported the ADA. Ultimately, President Bush instructed his administration to work with Congress to enact disability legislation. Enactment of the ADA may therefore be credited, in part, to Reagan's "invalid" statement.

Representative Major Owens (D-N.Y.) spoke in favor of the ADA on August 11, 1988. He said that both parties "are in agreement on at least one major item on our agenda for future legislation. While the Democratic convention will endorse this piece of legislation, both candidates are on record for having endorsed it also."[37] His comment reflected candidate Bush's endorsement of the ADA.

II. May 9, 1989, Bill: Important Compromises

Acquiescing in part to the reservations from some of the sponsors of the 1988 bill, Senator Harkin introduced a revised ADA bill on May 9, 1989. (Weicker was no longer in the Senate.) Like Weicker, Harkin has a personal connection to disability issues. His brother, Frank, is deaf, and his nephew is a quadriplegic. On the day that the Senate passed the ADA, Harkin began his remarks by using sign language to thank his brother.)[38] Coelho again introduced the House version.[39] As in 1988, Coelho supported the ADA through extended remarks in the *Congressional Record*; his comments were not offered live in the House.[40] At this stage in deliberations concerning the ADA, there was little discussion on the floor of the House.

The bill had strong bipartisan support. In the Senate, it was cosponsored by 25 Democrats and 9 Republicans.[41] In the House, it was cosponsored by 74 Democrats and 11 Republicans. Nonetheless, this version of the ADA did not have the support of Senators Dole or Orrin Hatch (R-Utah). Dole's absence from the list of sponsors is particularly important because he had sponsored the 1988 version of the ADA. Presumably, Dole understood that the ADA now stood a serious chance of passage and was withholding his support until some compromises were made on the bill's language. Both Hatch and Dole joined the list of sponsors on August 2, 1989—the day that the Senate Committee on Labor and Human Resources met to mark up the bill.[42] Dole's support as a cosponsor was presumably in exchange for concessions during the markup of the bill.

Attorney General Thornburgh spoke in favor of the new bill but made it clear that the accessibility title needed serious revision to limit its scope and protection. Nonetheless, the version of the ADA that was considered on May 9, 1989, was very similar to the version that was enacted. It was more conventional than the 1988 version in that it tracked the language of Section 504 but applied that language to the private sector. The findings section continued to reflect a broad mandate to protect individuals with disabilities. In fact, Congress now raised the estimate of the number of individuals with disabilities from 34 million to 43 million.[43] The definition of disability, however, was narrowed to reflect the definition in use under Section 504 of the Rehabilitation Act. The 1999 bill used the enacted language in which disability means: "a physical or mental impairment that substantially limits one or more of the major life activities of such individual."[44]

Like the enacted bill, the ADA was now divided into sections. Title I contained the general prohibition against discrimination. Title II was the employment title. Title III was the public services titles. Title IV was the public accommodations title. Title V was the telecommunications relay services title. Title VI was the miscellaneous title.

In acquiescence to Dole's request (even before he joined the list of sponsors), the undue hardship defense became a part of this version of the bill, reflecting the case law and regulations under Section 504. The employment title contained an undue hardship defense.[45]

The public accommodations title was changed somewhat from the 1988 version. Here, Congress was writing on a virtual clean slate because Section 504 did not contain a parallel to the public accommodations title. The closest parallel was Title II of the Civil Rights Act of 1964, but that act's model of racial antidiscrimination to end *de jure* segregation did not have a close parallel to the ADA's need to make facilities accessible to individuals with disabilities.

The 1988 version of the public accommodations provisions had simply used the definition of public accommodations found in Title II of the Civil Rights Act of 1964. That definition, however, focused only on places like restaurants and hotels. The disability community, however, argued that it needed access to other types of facilities like supermarkets, pharmacies, doctors' offices, and recreational facilities. In response to these arguments, the 1989 version of the ADA *broadened* the definition of public accommodations that appeared in the 1988 version. Public accommodations were defined as all privately operated establishments "that are used by the general public as customers, clients, or visitors; or that are potential places of employment."[46] The bill then provided an inclusive list of covered entities, which was not intended to be a complete list.[47]

While broadening the definition of public accommodations, the 1989 version of the ADA also made a distinction between existing and new structures. Existing structures were required to meet only a "readily achievable" standard.[48] New facilities, however, were required to be accessible unless it was "structurally impracticable."[49]

Finally, the enforcement section in the 1989 bill for the public accommodations title was stronger than existed under Title II of the Civil Rights Act of 1964. Under the Civil Rights Act, plaintiffs can obtain only injunctive relief. The disability rights community argued that injunctive relief would not be sufficient to create accessibility at places of public accommodation. It therefore successfully argued for the public accommodations title to contain the stronger remedies found in the Fair Housing Act.[50] Compensatory damages were available under this enforcement scheme.

The most important weakening compromise in the 1989 version of the ADA came in the telecommunications title. It was changed such that it made no reference to TDD's or other alternative communication devices. Instead, the telecommunications title required only the provision of telecommunication relay services.[51]

Although Congress would make further changes before enacting the ADA, the basic framework was set in the 1989 version, which was supported by the Republican administration and Democratic Congress. The most significant changes would occur in the public accommodations title. In the 1989 version, the ADA contained the Fair Housing Act remedies, which included compensatory damages. At passage in 1990, it contained the remedies found in Title II of the Civil Rights Act, which included only injunctive relief in private causes of action. The 1989 version contained a very broad definition of public accommodations, broader than the definition in Title II of the Civil Rights Act. The 1990 version still contained a broader definition of public accommodations than existed under CRA Title II, but the definition was somewhat narrower than the definition in the 1989 version of the ADA.

The legislative debate on May 9, 1989, reflected the legislative debate throughout the consideration of the ADA in that there was no real opposition to enactment. Harkin introduced the ADA in the Senate with 33 cosponsors, about one-fourth of whom were Republicans. Some of the points that he emphasized were that the ADA would make public transportation more accessible so that individuals with disabilities could be mainstreamed into public life. Further, he noted that there was considerable discrimination against individuals who were HIV-positive and that the ADA should help to remedy that discrimination. Finally, he emphasized that the average cost of reasonable accommodations is modest and that the ADA should help reduce people's dependencies on public benefits by allowing them to enter the workplace.

After Harkin introduced the ADA and Kennedy offered his support, Senator David Durenberger (R-Minn.) spoke, offering more moderate support. He emphasized the importance of ending discrimination at the workplace and providing accessible transportation. Nonetheless, he expressed modest reservations. He asked whether rural areas might have trouble complying with some aspects of the ADA. (McCain spoke later, agreeing with this concern.) Durenberger also stressed that the federal government should not impose mandates on state and local government without providing fiscal assistance. Finally, he suggested that it was important that the ADA not impose rules on religious entities. Of the three concerns raised by Durenberger, one was ultimately addressed by Congress when it provided various religious exceptions to the ADA in the version that was reported out of committee and enacted into law.

III. August 1989 Version of the Bill

The ADA bill was referred to the Senate Committee on Labor and Human Resources, which held four days of hearings. On August 2, 1989, the committee met to mark up the bill. Harkin offered a substitute version that included an amendment proposed by McCain concerning technical assistance.[52] Hatch offered and then withdrew an amendment that would have extended the scope of coverage to include Congress. This version was reported favorably from committee in a 16-0 vote, with no opposition. The committee submitted a report on the ADA. (The coverage of Congress, however, proved to be a thorny issue that stalled passage of the ADA by a few weeks. The issue had emerged more than a year before passage.)

Representatives Steny Hoyer (D-Md.) and Norman Mineta (D-Calif.) spoke in favor of the ADA in the House on August 3, 1989. They indicated that it had 220 cosponsors in the House, as well as the support of the president, and hence was likely to become law.[53]

The August 1989 version of the ADA contained some important changes from the May 1989 version. Senator Durenberger summarized the changes, which included

—the new version eliminated rules which would have arguably permitted individuals to file lawsuits because they speculated that they might face discrimination;
—the new version weakened the reasonable accommodation language so that entities making good faith efforts to provide reasonable accommodations would not be penalized;
—the new version provided clearer definitions of terms such as reasonable accommodation, undue burden and readily achievable;
—the effective date for the employment provision was extended from 12 to 18 months; the effective date was phased in for employers with fewer than 25 employees;
—the penalties for the public accommodation title were reduced to injunctive relief for private lawsuits;
—the time period for accessible buses was extended.[54]

Private clubs and religious organizations were also exempted, as had been requested by Durenberger in earlier remarks.

None of these changes were substantial. They did not undermine the drafters' basic intentions to provide clear and comprehensive coverage against disability discrimination. The report of the Senate Committee on Labor and Human Resources (along with the floor debate) made it clear that Congress maintained its intention to provide broad coverage. For example, the committee report made manifest that it intended the term "disability" to be interpreted broadly. It specified that the term includes "orthopedic, visual, speech, and hearing impairments, cerebral palsy, epilepsy, muscular distrophy, multiple sclerosis, infection with the Human Immunodeficiency Virus, cancer, heart disease, diabetes, mental retardation, emotional illness, specific learning disabilities, drug addiction, and alcoholism."[55] The courts, however, have not consistently held that each of the categories comprises individuals who are disabled.[56]

The report also commented on the meaning of the term "major life activity," noting that it includes functions such as "caring for one's self, performing manual tasks, walking, seeing, hearing, speaking, breathing, learning, and working."[57] Nonetheless, the Supreme Court has questioned whether "working" should be considered a major life activity for the purposes of the ADA.[58]

Because the committee vote was unanimous, there was no minority report. Hatch submitted additional views as part of the committee report. His statement reflected that the current version of the ADA reduced the penalties, narrowed the breadth of coverage of public accommodations, and relaxed the standards imposed on the private bus industry.[59] He noted, however, that he reserved the right to pursue further changes on the floor.

Hatch voiced some concerns that did not lead to any changes in the bill, for example, that a small grocery store would not be covered by the ADA with respect to employment but would be covered with respect to its treatment of its customers. He indicated that he favored a small business exemption for the public accommodations title. That change, however, was never accepted by Congress. Ultimately, Title III did include a phase-in provision for small businesses. He also objected to the provision that permits the attorney general to seek civil penalties. That provision remained in the bill, nonetheless. Moreover, Hatch objected to the requirement that the private bus industry purchase lift-equipped vehicles (over a specified time period). Although the time period for compliance was relaxed, the basic rules were not changed during consideration of the ADA.

IV. September 7, 1989: Bill Passes Senate

On September 6, 1989, debate resumed in the Senate on the committee's version of the ADA, with no substantive discussion occurring on that day. Nonetheless, the bill received negative publicity in a *New York Times* editorial, which asked whether the ADA was a blank check for the disabled.[60] The editorial did not actually oppose the ADA but encouraged the Office of Management and Budget to estimate the costs and benefits of the legislation before final passage. It also encouraged Congress to be more precise about the accessibility obligations that it was imposing on businesses. In the days that followed, the editorial was frequently cited by the bill's opponents to argue that the ADA was unduly expensive and vague. The final committee reports on the ADA did include extensive cost estimates.

The Senate debated, amended, and voted on the ADA on September 7, 1989. Its basic outline was reflected in the Committee on Labor and Human Resources report. Harkin explained that all the key compromises were already reflected in this version of the ADA and no further, substantial changes were expected:

> Senator Kennedy and I are committed to this compromise. We will oppose all weakening amendments. We will also oppose any amendments that are intended to strengthen the substitute, if these amendments do not have the support of the administration and Senator Dole. We are pleased that the administration and Senator Dole share this commitment. We hope that other Senators will understand how fragile this compromise is and will support it.[61]

Senator Hatch shared the statement of the ADA's underlying purpose. He stated that he was a cosponsor of the legislation because "I firmly believe in its objective—establishing a clear, comprehensive prohibition of discrimination on the basis of disability."[62] Hatch sought to amend the ADA by providing a refundable tax credit for the costs incurred by small businesses to comply with the public accommodations requirements.[63] Although the amendment was rejected on a point of order, Hatch had offered it in good faith. He did not seek to undermine the basic purpose underlying the ADA. Throughout the debate surrounding the ADA, Hatch demonstrated a strong commitment to passage of the legislation and helped secure some important compromises to secure strong bipartisan passage. Senator McCain then spoke about one important amendment that emerged from the committee process: the communication requirements contained in Title IV of the ADA that include the existence of a telephone relay system that enables individuals with disabilities to use the telephone system.[64,65] Although the communication requirements were more stringent in the 1988 version of the ADA, it is clear that the telephone relay system had strong bipartisan support. McCain and Harkin cosponsored the amendment in committee.

Senator Durenberger noted the consistency of the purpose underlying the ADA as it was modified during the legislative process:

> The bill's genesis is in the proposals by the National Council on the Handicapped—a 15-member commission appointed by President Reagan. They were introduced as a bill last year by Senator Weicker. The changes since then have been many. We have eliminated many of the cost concerns that were troublesome to small businesses. In doing so we have won the support of President Bush. We were able to do this while still maintaining the basic principle of this legislation—to provide a clear and comprehensive prohibition against discrimination against persons with disabilities.[66]

Although the 1989 version of the ADA contained changes from the 1988 version, many senators made mention of Weicker's earlier work on the 1988 version as foundational to the ultimately enacted version.[67]

When Cranston spoke in favor of the bill, he made special mention of the fact that the ADA would cover individuals with HIV infection.[68] He also noted that the bill contained a "direct threat" defense that would permit an employer to exclude someone from employment if his or her medical condition posed a significant risk of transmitting the infection to others. But he concluded with this statement: "As medical evidence concerning HIV has shown, however, AIDS carries very low risks of transmission. Therefore, the applicability of such a standard to an individual infected with the HIV virus should be rare."[69] No senator objected to the accuracy of his statements.

Later in the day on September 7, the Senate considered various amendments to the ADA. Hatch offered an amendment requiring the National Council on Disability to conduct a study and report on the accessibility of wilderness areas to individuals with disabilities. That amendment was supported by Kennedy and agreed to.[70]

Hatch and Harkin entered into a colloquy to "clarify some of the mechanisms created in S. 933 to prohibit discrimination against people with disabilities in various employment settings."[71] The main point of the colloquy was to clarify that employers at temporary and changing construction sites would not necessarily be expected to create accessible paths of travel throughout work on a site. "[T]o make constant different accommodations at different points on the site as would often be the case on temporary worksites, [would] be a factor taken into consideration in assessing which accommodations would pose an 'undue hardship' for an employer."[72]

Harkin introduced two technical amendments. The first added a comma to the bill. The second allowed telecommunication carriers to have three, rather than two, years to comply with the bill.[73] Hatch agreed to these amendments and they were approved.

Hatch offered the amendment that he had previously mentioned, which would provide a refundable tax credit for the costs of a small business's compliance with the ADA.[74] The amendment was cosponsored by McCain, Mitch McConnell (R-Ky.), Strom Thurmond (R-S.C.), and Robert Kasten (R-Wisc.). Hatch argued that the amendment would allow the ADA to cover small businesses while also protecting them financially from the ADA's requirements.

Senator Lloyd Bentsen (D-Tex.) opposed the amendment, calling it a "killer amendment" because of its being an "S-numbered bill."[75] The House is supposed to initiate tax legislation, and Bentsen was concerned that it would "blue-slip" the bill because the "House is very jealous of its jurisdiction."[76] He also noted that "the Budget Act clearly stipulates that it is not in order for the Senate to consider any amendment that reduces revenues below the level in the budget resolution."[77] Bentsen was also chair of the Finance Committee, which should have had jurisdiction over this tax credit idea, and appeared to be protective of his turf. Packwood also objected to the amendment and suggested that Hatch normally would have been opposed to such an amendment had he not taken a "paternal interest" in the ADA.[78]

Senator Mark Pryor (D-Ark.) then negatively commented on the bill itself—somewhat surprisingly because he had become a cosponsor on August 3, more than a month earlier. (Pryor was absent for the Senate's vote on this version of the ADA, so he voted neither for nor against it.) He acknowledged that he had decided to cosponsor the bill before having read it or the committee report. Having now read both items, he had "many questions."[79] His objections were as follows. First, he objected to the definition of disability because it "is extremely loose [and] . . . is going to be the subject of literally countless issues of litigation in the courts across the country."[80] Second, he criticized the scope of the bill, noting that it covers 43 million disabled Americans and 3.9 million private businesses. Because of the broad scope, the penalties were too harsh. In particular, he took issue with the remedies under Title III: an injunction, attorney's fees, and possible civil penalty by the attorney general. He described the bill as a "lawyer's dream."[81]

Hatch responded by saying that the civil penalty is available only in an action brought by the attorney general and that he hoped that the senator would still support the bill. He emphasized that the private action for damages that existed under a previous version of the bill was eliminated. Kennedy also responded to Pryor, reminding him that the remedies found in Title III were actually a compromise and that he, Kennedy, would have preferred stronger remedies.[82]

The discussion then returned to Hatch's tax credit proposal. Dole had conferred with members of various committees and now opposed the tax credit amendment. He argued that section 190 of the Internal Revenue Code, which allows for a $35,000 tax deduction for the removal of architectural barriers, was a better solution to the problem than Hatch's tax credit. He said that he was working on a revision of the provision that would attain Hatch's objectives. The amendment failed on a point of order after Hatch sought to have a waiver of the Gramm-Rudman-Hollings Act (a waiver required a three-fifths majority). The vote was 48 to 44 in favor of the waiver, but that was not enough votes for the waiver.[83]

The discussion of the tax credit lasted more than two hours. Throughout the debate, Hatch insisted that he was not pushing the amendment to kill the ADA.

> I am happy to lick my wounds and admit I lost. I do not care; that is the way life is around here. If you want to win, you want to win; do not tell me it will kill this bill. I would not let it kill the bill. Before I let that happen in conference, I would have stripped it out myself, if that were the case. But it could not possibly be the case.[84]

After defeat of the tax credit amendment, general debate continued. Senator William Armstrong (R-Colo.) initiated a discussion concerning the definition of disability, which led to some of the exclusions found in the ADA. Armstrong first inquired as to whether the bill covered drug users and alcoholics. Harkin informed him that they were working on some clarifying language for those disabilities. Armstrong then said he wanted to provide a list for consideration of questionable disabilities that should not be covered by the ADA, such as "alcohol withdrawal, delirium, hallucinosis, dementia with alcoholism, marijuana, delusional disorder, cocaine intoxication, cocaine delirium, [and] disillusional disorder."[85] He also inquired about "homosexuality and bisexuality," about "exhibitionism, pedophilia, and voyeurism," and about "compulsive kleptomania, or other impulse control disorders." The list was reportedly derived from court cases regarding similar legislation. In each instance, Harkin responded that those categories were not already covered by the ADA. Ultimately, however, Armstrong was not satisfied unless the bill was amended to exclude these groups from coverage.

Helms later returned the discussion to the definition of disability. (Helms was one of eight senators who voted against this version of the ADA.) In response to questions from Helms, Harkin replied that the bill did not cover pedophiles; it did cover schizophrenics; he wasn't sure whether it covered kleptomaniacs; it did cover manic depressives, people with very low IQ's, and individuals with psychotics disorders; did not cover homosexuals; he wasn't sure about transvestites but would accept an amendment to exclude them from coverage. Helms repeatedly stated that he objected to individuals who are HIV-positive being covered by the statute because of the "people who are HIV positive, most . . . are drug addicts or homosexuals or bisexuals."[86] Harkin kept responding by saying that they were making good legislative history by agreeing that people who are HIV-positive are covered by the ADA.

Later in this discussion, Kennedy reiterated the point about people who are HIV-positive being covered by the ADA and asked to have some letters printed in the *Congressional Record* from the National Commission on AIDS that were consistent with that point.[87] Despite the clarity of this legislative history, some lower courts initially concluded that HIV infection was not covered by the ADA.[88] Had judges made any inquiry into the ADA's legislative history, they would have seen a unanimous understanding that Congress intended HIV to be covered. Helms objected to that coverage and ultimately voted against the bill. But the supporters of the bill understood it covered individuals with HIV infection.

Armstrong continued the discussion about the breadth of the definition of disability, arguing that "voyeurism" would be covered by the ADA because it is a listed disability in the DSM III,[89] and requesting an amendment to exclude voyeurism and other conditions from coverage under the ADA. After further discussion about the definition of disability, Helms offered an amendment that limited coverage of individuals who engage in the illegal use of drugs or are alcoholics under Section 504 of the Rehabilitation Act. The ADA, however, had already been amended to reach that result. Harkin complained that Helms was seeking to amend a bill other than the ADA but acquiesced to the amendment.[90] The Senate agreed to the amendment.

Referring to the 1986 Rehabilitation Act case involving coverage of transvestites, Helms then offered an amendment excluding them from coverage.[91] As noted earlier, that result had already been agreed to under the Fair Housing Act Amendment. Harkin accepted this amendment, and the Senate agreed to the amendment.

Supporters of the statute also suggested language clarifying whether certain individuals would be covered by the ADA. Harkin offered an amendment to exclude current users of illegal drugs as well as alcoholics from the definition of disability in certain situations.[92] Senator Dan Coats (R-Ind.) supported the amendment and asked some clarifying questions. Coats indicated that he had supported a similar exclusion in committee and was satisfied with Harkin's amendment. In response to Coats's questions, Harkin indicated:

—an employer can refuse to hire a job applicant or discharge an employee who is a current user of illegal drugs;

—an employer can refuse to hire a job applicant or discharge or discipline an employee who is an addict who is also currently using illegal drugs or alcohol;

—an employer may fire or discharge an employee who is a casual illegal drug user;

—an employer may use drug testing as a means of determining whether the employee is currently using illegal drugs;

—an employer may fire or discipline the employee if through testing it is determined that the employee is using illegal drugs;

—an employer may use drug-testing as part of the pre-employment screening process and then refuse to hire the applicant if it is found that he or she is using illegal drugs;

—a rehabilitated drug user, however, can not be fired;

—an employer is under no legal obligation to provide rehabilitation for an employee who is using illegal drugs or alcohol.[93]

In response to a question from Senator John Danforth (R-Mo.), Harkin offered further clarification of the drug-users provision in the bill.

(Danforth was not a sponsor of the ADA but did vote for this version of the bill.) The amendment (no. 718) was set aside while the senators proceeded with other amendments. The discussion then returned to amendment no. 718, concerning drug users and alcoholics. In response to a question from Armstrong, Harkin indicated that an employer could take into account off-site drinking as a factor in employment or promotion "because it might bring disgrace" to the employer.[94] (In fact, it is not clear that an employer could consider off-site drinking if it did not impair job performance. The "disgrace" language was Armstrong's. Harkin simply agreed with it.) The amendment was agreed to.[95]

Senator Gordon Humphrey (R-N.H.) also objected that drug addiction is a covered disability under the ADA. He offered amendment no. 721, supported by Harkin and Kennedy, which clarified that current users of illegal drugs are not covered by the ADA.[96] Humphrey sought assurance that the amendment would not disappear in committee. Harkin assured Humphrey that the language would stay in the bill in committee. (He also noted that the language was redundant because other language in the bill already achieved this purpose. At this late hour, several of the amendments appear to have been redundant.) Hatch also offered his assurance that the language would survive the conference. The amendment was agreed to. (It did survive the conference.)

Debate then turned to amendment no. 722, which excluded various conditions from the definition of disability. Kennedy supported the amendment while making it clear that it was a compromise that he would have preferred not to make. He also pointed out "that some of the behavior characteristics listed such as homosexuality and bisexuality are not, even without this amendment, considered disabilities."[97] Armstrong spoke in favor of the amendment while also noting that it should not be assumed "that because we have failed to exclude something that it is necessarily included."[98] Hatch asked to be added as a cosponsor of the amendment. Hatch, like Kennedy, argued that the amendment was unnecessary but agreed to support it as a compromise. The Senate agreed to the amendment.[99]

The foregoing agreement is among the most interesting deals that helped make passage of the ADA possible by a strong bipartisan majority. Throughout the debate over the ADA, there are homophobic comments about the "sodomy lobby" that was supporting passage of the ADA. Many of these comments were also insensitive on HIV issues. Kennedy and other liberals, however, never intended the ADA to protect individuals merely because they were homosexual. They therefore disarmed Armstrong and Helms by readily agreeing to an amendment to exclude homosexuals from coverage but refused to go so far as to exclude individuals who are HIV-positive from coverage because they genuinely did believe that the ADA would assist some individuals who faced discrimination because of HIV status.

The language achieved under amendment no. 718 was key to the passage of the ADA because it offered a compromise between those who wanted drug users to be unprotected by the statute and those who wanted drug addiction to be recognized as a disability. By creating the category "rehabilitated drug user," the drafters of the ADA would be able to be responsive to both constituencies. As with any compromise, there were still some ambiguities. Courts have, for example, struggled with the meaning of "current" drug user. How "current" is "current"? Does the person have to be using drugs illegally at the moment of discharge? Congress did foresee that ambiguity but offered no specific guidance on the meaning of the term.

Although most of the debate that day concerned the definition of disability, transportation issues received significant discussion during that time. Senator Fritz Hollings (R-S.C.) (who had become a cosponsor on June 6) offered an amendment that related to the study required by the bill on the access needs of individuals with disabilities to intercity buses. The amendment provided for a one-year delay in implementing the lease/purchase requirement of accessible buses under the ADA. Kennedy and Harkin supported the amendment, and it was agreed to. Senator Dale Bumpers (R-Ark.) then sought clarification on some issues. He declared that he was going to vote for the bill and was a cosponsor.[100] In fact, he is not listed as a cosponsor although he did vote for this version of the bill. He also indicated that he became sensitized to disability issues when his daughter was paralyzed and in a wheelchair for six months.[101] He sought reassurance that public entities would have to purchase accessible buses only thirty days after the enactment of the ADA; buses ordered before that date need not comply with the accessibility requirements. Harkin provided Bumpers with that reassurance, reading from page 47 of the committee report in support of his answer.[102] (It is interesting that the committee report is often used to reply to questions rather than the text of the statute, showing how much members of Congress rely on committee reports.)

Bumpers entered into a colloquy with Harkin concerning the meaning of the term "readily achievable" in the transportation context. Harkin reassured Bumpers that the term does not apply to private buses purchased prior to thirty days after the enactment of the bill. He also explained that if it is too expensive for the owner of an establishment to provide access, the owner has to consider alternative means of access. Again, Harkin read extensively from the committee report to reply to Bumpers's questions.[103]

A discussion ensued about the cost of lifts on buses. Greyhound had taken the position that a lift would cost about $30,000 and increase the cost of a bus ticket by 25 percent. Harkin disputed that assertion, arguing that the price of a lift in Denver was only $12,000 and it would be lower in the near future.[104]

The Senate also debated whether Congress should be covered by the ADA. Details concerning congressional coverage ultimately delayed passage of the ADA. Senator Chuck Grassley (R-Iowa) introduced an amendment, supported by Dole, Arlen Specter (R-Pa.), and Humphrey, which would require Congress to be covered by the act.[105] (Humphrey's sponsorship of this amendment is odd because he did not vote for this version of the ADA.) Senator Wendell Ford (D-Ky.) objected to the amendment because it would mean that the executive branch would have some control over the legislative branch. (Ford did not sponsor the ADA, but he did vote for this version.) Ford asked that the amendment be withdrawn and that acceptable language be worked out in committee. Grassley responded that he was willing to work out something in conference but that he wanted the amendment accepted at that time. Ford was not happy with that solution: "I understand that we are pushed for time. It is a quarter of 10 at night. So we want to get it over with and go on and make a mistake and hope that we can take care of it at the conference. I think that I brought it to the attention of my colleagues, and apparently my colleagues are so anxious to get the bill passed tonight, they will swallow camels and choke on gnats."[106] The amendment was agreed to. (The text of the amendment proved controversial in the final weeks of consideration of the bill.)

Humphrey then delivered a lengthy speech against the ADA. He objected to the potentially "monumental" price tag that would accompany its passage, citing the *New York Times* editorial.[107] He objected as well to the scope of reasonable accommodations required in the employment section. "In fact, the definition of protected 'disabilities' in this bill is so broad that virtually any mental or physical shortcoming can be invoked as grounds for demanding the special 'accommodations' which the bill requires employers to provide."[108] He argued "that these unprecedented Federal restrictions on employee qualifications will deter employers from preserving high standards of fitness, safety, and efficiency within their work force."[109] He opposed the requirement that all businesses become accessible because the design changes would greatly increase the cost of new construction. He criticized the legal standards under ADA Title III as "riddled with vague terms and requirements which make compliance virtually unachievable."[110]

Before the Senate voted to approve this version of the bill, various members spoke in support. During Kennedy's speech, he reiterated the importance of the bill to individuals who are HIV-positive.[111] It is interesting that none of the amendments that sought to exclude certain individuals from coverage sought to exclude HIV-positive individuals. No one hid that they would be covered by the bill; a fact repeatedly mentioned on the floor of the Senate.

The Senate vote on this version of the bill: 76 in favor and 8 against (16 senators were not present).[112] The most interesting votes were Armstrong's and Pryor's. Armstrong got the amendments he wanted but voted against this version of the bill anyway. Ultimately, however, he voted for final passage of the ADA.[113] Pryor did not vote on the version although he was present but, like Armstrong, he voted for final passage. The *New York Times* editorial may have been correct in predicting that "[n]o politician can vote against this bill and survive." Both Armstrong and Pryor appear to have had serious reservations about the ADA yet they voted for the legislation.

V. Bill Returns to the House

After lengthy discussion of the bill in the Senate, it returned to the House. It now had some momentum, with the support of the Bush administration. Representative Conte reflected on that fact when he spoke on September 12, 1989, urging passage: "The Senate-passed bill is a good bill, the product of countless hours of negotiation. We ought to use it as our vehicle for the slight changes that may still be need to be made, or go ahead and pass it as is. The President and the congressional leadership are committed to enactment of this legislation. Let us get on with it."[114]

One of the few objections to the ADA in the House was offered by Representative Norman Shumway (R-Calif.) who included an editorial from the *Wall Street Journal* in extended remarks (that were not spoken on the House floor). The bill was criticized as being vague and contradictory.[115] In even stronger language on October 2, 1989, Representative Dan Burton (R-Ind.) said: "The ADA is the last ditch attempt of the remorseless sodomy lobby to achieve its national agenda before the impending decimation of AIDS destroys its political clout. Their Bill simply must be stopped. There will be no second chance for normal America if the ADA is passed."[116] Burton's comments reflected the homophobia that was used to prevent passage of the ADA.

Work on the ADA continued as the legislative session came to a close. Representative Steny Hoyer (D-Md.) reported on November 15, 1989, that the Education and Labor Committee approved the ADA on a 35 to 0 vote.[117] Representative Newt Gingrich (R-Ga.) also made positive comments (in extended remarks) about the ADA and the work of the Education and Labor Committee on November 15, 1989.[118]

VI. House Committee Reports

Four House committees considered the ADA and made modifications in committee. In general, their work created eighty discrepancies with the Senate version of the ADA. Few of the discrepancies would prove to be controversial. The Senate largely receded to the House amendments. Hence, the work of these four committees is crucial because they laid out the fine details in the statutory language.

The House resumed consideration of the ADA on March 7, 1990. Representative Major Owens (D-N.Y.) expressed concern that the bill was moving very slowly through the House and that the administration was "no longer interested in the bill,"[119] and that the Committee on Public Works "passed an amendment which seemed to water down one of the provisions of the act."[120] He added:

> Will the President lift a finger to get this legislation passed in a worthy and effective form, or will he continue to be distracted by whatever the White House's issue of the week happens to be?
>
> Will the White House lead on this issue or will it continue to drift? I think the disabled community knows the difference between rhetorical

commitment and a real commitment to their civil rights. They want to know where the President stands and what is the true depth of his commitment on the most important piece of legislation affecting them that the Federal Government has ever considered.

They have little regard for Republican Members of Congress who posture by offering amendments to strengthen the bill in committee that they know will not pass, and which they unalterably oppose behind closed doors. . . . The White House chooses to roll the dice and risk losing the credibility and good will it has created with Americans with disabilities.

I call upon my colleagues in the House to take a firm stand against the White House's shenanigans, to assert our commitment to freedom, opportunity, and full civil rights protection for Americans with disabilities, and a strong America that such an act will bring about.[121]

The Committee on Public Works had approved an amendment that would allow community rail services to make only one car per train accessible. The Energy and Commerce Committee approved different language. The language of the Committee on Public Works was not the language considered by the House when the bill came to it for consideration. An attempt to substitute the Public Works language for the Energy and Commerce language was unsuccessful on the floor of the House.

The second, and most complete, report was the report of the Committee on Education and Labor.[122] It summarized the extensive hearings that had been held on the ADA, describing the need for broad-reaching legislation in this area. Of the definition of disability, it says:

Whether a person has a disability should be assessed without regard to the availability of mitigating measures, such as reasonable accommodations or auxiliary aids. For example, a person who is hard of hearing is substantially limited in the major life activity of hearing, even though the loss may be corrected through the use of a hearing aid. Likewise, persons with impairments, such as epilepsy or diabetes, which substantially limit a major life activity are covered under the first prong of the definition of disability, even if the effects of the impairment are controlled by medication.[123]

Despite the clarity of this statement in the legislative history, the Supreme Court ruled otherwise, concluding that a court should consider mitigating measures in determining whether an individual is disabled under the ADA.[124]

The Minority Report of the Education and Labor Committee did not dispute the accuracy of this description of the definition of disability. It merely emphasized the changes that were made in committee to the Senate version of the ADA. These include (1) the Title VII relief mechanism was created for ADA Title I, (2) a phase-in period for coverage was created for ADA Title I, (3) the prohibition against anticipatory discrimination was eliminated, (4) current users of illegal drugs were eliminated from coverage, (5) contract liability was clarified in ADA Title I and Title III, (6) more specific guidelines were created for the meaning of reasonable accommodation and undue hardship, (7) clarification of the alteration requirements under ADA Title III, (8) restrictions of the attorney general's power under ADA Title III to seek damages, (9) clarification under ADA Title III that commercial facilities, rather than individual workstations, must be accessible, (10) clarification of good-faith defense, and (11) creation of flexibility in dealing with historical landmarks under ADA Title III.[125]

The third report, by the Judiciary Committee, described some modifications made to the bill by the Judiciary Committee.[126]

The Committee adopted 5 amendments to the bill ordered reported by the Subcommittee. An amendment added a new section to the bill, Section 513, to encourage the use of alternative dispute resolution where appropriate and to the extent authorized by law. An amendment added additional factors to be considered in making a determination of what constitutes an undue hardship under title I and what is readily achievable under title III. An amendment clarified that the remedies incorporated by reference in titles I, II and III are the remedies that the ADA provides, and that the incorporated remedies are the remedies currently available. If those remedies are amended in the future, such remedies also apply to the ADA.

An amendment clarified the "direct threat" provision, the phrase "essential functions" of a job, and the "anticipatory discrimination" provision. This amendment also clarified what entities are covered under the general rule of title III, that commercial facilities are covered by the alterations provisions, and that exams and classes relating to applications, licensing, certifications, or credentialing must be held in an accessible place and manner. An amendment made technical changes to the interim accessibility standards under title III.[127]

Of these amendments, the most controversial was the rule that made Title VII remedies applicable to ADA Title I, with the understanding that those remedies would change in the future if Title VII's remedies were to change. In a report with "Additional Views," Representatives James Sensenbrenner (R-Wisc.), Bill McCollum (R-Fla.), George Gekas (R-Pa.), William Dannemeyer (R-Calif.), Lamar Smith (R-Tex.), and Craig James (R-Fla.), argued that it was wrong to tie the two statutes together because the pending Civil Rights Act of 1990 would strengthen the remedies available under Title VII, and thereby strengthen the remedies available under the ADA. They objected to the modification because it would make compensatory and punitive damages available under ADA Title I. It was contrary to an earlier agreement reached between the Senate and the Bush administration in which punitive damages were deleted from a draft of the ADA.[128] It was an issue that would remain controversial as the ADA was considered in Congress, but the view of the House committee would ultimately prevail.

The Judiciary Committee report also agreed with the report of the Committee on Education and Labor with respect to the definition of disability.

> The impairment should be assessed without considering whether mitigating measures, such as auxiliary aids or reasonable accommodations, would result in a less-than-substantial limitation. For example, a person with epilepsy, an impairment which substantially limits a major life activity under this test, is covered under this test, even if the effects of the impairment which substantially limits a major life activity, is also covered, even if the hearing loss is corrected by the use of a hearing aid.[129]

The final committee to report on the ADA was the Committee on Energy and Commerce.[130] Its amendments were limited to matters within the committee's sole or shared jurisdiction: provisions affecting rail transportation services provided by Amtrak, commuter authorities, and private entities; provisions affecting telecommunications services for individuals with speech or hearing impairments; general provisions relating to the entire bill. The minority report characterized the ADA as a "homosexual rights" bill even though homosexuals were specifically exempted from statutory coverage. The report was characteristic of some of the homophobia that underlay opposition to the ADA:

Sixty percent of the 119,500 adults who have been diagnosed with full blown AIDS as of February 1990 contracted the fatal virus through homosexual activity. An additional 7 percent list homosexual activity as one of their risk factors. It does not require a particularly shrewd attorney to argue that the protections available in the ADA are available to *all* male homosexuals by virtue of the perception that homosexual males "are regarded as" being infected with HIV. Indeed, a New Jersey court has interpreted a similar state law in exactly this fashion. . . . [W]e believe that the ADA is a homosexual rights bill in disguise.[131]

In general, the reports of the four House committees made careful technical corrections to the ADA, which did not prove to be controversial when the bill went to a conference to resolve the discrepancies. The reports highlight that it was well understood by supporters and detractors that the bill would cover individuals with HIV infection. Two of the reports also reflect that some members of Congress did consider the mitigating-measures issue and concluded that whether someone was disabled should be determined without taking into account the use of mitigating devices. Nonetheless, the Supreme Court ruled otherwise. The reports also foreshadow the controversy about remedies that would continue until final passage of the ADA. The House view, however, eventually prevailed despite an earlier agreement between the Senate and the Bush administration concerning damages remedies.

VII. Floor Debate Resumes

House consideration of the ADA resumed on May 1, 1990. Roscoe Bartlett (R-Md.) answered some frequently asked questions about the ADA on the floor of the House.[132] On May 8, 1990, Tom DeLay (R-Tex.) spoke in favor of a tax credit for businesses to assist compliance with the ADA.[133] (The tax credit was one of the most controversial aspects of ADA consideration.) DeLay repeated his comments on May 15, 1990,[134] and then spoke at length in opposition to the ADA.[135] He complained that the bill was costly and vague because it relies on "case law" rather than statutory language to define who is disabled. He declared that there had been insufficient discussion of the bill in the House and that members of Congress were afraid to speak against it. Dan Burton (R-Ind.) agreed with DeLay and argued that the ADA would raise the cost of housing for everyone by requiring accessibility.[136] Lamar Smith (R-Tex.) then argued for the importance of a credit for small businesses to assist with ADA compliance.[137]

Representative Charles Douglas (R-N.H.) then indicated that DeLay, Burton, Smith, and he had gone to the White House the previous week to argue that the remedies under the ADA had to be weakened under ADA Title III and that the Committee on the Judiciary had approved a narrowing amendment on the remedy issue.[138] He also said that he wanted an amendment to protect public safety under the ADA and a religious exemption under the ADA. (The ADA does contain a direct-threat exemption, which responds to his first concern, and exempts religious entities under ADA Title III, which responds to his second concern.)

Douglas was also against the medical examination rules; police departments should be able to conduct prescreenings before making offers of employment.[139] That language, however, was never changed in the ADA, although the issue was raised repeatedly during debate. (Nonetheless, the courts have been very lenient with police and fire departments in ADA cases,[140] interpreting the act as if it had been amended to achieve Douglas's desired policy outcome.)

Finally, Burton spoke about the ADA's purported coverage of "homosexuals." He was concerned that the ADA would cover homosexuals because it covers people who have HIV infection. He sought an amendment that "would clarify that the ADA is in effect homosexual rights legislation, but stating that homosexuals are not disabled because they are regarded as HIV positive."[141] Although Burton did not succeed in amending the ADA with such language, some courts have interpreted the ADA as if there were such an amendment.[142] Burton also was concerned that the bill could be used by homosexuals to assist them in adopting children.

DeLay offered into the *Congressional Record* an article entitled "Disabling the Disabled" by Maiselle Dolan Shortley. Shortley argued that child molesters would be considered disabled under the ADA and that the language of the statute is so vague that it should be considered the "Lawyers Full Employment Act." (That label was used frequently by the bill's detractors.)[143]

Serious consideration of the ADA took place in the House between May 17 and May 22, 1990, when an amended version of the ADA passed by a vote of 403-20. Bart Gordon (D-Tenn.), who was not a sponsor of the 1988 version of the ADA, called up the resolution in the House that established the rules for debating the ADA.[144] He indicated that the bill had 249 cosponsors in the House, and had passed the Senate by a vote of 76 to 8. Lynn Martin (R-Ill.) then spoke against the rule for debate, claiming that it was too restrictive. She also objected to section 509 of the bill, which made it applicable to Congress but subject to its own internal rules and enforcement.[145] This issue would be a source of disagreement until final passage. (Martin ultimately voted for the ADA.) Bart Gordon argued that the rule for debate was fair because the bill had already been subjected to extensive consideration by subcommittees and committees. "To talk about having an open rule of the floor now, after all this kind of earlier scrutiny of the bill, would make a mockery of the whole committee system."[146] His comments reflect the respect that is generally accorded to the committee system and why it is often reasonable for courts to give weight to the work of those committees.

Robert S. Walker (R-Pa.) supported Martin's remarks, arguing that some important amendments would not be considered under the rule proposed for the bill's consideration. Glenn Anderson (D-Calif.) spoke in favor of the rule, adding that it would allow consideration of amendments that he would oppose. DeLay also spoke against the rule, indicating that he had offered eleven amendments in the Rules Committee, not one of which would be considered under the rule for consideration of the ADA.[147] (He ultimately voted against the bill.)

Charles Bennett (D-Fla.) spoke passionately in favor of the bill, indicating that he became disabled when he contracted polio during World War II. He spoke about the importance of buildings being accessible and individuals with disabilities having an opportunity to be employed. Bill McCollum (R-Fla.) spoke against the rule, although he favored the bill itself.

Debate in the House continued on May 17. H. Martin Lancaster (D-N.C.) spoke against the rule, although he ultimately voted for the ADA. His proposed amendment to Title III would not be considered by the House. Newt Gingrich (R-Ga.) also spoke against the rule.

William E. Dannemeyer (R-Calif.) spoke against the definition of disability under the ADA, focusing on its coverage of HIV infection:

> With this bill, in the form that it is now to be considered by the House, if it is adopted, every HIV carrier in the country immediately comes within the definition of a disabled person. . . . Is that sound public policy? And since 70 percent of those people in this country who are HIV

carriers are male homosexuals, we are going to witness an attempt or utterance on the part of the homosexual community that, when this bill is passed, it will be identified by the homosexual community as their bill of rights.[148]

Burton agreed with Dannemeyer, arguing that amendments to protect the public against communicable diseases needed to be discussed or debated on the floor of the House. Steve Bartlett (R-Tex.) also agreed that the rule should be opposed so that full debate of the ADA could occur.[149] He opposed the rule but voted for the ADA.

Despite the vigorous opposition to the rule, it passed by a vote of 237 to 172, with 23 not voting. Debate, pursuant to the rule, then proceeded on the bill itself. Representative Steny Hoyer (D-Md.) offered the first major speech in favor of the bill.[150] He stated: "Whenever possible, we have used terms of art from the 1964 Civil Rights Act and from the Rehabilitation Act of 1973 phrases already interpreted in courts throughout this land so that business can know exactly what we mean."[151] Representative Major Owens (D-N.Y.) emphasized the same point: "None of the fundamental concepts in this legislation are new. Rather, they are derived largely from section 504 of the Rehabilitation Act of 1973 and its implementing regulations, and the Civil Rights Act of 1964. As such, there is a history of experience in implementing the concepts in this bill which will greatly facilitate the task of informing those with rights and responsibilities under this legislation as to what its provisions mean."[152]

Representative Bartlett spoke in favor of the bill, after an exchange with Representative Hoyer to clarify the meaning of the "direct threat" defense under the bill. He defined some of the phrases in the statute, such as "undue hardship" and "readily achievable" in ways that were consistent with the committee reports. He also offered his support of some forthcoming amendments regarding remedies and food workers.[153] There was further general debate before the House considered the amendments that were permitted under the rule for debate. (Members of each of the committees that considered the legislation were given an allotted amount of time for general comments.)

Representative John J. LaFalce (D-N.Y.) offered the first amendment. (He voted for the bill.) The amendment phased in coverage of small businesses under ADA Title III. It was cosponsored by Tom Campbell (R-Calif.). No one spoke in opposition to the amendment. The amendment passed unanimously, 401-0, with 31 not voting.[154] (With a minor amendment, this language is part of the Conference Report, and became a part of the enacted bill.)

McCollum then offered an amendment to ADA Title I, stating that "if an employer has prepared a written description before advertising or interviewing applicants for the job, this description shall be considered evidence of the essential functions of the job."[155] Without the amendment, the bill already gave deference to the employer's judgment but did not specify that deference would be particularly important when that job description was in written form. There was no opposition. The amendment was agreed to.[156] It became part of the final bill.

Representative Jim Olin (D-Va.), who would vote against the ADA, offered the third amendment. It provided that an expense is presumed to be an undue hardship under ADA Title I "if an employer incurs costs in making an accommodation which exceeds 10 percent of the annual salary or the annualized hourly wage of the job in question."[157] The amendment was opposed. Some in opposition were concerned that it would encourage or permit accommodations so long as they did not exceed 10 percent of salary, thereby raising the ceiling on reasonable accommodations. Others objected that the 10 percent figure was arbitrary. The argument was also made that the amendment was harmful to low-wage employees, whom the bill should be seeking to assist. The amendment failed on a vote of 187 ayes, 213 noes, and 32 members not voting.[158]

The fourth amendment, concerning access to wilderness areas,[159] was offered by Representative James Hansen (R-Utah), who agreed to a substitute version offered by Bruce Vento (D-Minn.). There was no opposition. The amendment, as modified, was agreed to;[160] it became part of the final bill.

The fifth amendment was offered by Representative Jim Chapman (D-Tex.), who would vote for passage of the ADA. Some congressmen declared that the bill would bankrupt the restaurant industry by forcing employers to hire HIV-positive individuals, which would cause the public to perceive that their food was unsafe. The Chapman amendment responded to this concern and became a bone of contention in the Senate. It read:

> Food Handling Job.—It shall not be a violation of this Act for an employer to refuse to assign or continue to assign any employee with an infectious or communicable disease of public health significance to a job involving food handling, provided that the employer shall make reason-

able accommodation that would offer an alternative employment opportunity for which the employee is qualified and for which the employee would sustain no economic damage.[161]

In supporting the amendment, Chapman suggested it could be used by food service employers to deny employment to people who are HIV-positive even though "I am not here to say that there is any evidence that AIDS can be transferred in the process of handling food."[162] He added that the amendment was needed "in the real world with real people who have real businesses that create real jobs."[163] (The amendment does not specifically mention HIV and does give rise to ambiguity as to whether HIV should be considered an infectious or communicable disease.)

Representative J. Roy Rowland (D-Ga.) suggested that the amendment be modified to say "as specified by CDC" so that there would be no ambiguity about what infectious or contagious diseases are affected by this amendment.[164] (That language was part of the compromise reached by the two houses.)

Opponents of Chapman's amendment argued that it perpetuated discrimination against people with HIV infection by suggesting, contrary to medical evidence, that they can spread HIV through the food supply. Supporters of the amendment recognized that there was no medical evidence that HIV could be transmitted by food handlers, but they also reasoned that the amendment was necessary to protect the restaurant industry from the public's false perceptions.

The House approved the amendment by a vote of 199-187, with 46 representatives not voting.[165] The amendment was controversial until passage because the Senate deemed it unnecessary. The House approved a weaker version in the final bill, following two conference committee reports, although the Sixth Circuit has interpreted the ADA as if the Chapman amendment had prevailed.[166]

Three more amendments were considered on May 22, 1990. Representative William Lipinski (D-Ill.) and Dennis Hastert (R-Ill.) offered an amendment that would allow commuter rail services to make only one car per train accessible. But if continuing demand were not met by the one car, additional cars must be made accessible. Although this amendment required fewer accessible cars than did the pending ADA, it also created a higher standard of accessibility for the cars. The approach had been approved by the Public Works and Transportation Committee, and the existing language had been approved by the Energy and Commerce Committee.[167] The amendment was opposed by many representatives who argued that the existing language had been worked out between the administration, the disability community, and the Energy and Commerce Committee. The amended version would promote segregation rather than integration of the entire transportation system. Supporters argued that it would be more financially feasible. The amendment was defeated on a vote of 110 ayes, 290 noes, and 32 not voting.[168]

Representative Bud Shuster (R-Pa.), who voted against ultimate passage of the ADA, offered the next amendment. It would permit the secretary of transportation to waive application of the transportation section on an annual basis if certain conditions were met.[169] Opponents of the ADA contended that the amendment would exempt 80 percent of U.S. cities and undercut the goal of providing accessible transportation. The amendment was defeated on a vote of 148 to 266, with 18 not voting.[170]

The last amendment considered by the House was introduced by F. James Sensenbrenner (R-Wisc.) and related to enforcement of the ADA. His concern was that the pending Civil Rights Act of 1990 would amend Title VII to provide for jury trials and for compensatory and punitive damages. Because the ADA linked its remedial structure to Title VII, the pending bill would also expand the remedies available under the ADA. Sensenbrenner sought to "delink" the remedies available under the ADA from the remedies available under Title VII so that the 1990 Civil Rights Act would not apply to the ADA. As Sensenbrenner had pointed out previously, Congress had been assured that punitive and compensatory damages would not be available under the ADA.[171]

Opponents of the Sensenbrenner amendment argued that it was important for the ADA to offer the same remedies as Title VII. If Title VII were to be expanded to include compensatory and punitive damages, then the ADA should follow suit.[172] After a spirited debate, the amendment lost by a vote of 192 to 227, with 13 members not voting.[173]

Despite the fact that there were supposed to be no more amendments considered before the vote in the House on the bill, DeLay, who voted against final passage, moved to recommit the bill to the Committee on Rules with various amendments. These amendments included an exception for individuals with a history of drug addiction or alcoholism, as well as rules to include the executive and judicial branches under the ADA. The motion failed by a vote of 143 to 280, with 9 members not voting.[174]

The House then voted on this version of the ADA. It passed by a vote of 403 to 20, with 8 members not voting.[175]

In all, the House passed three amendments before passage in that chamber: the small business amendment for ADA Title III; the written job-description amendment for ADA Title I; and the food-handling amendment for ADA Title I. Of the three, the last would prove to be the most controversial, causing a slight delay in the passage of the ADA.

VIII. First Conference Report

Because the House and Senate had passed different versions of the ADA, it would go to a joint conference for consideration. Before that, each chamber met to discuss the instructions that it wished to give its conferees. On May 24, the House conferees were instructed to insist upon the three amendments that had been passed in the House.

In the Senate, Helms made a motion to insist that the conferees agree to the House's food-handling amendment (the Chapman amendment).[176] Harkin disagreed, and Kennedy also objected, pointing out that there was no medical basis to the Chapman amendment and that Chapman, himself, had acknowledged that fact.[177] A motion was made to table the Helms motion; the motion lost on a vote of 40 to 53.[178]

Grassley then spoke about the importance of the ADA's creating a cause of action against members of Congress. He did not offer a formal amendment, but Harkin offered his support for a cause of action against the Senate. There was discussion about how to do so within constitutional limits because it did not seem appropriate for the Equal Employment Opportunity Commission (EEOC) or the attorney general to have authority over the legislative branch.[179] Last, Senator Rudolph Boschwitz (R-Minn.) indicated his support for the small-business amendment to ADA Title III, as did Harkin.[180] There was no discussion of the written job-description amendment from the House, and the amendment did not prove controversial in the joint conference, where the Senate agreed to the House language.

The conference report (June 26, 1990) carried its suggested language.[181] It indicated that the House receded to the Senate's version of the bill with respect to the food-handling issue. It noted that the undue hardship and direct-threat rules had already taken care of any potential problems with contagious food handlers, rendering the Chapman amendment unnecessary.[182] With respect to the small-business exemption, the Senate receded as well, although the conferees made some modest language changes to the House wilderness amendment.[183] With regard to this amendment, the Senate also receded, although the language again was changed slightly.[184] The House receded to the Senate's amendment to have the Senate covered under the ADA. The House chose a different mechanism for its own coverage.[185]

Both the House and Senate versions had various exceptions from the definition of disability within Title V (miscellaneous title). The Senate had exempted a list of potential disabilities from coverage. The House had various exclusions by category. The Senate receded to the House version. The Senate version arguably contained more exemptions because it included an exemption for current psychoactive substance-induced organic mental disorders (as defined by DSM-III-R; they are not the result of medical treatment).[186] That general exclusion was not in the House version. Before the House or Senate met to discuss the conference report, Representative Bartlett noted that the conferees did not follow the Senate's instructions with respect to the food-handling amendment.[187] Senator Hatch also noted that there was a problem with the language with regard to enforcement that would be used against the Senate, and he agreed that there was a problem to be resolved with respect to the food-handling amendment.[188] Hatch indicated that he signed the conference report "but withheld a right to be able to vote whichever way I wanted to on the Chapman [food-handling] amendment."[189] In an exchange with Kennedy, Hatch indicated that his staff had mistakenly signed off on the language with respect to Senate coverage, and the language needed to be changed. Because the food-handling and senatorial-coverage issues still had to be resolved, Congress could not vote on the ADA before the July 4th recess.

IX. Civil Rights Act of 1990

The Senate delayed further consideration of the ADA while it considered the Civil Rights Act of 1990 on July 10, 1990. Discussion of the Civil Rights Act discussion was relevant to the ADA because the remedial rules that Congress was creating would also apply to the ADA.

First, the Senate considered an amendment to the Civil Rights Act that was a bipartisan rule that would apply the various civil rights laws to the Senate while also protecting separation of powers principles.[190] Wendell Ford (D-Ky.) proposed the amendment and Kennedy supported it.[191] Harkin indicated that it would also apply to the ADA.[192] As Grassley later explained, the language of the amendment was somewhat controversial. The supporters of the ADA had not yet worked out acceptable language on coverage of the Senate, and the language in the Civil Rights Act was apparently weaker than the language being considered by the Senate for the ADA. (Under the Civil Rights Act language, the Senate, rather than the courts, would resolve complaints.) By approving the language in the Civil Rights Act, further debate about this issue would be effectively foreclosed under the ADA.[193]

Grassley moved to table the pending amendment (concerning congressional coverage), a motion defeated in a vote of 18 to 74.[194] (Harkin voted in favor of tabling the motion; he apparently preferred the Grassley amendment under which there would be a stronger cause of action than under the Ford amendment. But Kennedy and Hatch voted against the motion to table, apparently having agreed to the Ford amendment.) The Senate then approved the Ford amendment.

Despite the vote, Grassley and Hatch continued to try to modify the language. Grassley offered an amendment that would give an aggrieved individual a private right of action against the Senate if he or she were a victim of discrimination.[195] Hatch offered an amendment to the Grassley amendment.[196] The Hatch-Grassley amendment gave individuals a private right of action; the previously approved Ford amendment would not have done so. Hatch indicated that he voted no to table the Ford amendment because it provided, in general, for a good underlying structure. Nonetheless, he believed that his amendment offered further improvement by providing for a private right of action. At the conclusion of the debate, Warren Rudman (R-N.H.) moved to table the amendment. That motion passed by a vote of 63 to 26.[197] Hence, the Ford amendment contained the language ultimately used in the ADA, the Hatch-Grassley mechanism having failed to pass the Senate.

X. *Further Senate Consideration of First Conference Report*

Having considered the Civil Rights Act of 1990, the Senate then returned to consideration of the First Conference Report on the ADA (July 11, 1990). At conference, the Senate had agreed to most of the language changes proposed by the House, but there were a few areas of ongoing disagreement. Senator Ford moved to have the conference report language with respect to remedies against the Senate replaced by the language approved the previous day with regard to the Civil Rights Act of 1990.[198] Harkin accepted the Ford amendment, given the vote of the previous day, although he indicated his continued preference for an approach under which a private right of action against the Senate would be available.[199] Given that the Senate-remedy issue had been resolved, Harkin indicated that the remaining point of disagreement concerning the conference report involved the food-handling situation.

Hatch proposed an amendment to resolve the food-handling controversy. Under the amendment, the secretary of health and human services would publish a list of "infectious and communicable diseases which are transmitted through the handling [of] the food supply."[200] Also under the amendment, a restaurant could not discharge someone merely because of public fears and misperceptions about the contagiousness of a disease. For a restaurant to act adversely, the CDC must have indicated that there was a genuine risk of contagiousness. The amendment "is not based on fear. It is based on sound science."[201]

Helms opposed the Hatch amendment, asserting that it would "gut the Chapman amendment."[202] Dole supported the Hatch amendment (with one minor language change that Hatch accepted). In supporting the Hatch amendment, Dole specifically mentioned that the ADA covers people with mental retardation, cerebral palsy, deafness, blindness, or HIV infection.[203] Like everyone else who commented on the food-handling amendment, Dole presumed that individuals with HIV infection were covered by the ADA. Ultimately, the Hatch amendment passed on a vote of 99 to 1, with only Helms voting against it.[204] Before the Senate completed its discussion of this matter, Dole and Hatch had a colloquy in which Hatch agreed that HIV infection would be one of the diseases the CDC would consider including in its list of diseases that could be spread through the food supply. Because the Senate had not accepted all the language from the conference report, a second conference was necessary.

XI. The Second Conference Report

Following the instructions from the House and Senate conferees, there was a second conference report.[205] The House receded to the Senate version of the food-handling amendment. With respect to coverage of the Senate, the House receded to the Senate version with a minor amendment. The bill then went to both houses for final approval. The bill, along with the second conference report, appeared in the *Congressional Record*.[206]

Representative William Dannemeyer (R-Calif.) spoke on the floor of the House in opposition to the rule that was supposed to govern consideration of the ADA. He indicated that he had repeatedly requested an amendment to the ADA that would have excluded individuals with communicable diseases from coverage; the amendment was defeated.[207] Representative Burton also opposed the bill because of the scope of the definition of disability: "There [are] going to be about 900 classes of disabled or handicapped people because of this bill, 900; 46 million people are going to fall under the definition of handicapped or disabled, 46 million. That is one out of every five Americans who is going to be considered disabled or handicapped."[208] He also objected to the removal of the Chapman amendment. "The AIDS virus is a time bomb ticking that will explode in the future. We have made it even more volatile because we are allowing people with active AIDS to work in close proximity to patients and to handle food."[209] Despite these two objections, the House approved the rule for debate by a vote of 355 to 58, with 19 members not voting.[210]

The House considered the second conference report. Representative Augustus Hawkins (D-Calif.) described the final bill as a compromise:

> The conference report which we consider today is also a compromise. When we went to conference on the bill, there were a substantial number of differences, over 80, between the House and Senate versions. Almost without exception, these differences were resolved in favor of the House position. I want to stress this again, that the Senate receded on almost every point of difference, particularly to those which amended the Senate-passed bill with provisions deemed important to business or other private interests.

With respect to the provision dealing with placement of individuals in food handling positions, the House receded to the Senate provision which was the result of a bipartisan and unequivocal compromise fashioned by Senator Hatch. The House also receded to the Senate provision concerning the applicability of the legislation to Senate employees.[211]

In the discussion of the food-handling issue, various representatives said that they preferred the Chapman amendment to the Hatch amendment, but they did not want to hold up final passage of the ADA over this relatively minor issue. They noted that the ADA affected many individuals with disabilities who do not have HIV and do not have jobs in the food-handling industry. Passage of the ADA was needed to protect the larger category of individuals with disabilities.

Representative DeLay then raised the relief issue. He noted that the 1990 Civil Rights Act was being considered by Congress, and under that bill, individuals who bring suit under Title VII of the Civil Rights Act of 1964 could attain punitive and compensatory damages. Because the ADA borrows Title VII's enforcement scheme, the effect of that legislation would be to incorporate punitive and compensatory damages into the ADA. Although Hawkins had described the bill as a compromise, DeLay disagreed. He argued that the bill was too proplaintiff:

> I think that this bill is probably the most closed piece of legislation that I have ever seen and ever witnessed and ever been a part of in my 12 years in the legislative body. Because of support from the White House for the bill, the Democrats for this bill and many of the Republicans for this bill, Members of this House on committees and in the full House have had the political cover to resist any reasonable amendments to this bill.[212]

Representative Burton also spoke against the bill, complaining about its broad scope:

> [T]hey tell us there are going to be 43 million plus people defined as handicapped or disabled by this bill. That is one out of five or six Americans. When we start talking about the massive amounts of litigation this is going to cause over the next few years, just think about what that is

going to do to the economy and the commerce of this Nation. It is going to cause severe problems.[213]

At the end of the debate, Dannemeyer moved that the conference report be recommitted with instructions to adopt the Chapman amendment. That motion failed by a vote of 180 to 224, with 28 members not voting.[214] The House then voted on the ADA itself. The vote was 377 to 28, with 27 members not voting. (Ford, who had participated extensively in the debate, did not vote.)

The Senate then took up consideration of the conference report. Kennedy agreed with Representative Hawkins's description of the legislation.

> During the process, the House made a number of modifications in the Senate bill to clarify certain aspects of the legislation and to allay the opposition of the business community. The House has been productive in its deliberations and has included the disability community in shaping its refinements. Senate conferees have accepted almost all of these clarifications.[215]

After further debate, which mostly consisted of senators acknowledging the hard work that underlay enactment of the ADA, the bill passed the Senate on July 13, 1990, by a vote of 91 to 6 with 3 members not voting. The president signed the bill into law on July 26, 1990.

The president's signing statement correctly described the agreements reached under the ADA. He expected the ADA to be interpreted consistently with the Rehabilitation Act, which had been in effect for seventeen years. Business interests were protected by phase-in periods and cost defenses. No mention was made by the president or any member of Congress of protecting the business community through a narrow definition of disability. Instead, the president predicted that the ADA "promises to open up all aspects of American life to individuals with disabilities—employment opportunities, government services, public accommodations, transportation, and telecommunications."[216]

XII. Conclusion

What do we learn from this legislative history? At least four important points emerge. First, the committee reports were considered extensively and relied upon as an accurate statement of the meaning of the ADA. Whenever members quoted from the committee reports, there was agreement that the principles in the reports reflected the intent of Congress. There was no attempt whatsoever to hide controversial items like the coverage of individuals with HIV-infection in the bill. The courts made some of these issues more difficult to resolve by ignoring this legislative history. Although it may be true that legislative history can be sneaky and conniving, the ADA's history reflects a very open and honest legislative debate. Ignoring this material is disrespectful to Congress's hard work.

Second, it is clear that Congress had a very strong intent to use the ADA to help respond to the AIDS crisis. One historical origin of the ADA was the President's Commission on HIV Infection. In the key committee reports and in comments by the key sponsors (as well as detractors), it was acknowledged that the ADA would cover individuals who are HIV-positive. The courts, by contrast, have acted as if it were hard to discern Congress's intent on this issue.

Third, proponents and opponents of the ADA understood the definition of disability to have a very broad scope. The proponents proudly proclaimed that the bill would cover more than 43 million Americans with disabilities. The opponents complained that the bill covered 900 categories of disabilities, which encompassed one in five Americans. There were some attempts to narrow the definition of disability by, for example, excluding individuals with contagious diseases or individuals with a history of drug abuse. None of these efforts succeeded. The compromises that were achieved with respect to the ADA involved further protections for the business community by phasing in its coverage and limiting remedies that could be sought against it under ADA Title III. The definition of disability, however, was not a source of compromise except to exclude certain categories of individuals such as homosexuals, whom the bill's supporters never claimed the bill covered.

The primary source of controversy under the ADA was an exemption for restaurants so that they could fail to employ individuals who were HIV-positive. The Senate succeeded in obtaining the language it desired. It refused to permit restaurants to fail to hire individuals who are HIV-positive merely out of unfounded fears that they might infect the food supply. Hatch was crucial in holding the line against AIDS hysteria.

There were predictions by a small minority of senators that the judiciary would find the ADA to be a vague document that is hard to interpret. The predictions turned out to be accurate because the judiciary has refused to consider the documents that Congress created to clarify its intentions. It has insisted that the plain language resolves all controversies rather than interpreting the ADA in the context of its two years of consideration. Justice Sandra Day O'Connor may choose to blame Congress for this state of affairs; I argue that the blame lies with a judiciary that has refused to educate itself about the history of the statute.

Last, we learn that in 1990 even liberal members of Congress knew that there was no chance that a federal statute could be used to protect sexual minorities. But there was also en interesting policy question for the gay rights community of whether it should even *seek* to fight the exclusions because the American Psychiatric Association has taken the position, since the 1970s, that being gay, lesbian, or bisexual is *not* a mental health impairment.

In an ideal world, the gay community would have fought these exclusions because the manner in which the exclusions were considered was offensive. As written, the ADA lumps gay men, lesbians, and bisexuals with "voyeurs," as if these groups have something in common. The language concerning transvestites and transsexualism is also extremely derogatory. Transvestite and transsexual individuals are lumped with individuals who have "sexual behavior disorders." Certainly, many individuals who are transgendered do not consider themselves to have a "sexual behavior disorder." Additionally, transvestites are excluded from coverage twice, in section 12,208 and in section 12,211. That redundancy is itself derogatory because it highlights the legislators' extreme desire to prevent this group from having legal protection. In sum, the language is deeply insulting to sexual minorities even if we agree that they should have no claim for coverage under the ADA. But with the right wing clamoring about the "sodomy lobby," there was no room in which to argue that the exclusions were harmful and degrading. The best that the gay rights community was able to achieve was to take "homosexuality" and "bisexuality" out of the sentence that listed "sexual behavior disorders." This was not much of a victory.

The articulated homophobia during the ADA's consideration was standard fare during legislative debate at that time. Senator Helms made repeated homophobic comments as Congress considered the AIDS Control Act of 1989, and during consideration of the Ryan White CARE Act, he argued that federal funds should be used to assist only women and children, not homosexuals. Helms also blamed the "homosexual community" for the AIDS epidemic. His comments were so inappropriate that Senator Hatch felt compelled to respond to correct his errors. Nonetheless, no one suggested that Helms be reprimanded or censured because of his homophobic comments.

One must wonder if anything has really changed in society. Would those comments be tolerated today? Or might homophobic remarks be considered as inappropriate as are racially insensitive remarks? On December 5, 2002, former Senate Republican leader Trent Lott (R-Miss.) publicly stated that Republicans should have endorsed South Carolina Senator Strom Thurmond's segregationist bid in 1948 for the presidency. Although President George W. Bush initially declined to comment, within a week he sharply criticized Lott, saying his remarks did not reflect the beliefs of the Republican Party. By December 20, Lott had stepped down from the party leadership role.

Approximately five months later, Senator Rick Santorum (R-Pa.) made the following comment regarding the Supreme Court's decision in *Lawrence v. Texas*:

> If the Supreme Court says that you have the right to consensual [gay] sex within your home, then you have the right to bigamy, you have the right to polygamy, you have the right to incest, you have the right to adultery, you have the right to do anything.[217]

The president refused to criticize Santorum for his remarks and, instead, said, "The president has confidence in the senator and believes he's doing a good job as senator." Senator Lincoln Chafee (R-R.I.) deplored Santorum's remarks, as did the Log Cabin Republicans. Otherwise, Republicans stood behind Santorum. There were no calls for his resignation. Although Santorum clarified his comments later, "I have no problem with homosexuality. I have a problem with homosexual acts," he saw no need to offer an apology.

So where have we come with respect to sensitivity on issues of civil rights? There might not be an ADA but for President Reagan's insensitive comments about the mental health of Senator Michael Dukakis. Those remarks helped spur presidential candidate Bush to endorse the concept of the ADA, and later, to instruct his attorney general to seek its passage in Congress. Further, there might not be strong protection for individuals with HIV infection were not some conservative Republicans, like Hatch, aware of the importance of nondiscrimination protection for this class of individuals. But homophobia still can underlie Congress's handiwork. A decade after enactment of the ADA, there is little sign that such blatant homophobia has abated in Congress.

3

ADA Title I
An Empirical Investigation

When Congress was considering the ADA, it heard considerable testimony about the poverty rate and unemployment problems of individuals with disabilities. Such persons have been and continue to be one of the poorest groups in society.

Only 32 percent of people with disabilities are employed full- or part-time compared with 81 percent of individuals without disabilities.[1] Two-thirds of unemployed persons with disabilities report that they would prefer to be working. Twenty-nine percent of people with disabilities are living in poverty (household incomes of $15,000 or less), compared with 10 percent of the nondisabled population. People with disabilities also lag in education. Twenty-two percent of individuals with disabilities fail to complete high school, compared with 9 percent of the nondisabled population. Twelve percent of individuals with disabilities graduate from college, compared with 23 percent of the nondisabled population. People with disabilities are more than twice as likely to postpone needed health care because they cannot afford it (28 percent compared with 12 percent). Access to transportation is also a greater problem for people with disabilities than others (30 percent versus 10 percent).

Some people may have naively thought that enactment of the ADA would begin to correct the economic imbalance. No study has been able to establish that the ADA has had any positive impact on the employability or poverty rate of individuals with disabilities. Daron Acemoglu and Joshua Angrist have sought to investigate the effectiveness of the ADA by examining data from the March Current Population Survey (CPS) for 1988–1997.[2] Their data show a post-ADA decline in the relative employment of men and women with disabilities aged 21–39, with no change in relative wages. The deterioration began when the ADA went into effect, two years after passage. Similarly, Thomas DeLeire sought to assess the impact of the ADA on men with disabilities using data from the Survey of Income and Program Participation.[3] Like Acemoglu and Angrist, he found a decline in the relative employment rates of men following passage of the ADA but that the trend began in 1990, two years before ADA Title I became effective. Christine Jolls has argued that the ADA's "accommodation mandates" have contributed to the declining employment rate for individuals with disabilities in the 1990s by raising the apparent cost of hiring individuals with disabilities.[4]

The situation for individuals with disabilities was very grim in 1990 and continues to be grim, more than a decade after the ADA became effective. It was naive of Congress or others to have expected that the ADA would have a significant impact on the employment patterns of individuals with disabilities. People are able to benefit from ADA Title I only if they are both "disabled" and "qualified" for employment. Because the courts have narrowly construed the definition of "disability" in conflict with Congress's intent in enacting the ADA, few of the 11.3 million working-age adults with disabilities qualify for ADA protection. Moreover, nearly every state had a law banning employment discrimination against individuals with disabilities before the ADA was enacted in 1990. In the employment area, the ADA simply created a uniform national standard but did not necessarily raise the existing standard above the one already imposed by state law.

More fundamentally, the ADA is only an antidiscrimination statute. It does not deal with the fundamental aspects of many individual's lives that may lead to poverty. Discrimination may be one factor that contributes to poverty, but it is not the most significant factor cited by individuals with disabilities for the problems they experience finding or maintaining suitable employment.

The Urban Institute commissioned a study in 2001 to better understand what exactly are the barriers to employment faced by individuals with disabilities.[5] Of the six factors that individuals with disabilities cite as creating barriers to work, discrimination was only a minor factor. The other factors included

—not aware of any available jobs due to social isolation
—family responsibilities
—lack of transportation
—lack of adequate training
—fear of loss of benefits, such as Medicaid or SSDI

Some columnists have described the ADA as producing an inappropriate windfall for plaintiffs. Ruth Shalit, for example, asserted that the ADA was creating a "lifelong buffet of perks, special breaks and procedural protections" for people with questionable disabilities.[6]

What is the truth? Has the ADA been relatively useless in improving the employability of individuals with disabilities? Or has it been a windfall for ADA plaintiffs? The ADA has had little or no impact on the overall employability of individuals with disabilities. In addition, as we will see, ADA plaintiffs have fared very poorly in the courts of appeals. Nonetheless, the ADA has benefitted some ADA plaintiffs, and we should not overgeneralize from the appellate statistics to conclude that virtually no ADA plaintiffs ever succeed.

Unfortunately, commentators have misused win-loss statistics in discussing the effectiveness of the ADA. In reaction to the claims by Shalit and others that the ADA was generating a windfall for plaintiffs, I collected some statistics on appellate cases that suggest that plaintiffs were faring very poorly in appellate litigation.[7] From my data and data collected by the American Bar Association, the media and various academics began reporting that plaintiffs were losing more than 90 percent of ADA cases at the trial court level.[8] Unfortunately, these accounts were as inaccurate as the original accounts of a windfall for plaintiffs. The pendulum first swung extremely in one direction, with the media declaring that the ADA was creating a lifelong buffet of perks for plaintiffs and then swung extremely in the other direction with the media declaring that ADA plaintiffs rarely win.

This chapter will attempt to provide some balance to these two extreme accounts of win-loss rates under the ADA. Conservative Supreme Court decisions have certainly prevented many plaintiffs from prevailing under the ADA and may have caused employees to become more cautious in even filing charges of discrimination under the ADA. Nonetheless, there is some evidence that plaintiffs are prevailing in roughly one-third of ADA cases when their cases get to the jury (or a judge in a bench trial). The primary problem for plaintiffs at the trial court level is that they lose their cases at the summary judgment stage. Judges frequently grant motions by defendants for summary judgment, precluding their cases from ever getting to the jury. Although plaintiffs may fare reasonably well before juries, they fare very poorly before judges at the summary judgment stage.

An important note of caution is that win-loss data are not the only way to think about litigation outcomes. Win-loss data are affected by settlement decisions. Successful settlement outcomes are beneficial to plaintiffs but are not counted in judicial-outcome statistics. Nonetheless, settlement decisions are made in the shadow of litigation outcomes. Lawyers can be expected to watch litigation outcomes closely in deciding which cases to take and which cases to settle, as well as which cases to take to trial. If all the reported cases, for example, are prodefendant, then we would expect the plaintiff bar to respond by being very cautious in accepting new cases. Moreover, we would expect the defense bar to take a firm stance in settlements. Thus, win-loss data tell an incomplete story but may have a profound impact on litigation conduct, including settlement negotiations. I will examine the available settlement data.

In addition to win-loss data, it is also interesting to consider the third question: which factors predict a successful outcome for plaintiffs? What are the characteristics that a lawyer might identify as predictive of a successful judicial outcome? In this chapter, I will report the results of a regression analysis to consider which factors predict successful judicial outcomes at the appellate level.

Before considering the available win-loss data under the ADA, one needs to understand the ADA's enforcement process. The ADA has a complex enforcement scheme that complicates empirical analysis. The ADA is divided into three main titles, each of which has its own enforcement scheme. ADA Title I is the employment provision of the act. Modeled after Title VII of the Civil Rights Act of 1964, it requires all complaining parties to file a charge of discrimination with the Equal Employment Opportunity Commission (EEOC) before receiving a right-to-sue letter. The EEOC has a statutory obligation to seek to resolve complaints amicably before the right-to-sue letter is issued. Hence, settlement attempts are an important part of ADA Title I enforcement. Nonetheless, most of the reported litigation under the ADA has been under ADA Title I.

ADA Title I lends itself to empirical analysis because the EEOC reports some data with respect to the conciliation process. Further, trial court outcomes under ADA Title I are reported, along with other civil rights employment discrimination cases, in the data made available by the U.S. Administrative Office. It is therefore possible to track, in part, the resolution of ADA Title I cases from the stage of filing a complaint to resolution in a federal court. (ADA cases can also be filed in state courts, but there is no easy way to track the resolution of those cases.)

To assess the effectiveness of ADA Title I, one would ideally have access to all judicial outcomes and settlements under the statute. Because of the administrative apparatus that exists under ADA Title I, which seeks to encourage voluntary resolution of complaints, it seems particularly important to have access to settlement data, along with trial and appellate data. As I will discuss below, however, problems exist with settlement, trial, and appellate data. In this chapter, I will assess what we can learn from each of these information sources.

Part I of this chapter will present the available settlement data. Part II will discuss trial court data. Part III will discuss appellate data.

I. Settlement Data

Detailed settlement data are virtually impossible to acquire. As a condition of settlement, parties often insist upon confidentiality. Only the U.S. Department of Justice (DOJ) has a policy of making settlements publicly available, but DOJ plays a limited role in enforcing ADA Title I. The EEOC plays a significant role in the settlement process and makes some data available to the public, but the data give us only a limited snapshot of the settlement process. Because this is the only reliable source of information on settlement, however, it deserves our attention.

As stated above, all claimants must file charges with the EEOC before having a right to sue in federal court. The EEOC reports charge statistics on its Web site.[9] It has charge data available from the date the ADA became effective—July 26, 1992–September 30, 2002. This reflects approximately the first decade of enforcement data. Table 3.1 summarizes the data for the first decade of EEOC enforcement activity.

Table 3.1 shows that the EEOC's conciliation efforts were particularly successful in the first two fiscal years of statutory enforcement when the employment sector was adjusting to new legal requirements. After that, the success rate dropped consistently. It reached its lowest point in FY 1997, and rose slightly over the next five years. During the last three fiscal years, it hovered around 17 percent. Other than the first two years, those are the highest success rates since the enactment of the statute.

There appears to be an inverse correlation between the average monetary value of a successful charge and the number of successful charges. When the successful charge rate rises, the average monetary value declines, and vice versa. Hence, the years with the highest percentage success rate corresponded with the years with the lowest dollar value per successful charge.

TABLE 3.1.
EEOC ADA Title I Conciliation Process, FY 1992–FY 2002

Fiscal Year	Resolutions	Unsuccessful	Successful	Benefits (in millions of dollars)	Benefits/ Successful Charge (in dollars)
1992	88	70	18 (20.5%)	0.2	11,111
1993	4,502	3,457	1,045 (23.2%)	15.9	15,215
1994	12,523	10,542	1,981 (15.8%)	32.6	16,456
1995	18,900	16,729	2,171 (11.5%)	38.7	17,825
1996	23,451	21,290	2,161 (9.2%)	45.5	21,055
1997	24,200	21,927	2,273 (9.4%)	41.3	18,170
1998	23,324	20,819	2,505 (10.7%)	53.7	21,437
1999	22,152	19,334	2,818 (12.7%)	55.8	19,801
2000	20,475	17,098	3,377 (16.5%)	54.4	16,109
2001	19,084	15,787	3,297 (17.3%)	47.9	14,528
2002	18,804	15,622	3,182 (16.9%)	50.0	15,713
Total	187,503	162,675	24,828 (13.2%)	436.0	17,561

The number of successful resolutions has been falling slightly since 1997. The number of resolutions in 2002 was comparable to the number of resolutions in 1995.

When one looks at all these data, the following story emerges. It appears that plaintiffs became more selective in the second five years of enforcement in deciding whether to file charges of discrimination. That increased selectivity may have been a result of (accurate) media reports that the Supreme Court rendered numerous decisions that limited the scope of the statute. In particular, the Court narrowly interpreted the definition of disability. As plaintiffs became more selective in deciding whether to file charges of discrimination, they began to attain a higher success rate. Nonetheless, the dollar value of their charges declined.

It is hard to know why the dollar value of the average charge declined while plaintiffs became more selective in deciding what types of cases to file. Possibly, the dollar value declined because the defense bar became more aggressive about its litigation posture. Because parties settle in light of their expectations about judicial outcomes, the defense bar may have gained increasing confidence that judicial outcomes would be prodefendant; hence, it may make less-generous offers through settlement to avoid litigation.

Overall, the settlement data reflect that employers often settle ADA lawsuits for very modest amounts. A lawyer who has a contingency arrangement with his or her client is not likely to recoup his or her expenses with settlements around a $15,000 figure. A one-third contingency arrangement would yield only $5,000, which is not likely to finance more than very modest pretrial discovery.

A key benefit of the EEOC conciliation process is that charging parties can attain monetary settlements without hiring a lawyer. Of the 187,000 individuals who filed charges of discrimination with the EEOC in the first decade, 24,000 potentially attained the benefits of this free conciliation process. (Charging parties, however, are permitted to use an attorney during the EEOC conciliation process, and there is no way to know what percentage of the 24,000 claimants used paid attorneys.) Approximately 13 percent of individuals who file complaints with the EEOC may have benefitted from this conciliation process.

In sum, the EEOC conciliation process seems to encourage modest settlement results for 13 percent of the charging parties. These data reflect only settlements as part of the EEOC conciliation process. It is hard to estimate from these data whether private parties attain better outcomes, or more frequent, positive outcomes in their private settlement attempts.

II. Trial Court Outcomes

A. EEOC Litigation Outcomes

If the EEOC conciliation process is unsuccessful, then a charging party can receive a right-to-sue letter and file suit in federal (or state) court. In addition, when the EEOC finds reasonable cause, it may file a lawsuit on behalf of the charging party. The EEOC reports the results of its litigation activity. It is somewhat harder to collect data for lawsuits filed by private parties. Table 3.2 reflects that the EEOC has had an uneven record of filing ADA cases in court on behalf of plaintiffs. The commission's report of August 13, 2002, speaks of the situation:

> The number of suits alleging disability discrimination dropped in fiscal years 1999 . . . and 2000 . . . from a high in fiscal years 1997 . . . and 1998. . . . This drop is directly related to the Supreme Court's decisions in June 1999 in *Sutton v. United Airlines; Murphy v. UPS* and *Albert-sons, Inc. v. Kirkingburg*, in which the Court narrowed the definition of disability. . . . In the aftermath of these three decisions, the agency refocused its efforts and analysis of Americans with Disabilities Act (ADA) cases and has gradually rebuilt the litigation program.[10]

TABLE 3.2.
EEOC Litigation, FY 1992 through FY 2002

Fiscal Year	Direct ADA Lawsuits by EEOC
1992	0
1993	3
1994	34
1995	81
1996	38
1997	79
1998	79
1999	51
2000	23
2001	62
2002	41
Total	491

Although the EEOC filed fewer ADA cases after the Supreme Court's three decisions concerning the definition of disability, it continued to have a relatively high conciliation success rate in fiscal year 2000. Fiscal year 2001 is the most remarkable because the EEOC filed a significantly increased number of cases in court while also attaining a relatively high success rate through conciliation. The phenomenon could be explained by the fact that plaintiffs had already modified their behavior in light of the Court decisions narrowing the definition of disability. We have seen above that plaintiffs have modified their behavior by becoming more cautious in filing charges of discrimination with the EEOC. The EEOC may therefore have been trying to seek to resolve more-meritorious claims.

The EEOC litigation data reflect that the EEOC has not engaged in a great deal of litigation activity at the trial court level to enforce ADA Title I. Because thousands of lawsuits have been filed each year under ADA Title I, EEOC's enforcement activity probably reflects less than 10 percent of the ADA litigation (discussed below). Nonetheless, it is useful to examine the EEOC's success rate to ascertain the effectiveness of its litigation enforcement efforts.

The EEOC filed 491 lawsuits out of the 11,932 cases in which it found reasonable cause to believe that discrimination occurred. It does not provide direct tracking data for the 491 cases. Of the cases that did not result in consent decrees or settlements, it reported that 86 resulted in a favorable court order; 111 in an unfavorable court order; and 33 in a voluntary dismissal. Because consent decrees and settlement agreements are separately reported, I have to assume that the 33 cases that resulted in a voluntary dismissal would have resulted in an unfavorable court order had the EEOC not agreed to a dismissal. Characterizing the 33 voluntary dismissals as unfavorable court orders, then, results in a 37.4 percent success rate for the EEOC in cases that it took to trial during that time period.

The EEOC's success rate appears to be somewhat higher than the success rate for private plaintiffs (see below), although we can only estimate the success rate for private parties based on the limited data available. The EEOC's relatively high success rate makes sense when one considers that the EEOC gets "first crack" at all ADA cases. Because it screens those cases, it can determine which are most likely to result in favorable outcomes and pursue such cases through litigation. Further, as a government agency, the EEOC might be entitled to more respect than a private plaintiff who seeks to enforce the ADA.

Nonetheless, the results are also somewhat surprising. Although the EEOC has the "first crack" at cases, it also has a reputation for trying to pursue controversial claims in furtherance of the public interest. Because the EEOC does not receive attorney's fees under contingency fee arrangements, or as the prevailing party, it has fewer incentives than does the private bar to pursue only cases that appear to be meritorious. Further, the notion that the EEOC gets heightened deference or respect in trial courts is not consistent the EEOC's general treatment by the judiciary. As I have reported elsewhere, the courts are not typically deferential to the EEOC's policy positions as reflected in the regulations that the EEOC promulgates to enforce the ADA and other statutes.[11] Possibly, the EEOC receives more respect as attorneys than as policy makers. Finally, it is worth noting that the EEOC brings an enforcement action only if it finds "reasonable cause" to believe that discrimination has occurred. Private parties are not limited to that category of case. Hence, the EEOC is potentially bringing lawsuits in a more narrow band of cases than is the private bar. The EEOC data certainly suggest that charging parties benefit from the EEOC's enforcement efforts and that the defense bar should take seriously the possibility that the EEOC might bring an enforcement action.

B. Other Trial Court Data

1. DATA OF THE ADMINISTRATIVE OFFICE OF THE UNITED STATES COURTS

So far, I have discussed data collected by the EEOC. Two other sources are available to estimate overall trial court outcomes under the ADA: (1)

data made available by the Administrative Office of the United States Courts, and (2) data made available by the American Bar Association.

The Administrative Office of the United States Courts makes available data for all completed employment discrimination cases.[12] It also provides the plaintiff win rate for these cases. The employment discrimination category includes Title VII of the Civil Rights Act of 1964, the Age Discrimination in Employment Act, the Equal Pay Act, and Title I of the ADA. Completed cases include cases decided by summary devices in advance of trial, such as dismissals or successful motions for summary judgment, in addition to completed trials in which a decision was rendered by a jury or judge (in a bench trial). These data are available only through 2000. The Administrative Office makes data available for all completed cases, as well as all completed trials. From those data, one can calculate the results for cases that are completed through pretrial summary devices (rather than through completed trials). Table 3.3 reports the Administrative Office data for all completed cases, as well as completed trials, for 1992 through 2000 in employment discrimination cases.

Table 3.3 presents data for all employment discrimination cases, not only ADA cases. Even so, the data are indicative of two important trends during the time period. First, they show the importance of considering all case outcomes—not simply trials—in assessing the plaintiff win/loss rate. If we focused on only completed trials, we would conclude that plaintiffs had a 33.8 percent win rate in employment discrimination cases. If we also considered only cases decided through summary devices, the plaintiff win rate would be 13.3 percent. Moreover, we see that only a small percentage (18 percent) of all cases result in completed trials.

Second, the data reflect a trend over time for more cases to be decided by summary devices rather than by completed trials. In the final year for which statistics are available, only 10.7 percent of cases were resolved by completed trials. The trend is very important to plaintiffs because they fare much worse through the use of summary devices than completed trials. Unfortunately, the data are for all employment discrimination cases, rather than for only ADA cases. Accordingly, there is no way to know from the data if ADA cases correspond to the general trends found for employment discrimination cases.

Finally, it is worth noting that the overall plaintiff win rate for completed trials in all employment discrimination cases during this time period is comparable to the win rate reported by the EEOC during this time period for its ADA cases. (The EEOC win rate is modestly higher but in

TABLE 3.3.
Completed Employment Discrimination Cases, 1992–2000

Year	Plaintiff Win Rate, All Completed Cases	Plaintiff Win Rate, Completed Trials (Bench Trial or Jury Verdict)	Plaintiff Win Rate, Cases Resolved through Summary Devices
1992	20.0% (669 of 3,345)	29.3% (194 of 663)	17.7% (475 of 2,682)
1993	15.9% (478 of 3,005)	28.0% (195 of 697)	12.2% (283 of 2,308)
1994	14.9% (509 of 3,419)	31.2% (258 of 826)	9.7% (251 of 2,593)
1995	13.0% (511 of 3,942)	32.0% (274 of 855)	7.7% (237 of 3,087)
1996	12.9% (613 of 4,746)	35.5% (337 of 950)	7.3% (276 of 3,796)
1997	12.4% (646 of 5,199)	36.6% (358 of 979)	6.8% (288 of 4,220)
1998	11.5% (665 of 5,771)	36.5% (327 of 897)	6.9% (338 of 4,874)
1999	12.3% (702 of 5,725)	35.9% (306 of 852)	8.1% (396 of 4,873)
2000	11.1% (607 of 5,400)	37.2% (215 of 578)	8.1% (392 of 4,822)
Total	13.3% (5,400 of 40,552)	33.8% (2,464 of 7,297)	8.8% (2,936 of 33,255)

the same range.) We therefore have two independent sources confirming that if cases go to trial, plaintiffs have a reasonable chance of prevailing in ADA litigation. The problem for ADA plaintiffs appears to be the high percentage of cases that are resolved adversely through a summary device. This problem will be discussed further in chapter 4.

2. AMERICAN BAR ASSOCIATION DATA

The American Bar Association reported data that were available through on-line searches, particularly Westlaw and various media outlets.[13] It shared with me its trial court data from the first five years of judicial enforcement. The ABA had found that plaintiffs prevailed in 45 of 615 (7.3 percent) cases decided during the earlier time period, a much lower figure than one would estimate from the EEOC data or the Administrative Office database.

On closer examination, however, the ABA data suggest some selection-bias problems; more than half of the cases in the sample were decided by a trial on the merits. Yet, the Administrative Office data suggest that only 18 percent of all employment cases are decided by a completed trial. It is highly unlikely that ADA data differ significantly from this trend for all employment discrimination cases. Why is the ABA reporting such a high rate of completed trials for ADA cases? The answer stems from the problem of what kinds of cases get made available to the public through an electronic source—the public's primary tool for data collection. Trial court judges do not publish every disposition that is readily made available to the public. Summary dismissals often go unreported, as does the entry of a trial court verdict. The 615 cases collected by the ABA appear to be a very small slice of all ADA trial court outcomes for this time period. Based on the Administrative Office data, I estimate that there were 25,000 employment discrimination cases brought during this time period. ADA cases probably account for one-fourth of that number of cases—roughly 6,250. The ABA is therefore probably collecting data on only 10 percent of those cases. Disproportionately, it is collecting data on cases in which a decision was rendered by a bench trial or a jury trial and the judge entered a decision that was made publicly available.

What is odd about the ABA data, however, is that they are biased toward cases that are decided as a result of a completed trial; this should have *raised* the plaintiff win rate because the previous data suggest that plaintiffs typically fare relatively well in completed trials. Possibly, other selection-bias problems exist with the ABA data set. Judges may be more inclined to write opinions that are made available to the public when defendants, rather than plaintiffs, prevail. If a jury renders a favorable verdict for a plaintiff, there may be little reason for a judge to write an opinion. He or she will simply enter the verdict. But when a judge makes a ruling as a matter of law, he or she often has an obligation to issue an opinion. Legal rulings may tend to be more prodefendant than trial verdicts; by skewing the sample toward legal rulings, the ABA may have skewed the sample toward defendants.

The ABA data, however, do accurately reflect the information commonly available to lawyers about ADA outcomes. Because attorneys settle cases in light of what they can expect from litigation, the data may be giving plaintiffs' attorneys an unreasonably pessimistic attitude about litigation outcomes. Similarly, the data may cause the defense bar to feel unduly optimistic about its prospects at trial and lead to its taking a firm stance during settlement discussions.

III. *Appellate Outcomes*

A. Introduction

Trial court data give us only one perspective on the litigation process. Another perspective is the appellate perspective. Appellate cases set precedent and therefore influence behavior at the trial court level. In addition, courts of appeals most likely publish a higher percentage of their cases than do trial court judges because of their responsibility to create precedent. Settlement is also a somewhat lesser factor at the appellate level because the parties have already completed a trial process without settlement.

I decided to analyze appellate outcomes under the ADA by coding the appellate cases made available through Westlaw from 1992 through 1999. I generally coded these cases to calculate win-loss rates for plaintiffs, and additionally, to ascertain, through a logistic regression analysis, which factors predict a successful outcome for plaintiffs.

A victory on appeal means the reversal of the trial court decision. Sometimes, a remand will still be necessary, so the party is not assured a final victory. Nonetheless, the reversal of the trial court decision is certainly a victory for the party that brings the appeal (the "appellant").

I generally found that defendants are far more likely to attain a reversal on appeal than are plaintiffs. Defendants attained a reversal in 27 of 45 (60 percent) of the cases in my database; plaintiffs attained a reversal in 81 of 675 (12 percent) of the cases in my database. To determine if those results are statistically significant, I performed a Chi-square analysis of the differing rates of reversal for plaintiffs and defendants on appeals. The difference in reversal rates for plaintiffs and defendants was highly significant ($p < 0.01$). Because the significance level is below 0.001, factors other than chance should account for the differential success rate for the two cohorts on appeal.

When Professor Marc A. Franklin found a similar trend in defamation litigation, he concluded that such a differential result was surprising because "trial judges generally tend to rule in favor of defendants at pretrial stages to avoid possibly needless trial and to clear calendars of doubtful cases. If that were true, one would expect a lower affirmance rate in rulings for defendants than in cases in which trial judges rule for plaintiffs."[14]

Franklin, however, assumes that trial court judges have more of a docket-clearing motive than appellate court judges do, so that they would be more likely than appellate judges to render prodefendant outcomes. An appellate court judge, however, may have the same interest in docket clearing as a trial court judge, thereby making summary affirmances a popular device. Because summary affirmances tend to reflect affirmances of prodefendant trial court outcomes, it may not be surprising that the prodefendant bias in the trial courts is replicated in the appellate courts.

Although the overall win-loss statistics do suggest that plaintiffs are faring badly in the appellate courts, a closer examination of the statistics shows that defendants are rarely appealing cases from the trial courts. Only 45 of 720 (6 percent) of the cases in my database reflect situations in which the defendant appealed a proplaintiff outcome at trial. Researchers have mistakenly concluded from this statistic that my data reflect that plaintiffs won only 6 percent of the cases at trial.[15] In fact, there is no way to estimate the plaintiff win rate at trial from these statistics because my sample includes only cases in which a party decided to appeal an adverse trial court outcome and the appellate court made its decision available to the public. One can note only that defendants rarely appeal proplaintiff outcomes from the trial court. It is possible that the higher defendant win rate on appeal may be explained by the fact that defendants are more cautious than plaintiffs in filtering cases for appeal. Because defendants are usually paying their lawyers on an hourly basis, they may have more financial incentive to pursue only strong cases. By contrast, once a plaintiff's lawyer has assumed the financial risk of taking a case to trial, it may seem worthwhile to pursue the appellate process if a trial outcome is not satisfactory. If the appeal is *pro se*, it is virtually costless to the plaintiff. Even if a plaintiff has retained counsel, he or she may not incur any additional cost if there is a contingency fee arrangement. Thus, defendants may be deterred from pursuing appeals by built-in factors that do not affect plaintiffs. The huge disparity between the number of appeals by plaintiffs and defendants may reflect these differing incentives.

B. Comparison with Other Areas of the Law

I have compared my ADA data to data from comparable areas of law to see if such prodefendant results are typical in appellate litigation. Other researchers have collected data on published decisions in other areas of the law, such as defamation, nonprisoner constitutional tort litigation, prisoner constitutional tort litigation, and a control group of non-civil-rights litigation. The data did not include Title VII data for my time period of investigation. Consequently, I created a small data set to supplement the data made available by others to compare ADA data to Title VII data; the latter includes only the first six months of 1999. I gathered these data from the headnotes of published appellate decisions available on Westlaw from January 1, 1999, to July 1, 1999. I chose the time frame so that the ADA and Title VII cases would be covering a comparable period. Because headnotes are available only for published decisions, these are all published decisions. I found that judicial outcomes under Title VII appear to be much more proplaintiff than published judicial outcomes under the ADA. For this time period, I found that Title VII plaintiffs obtained reversals in 34 of 100 cases (34 percent) and defendants obtained reversals in 12 of 29 cases (41 percent).

Using this Title VII data, I was able to compare my ADA data to data from other areas of the law. I found that the prodefendant bias in my database is stronger than the pattern found by researchers in other fields who have examined published decisions (see table 3.4). Whereas plaintiffs obtained reversals in only 21 percent of ADA cases, they obtained reversals in 34 percent of Title VII cases, 26 percent of defamation cases, 38 percent of nonprisoner constitutional tort litigation, and 48 percent of prisoner constitutional tort litigation.[16] Similarly, whereas defendants obtained reversals in 60 percent of ADA cases, they obtained reversals in 41 percent of Title VII cases, 52 percent of defamation cases, 48 percent of nonprisoner constitutional tort cases, and 49 percent of prisoner constitutional tort cases. The ADA data look most comparable to the defamation data, which is somewhat surprising because the defamation data are from a much earlier time period (1976–1979), when one might expect judges to have been more liberally disposed toward plaintiffs. Possibly, liberal judges' biases were constrained by the First Amendment issues in these cases.

The area of law in which I would have expected to find the closest similarity to the ADA is Title VII. Yet, the Title VII data are much more proplaintiff than are the ADA data. Plaintiffs obtained reversals in 34 percent of Title VII cases, compared to 21 percent of ADA cases; defendants obtained reversals in 41 percent of Title VII cases, compared to 60 percent of ADA cases. There are many differences between ADA actions and Title VII actions, which may account for the different outcomes under the

TABLE 3.4.
Published Appellate Data

Litigation Category	Plaintiff Appeals Reversed	Defendant Appeals Reversed
ADA employment discrimination (1992–1998)	64 of 310 (21%)	21 of 35 (60%)
Title VII, Civil Rights Act of 1964 (1999)	34 of 100 (34%)	12 of 29 (41%)
Defamation (1976–1979)	82 of 315 (26%)	66 of 126 (52%)
Nonprisoner constitutional tort	150 of 395 (38%)	43 of 89 (48%)
Prisoner constitutional tort (1980–1985)	53 of 111 (48%)	11 of 16 (69%)
Control Group (Non-Civil-Rights) (1980–1985)	144 of 411 (35%)	73 of 222 (33%)

two statutes. One important difference is that Title VII actions include reverse discrimination actions brought by Caucasians or men on the basis of race or gender discrimination, respectively. ADA actions, by contrast, can be brought only by individuals with disabilities. The cases in my database that involve both ADA cases and Title VII claims do not include any Title VII reverse discrimination cases. Nonetheless, the reverse discrimination cases are not the predominant type of case in these Title VII appellate cases.[17] Title VII is also a much older statute than the ADA, so lawyers may have a stronger basis for making rational decisions about their chances in litigation under Title VII than under the ADA.

One explanation for the apparently low success rate under the ADA, along with the other civil rights statutes, may be the effect of the EEOC conciliation process. The EEOC conciliation process may be filtering out the weak cases so that they do not clog the court system. As one group of researchers has noted,

> There can be little doubt that many Title I charges are frivolous. It does not follow, however, that the charge process is failing or even that it is being widely abused. The administrative charge process is designed to provide a relatively inexpensive and quick means of resolving disputes between workers and employers. It is very easy for an employee who suspects discrimination to file a charge, even the employee who lacks

hard evidence to support the claim (as is often the case even in ultimately meritorious cases). There is no fee, no lawyer is required, and
charges can be filed by mail or faxed to agencies. The initial screening
of weak or malicious cases, that in standard litigation is performed by
lawyers and court clerks, comes after filing in the ADA charge system.[18]

Even so, the filter is not a big one. About 88 percent of the cases filed
with the EEOC are eligible to become court cases after the issuance of the
right-to-sue letter. More than half of those are cases in which the EEOC
found no reasonable cause to believe that discrimination has occurred.
Without accurate trial court data, it is hard to speculate on the effectiveness of the EEOC's filtering process.

In sum, plaintiffs appear to fare worse at the appellate level under the
ADA than in other areas of the law. In the next several sections, I will try
to understand why this is so.

C. Explanations for Unfavorable Appellate Judicial Outcomes

1. CHANGES OVER TIME

To understand why plaintiffs appear to be faring so poorly at the appellate level under the ADA, I explored several hypotheses. In this section, I
will explore one hypothesis; in the next, I will explore other hypotheses
through regression analysis.

My first hypothesis was that the ADA is a new statute with new issues,
causing a high rate of reversal during an initial period of judicial uncer-
tainty. In particular, the proplaintiff experience of many civil rights
lawyers under Title VII of the Civil Rights Act or Section 504 of the Rehabilitation Act may have caused them to overpredict their success rate
under the ADA. If this hypothesis were correct, then I would expect the
results to become more proplaintiff over time as plaintiff lawyers learn to
make better judgments about which claims may be meritorious on appeal. In other words, they would self-correct for their initial miscalculation.[19] That trend has not yet begun, possibly because the courts are rendering increasingly prodefendant decisions, thereby making it difficult for
plaintiffs to make accurate predictions about the successful nature of
their lawsuits. Table 3.5 displays ADA appellate outcomes from August
3, 1994, to July 26, 1999.

TABLE 3.5.
ADA Appellate Outcomes, 1994–1999

Year	Frequency, Prodefendant Results	Percentage
1994	5 of 6	83%
1995	35 of 42	83%
1996	96 of 114	84%
1997	158 of 178	89%
1998	189 of 219	86%
1999	140 of 161	87%
Total	623 of 720	87%

TABLE 3.6.
Title VII Appellate Outcomes, 1967–1972

Year	Frequency, Prodefendant Outcome	Percentage
1967	2 of 2	100%
1968	0 of 3	0%
1969	3 of 15	20%
1970	3 of 15	20%
1971	5 of 27	18.5%
1972	12 of 43	28%
Total	25 of 105	24%

The level of prodefendant outcomes has remained relatively constant since 1996. Therefore, it does not appear that the ADA is currently experiencing a period of fluctuations in appellate judicial outcomes. It has achieved a stable, although highly prodefendant, rate of judicial outcomes.

One explanation for the consistent, prodefendant outcomes in the early years of litigation is that plaintiffs have unrealistically high expectations for the ADA, and are therefore pursuing nonmeritorious litigation. I was interested to see if this purported problem also occurred in the early years of Title VII enforcement. I found exactly the opposite. I constructed a database with the early years of Title VII appellate cases that are available on Westlaw. I coded 105 cases from May 3, 1967, through December 31, 1972. These decisions were overwhelmingly proplaintiff. These results were also relatively stable over this time period (see table 3.6).

The comparative data suggest that judicial attitude toward a statute may be the most important predictor of litigation results. In the early years of Title VII enforcement, it appears that the appellate judges were often rendering more proplaintiff interpretations than were the trial courts (see table 3.7).

The 80 results that I characterized as proplaintiff were the 63 reversals of prodefendant trial court decisions and the 17 affirmances of proplaintiff trial court decisions. The appellate courts reversed 63 of 83 (76 percent) of the prodefendant trial court decisions and reversed only 5 of 22 (23 percent) of the proplaintiff trial court decisions. Given the high rate of reversal of prodefendant trial court outcomes, I would characterize the appellate courts as more proplaintiff than the trial courts.

The ADA results are exactly the opposite (see table 3.8). In the ADA cases, the appellate courts reversed only 91 of 675 (13 percent) cases in which the trial court had rendered a prodefendant result. By contrast, they reversed 28 of 45 (62 percent) cases in which the trial court had rendered a proplaintiff result. Thus, I would characterize the appellate courts as more prodefendant than the trial courts.

One explanation for my data is that ADA plaintiffs are facing a moving target. They may have initially miscalculated their chances of prevailing in the lower courts, based on their positive experience with disability discrimination claims under the Rehabilitation Act. When it became clear that the courts were narrowly interpreting the ADA, they may have adjusted their expectations and made more conservative decisions about litigation. But the tenor of the courts' decisions became even *more* prodefendant, so that they had not properly adjusted far enough in a prodefendant direction.[20]

I have some empirical support for this hypothesis from Rehabilitation Act data. I instructed a team of coders to code appellate cases under sec-

TABLE 3.7.
Title VII Appellate Court Outcomes, 1967–1972

Trial Court Outcome	Appellate Court Outcome, Affirmed	Appellate Court Outcome, Reversed	Total
Prodefendant	20	63	83
Proplaintiff	17	5	22
Total	37	68	105

TABLE 3.8.
ADA Appellate Court Outcomes, 1994–1999

Trial Court Outcome	Appellate Court Outcome, Affirmed	Appellate Court Outcome, Reversed	Total
Prodefendant	594	91	675
Proplaintiff	17	28	45
Total	611	109	720

TABLE 3.9.
Rehabilitation Act Appellate Court Outcomes, 1981–1992

Year	Frequency, Prodefendant Outcome	Percentage
1981	2 of 4	50%
1982	1 of 4	25%
1983	3 of 4	75%
1984	1 of 1	100%
1985	5 of 6	83%
1986	5 of 5	100%
1987	3 of 5	60%
1988	6 of 9	67%
1989	1 of 3	33%
1990	7 of 11	64%
1991	11 of 17	65%
1992	7 of 11	64%
Total	52 of 80	65%

tions 501, 503, or 504 of the Rehabilitation Act involving employment discrimination issues.[21] The team coded cases in the time period 1981–1992 in order that I could assess the perspective of a lawyer who was experienced with disability discrimination lawsuits on the eve of the enforcement of ADA Title I.[22] The team coded whether the trial court and appellate court outcomes in these cases were proplaintiff or prodefendant. The results suggest that a lawyer who read the available decisions on Westlaw would learn that defendants were successful in the appellate courts about 65 percent of the time (see table 3.9).

The prodefendant success rate on appeal under the Rehabilitation Act is considerably lower than it is under the ADA. As shown in table 3.5, the prodefendant success rate on appeal under the ADA has remained consistently at 87 percent throughout the period under investigation.

Until the case law under the ADA becomes more stable and consistent over time, plaintiffs may find themselves adjusting to a moving target. It is inconceivable that plaintiffs could continue to miscalculate their chances to such a large extent in litigation. The Title VII data show that massive adjustments can occur over time (application of the statute has evolved from proplaintiff to prodefendant in the appellate courts). The conditions for a major adjustment, however, have not yet occurred under the ADA because of the lag time between a Supreme Court decision and lower court litigation. The ADA cases in my database were decided before the Court rendered its narrow decisions on the definition of disability. It will take several years for a new generation of cases to be filed that have incorporated these new sets of rules. By then, however, the Court may have rendered other conservative decisions that the plaintiff bar has not yet anticipated. Thus, the predicate to "rational litigation" may not yet exist for the plaintiff bar.

D. Regression Analysis

1. GENERAL RESULTS

Having rejected my first hypothesis—that the ADA's status as a new statute explains the high prodefendant outcomes—I turned to other hypotheses that I could assess through regression analysis. To ascertain those factors, I coded various factors in my database of ADA appellate outcomes,[23] factors that related to various hypotheses that I had about ADA outcomes.

First, I coded background information about the origin of the cases, including the appellate court in which the litigation took place.[24] Second, I coded the plaintiff's occupation to determine if, for example, blue-collar workers fared worse under the statute than management employees. For these purposes, I used occupational classifications created by the U.S. military with one exception: I added the category "law enforcement" because I observed a significant number of cases with plaintiffs in that occupation.[25] I coded defendant characteristics by coding whether the defendant was a public or private entity. Third, I coded the type of disability alleged by the plaintiff. I wanted to see if individuals with uncontroversial disabilities, such as mobility impairments or hearing impairments, fared better than individuals with controversial disabilities such as back impairments or HIV infection. I used the EEOC's disability categories for this coding so that I also could observe how representative appellate cases are of cases originally filed with the EEOC. Are certain types of disabilities more likely to result in appellate litigation? Fourth, I coded the type of disability discrimination alleged by the plaintiff. I was particularly interested in seeing if individuals with reasonable-accommodation allegations fared worse than individuals who alleged an unlawful discharge. Finally, I coded whether EEOC participation in a lawsuit was a significant factor in predicting a successful outcome. EEOC participation could take two forms: participation as a party or participation as an amicus.

The three factors that I was fairly certain would predict appellate outcome are also contained in the regression model: lower court outcome, whether a party is appealing a verdict, and whether the plaintiff is proceeding *pro se*. The lower court outcome variable reflects whether the

TABLE 3.10.
Factors Affecting Appellate Court Outcomes,
Americans with Disabilities Act (ADA) Cases[26]

Variable	Coefficient
Lower Court Outcome	
Proplaintiff verdict	1.1608**
Prodefendant verdict	−.5470
Proplaintiff nonverdict	.5899***
Theories of Disability	.0870
Actually disabled	.1016
Record of disability	−.1445
Regarded as disabled	.0093
Not disabled	.9304
Major life activity, nonwork	.2324
Major life activity, work	−.5266
Major life activity, unknown	−.3967
Discrimination Alleged	
Demotion	1.6288**
Discharge	.0244
Harassment/hostile work environment	−.7843
Failure to hire	.2690
Medical examinations	.2218
Failure to promote	.1368
Otherwise qualified/essential functions	.4586
Reasonable accommodation	.1081
Failure to reinstate	.5014
Retaliation	−.0435
Suspension or involuntary leave (temporary)	.5513
Terms and conditions (monetary)	−.0536
Terms and conditions (nonmonetary)	−.1557
Defenses Alleged	
Judicial estoppel	.7328
No knowledge of disability	−.5684
Direct threat to health/safety of others	−.6163
Types of Physical or Mental Impairment	
Asthma	.4856
Back	−.0920
Blood disorder	−1.3416
Cancer	−.4488
Diabetes	1.2244*
Extremities	.7333*

plaintiff or defendant won at trial. Because appellate courts most typically affirm trial court outcomes, it was important that I control for the result at trial; otherwise, I would be overstating the tendency of appellate judges to render prodefendant results, in that the trial court results in my database were overwhelmingly prodefendant. The verdict variable reflects the type of decision that the party is appealing. The verdict variable was coded as a "1" for proplaintiff or prodefendant jury verdict, proplaintiff or prodefendant bench trial, proplaintiff preliminary injunction, and proplaintiff final injunction. It is coded "0" for all other outcomes. This variable reflects that the rules of law make it particularly difficult to overturn verdicts. Thus, I would expect a "verdict" outcome at trial to

TABLE 3.10. *(Continued)*
Factors Affecting Appellate Court Outcomes,
Americans with Disabilities Act (ADA) Cases[26]

Variable	Coefficient
Hearing	1.4190
Internal organs	.4505
Neurological	.6186
Other	.9674
Psychological	.5477
Respiratory	.5507
Substance abuse	−1.7884
Unknown	.3857
Visual	1.0282
Circuit Effects	
DC Circuit	1.8566**
1st Circuit	.9221
2d Circuit	1.4221**
3d Circuit	1.4208**
4th Circuit	−2.1329**
5th Circuit	−.5398
7th Circuit	.3233
8th Circuit	−.2654
9th Circuit	.5393
10th Circuit	−.3633
11th Circuit	.6207
Plaintiff Occupational Status	
Administrative	.6803
Blue collar	.2415
Clerical	.1114
Law enforcement	−.9982
Technical	.1656
Unknown	.4058
Other Factors	
EEOC as amicus	2.0238***
EEOC as participant	.8531
Other non–ADA issues	.0004
Pro se	−2.3288***
Public defendant	.5746
Constant	−3.7655***

Note: * p < .1, ** p < .05, *** p < .01, two-tailed tests

predict an unsuccessful appeal. Finally, the *pro se* variable reflects whether a party appealed the trial court outcome on a *pro se* basis. It is common knowledge that *pro se* plaintiffs are rarely successful in the appellate courts. The fact that an attorney has not been willing to take such cases for compensation may even suggest that many are frivolous. Hence, I would expect *pro se* outcome to predict an unsuccessful appeal. Having each of these three factors in my regression analysis enabled me to control for their effect on appellate outcome.

Table 3.10 displays the regression results in a logistic regression analysis in which appellate outcome is the dependent variable. A prodefendant outcome on appeal is a "0"; a proplaintiff outcome is a "1." Therefore, a positive coefficient means that the factor correlates with a proplaintiff outcome on appeal. If that coefficient is significant (or approaches significance), the number of asterisks indicates the degree of significance.[27]

E. Analysis

1. LOWER COURT OUTCOME

Many of the factors that I coded were statistically significant. As expected, a proplaintiff outcome at trial strongly correlated with a proplaintiff outcome on appeal. The coefficient for proplaintiff verdict is higher than the coefficient for proplaintiff nonverdict, meaning that a proplaintiff verdict has a higher probability of resulting in success for the plaintiff on appeal than a proplaintiff nonverdict. This is not surprising because we should expect appellate judges to defer to findings made by juries at trial.

2. THEORY OF DISABILITY

The type of disability was not a significant factor in predicting appellate outcome. It did not matter whether plaintiff alleged that he or she was actually disabled, had a record of disability, or was regarded as disabled in predicting appellate outcome. The small numbers of cases in the "record of" and "regarded as" categories may explain the lack of significance.

3. TYPE OF DISCRIMINATION ALLEGED

The type of discrimination alleged was a significant factor in predicting appellate outcome. A plaintiff who alleged a discriminatory demotion was significantly more likely to prevail than were other plaintiffs. The demotion data are somewhat surprising. It is certainly reasonable to expect people who hold jobs to fare better in discrimination cases than individuals who are merely seeking to be hired. Thus, I would have expected failure-to-hire cases to fare worse than demotion cases. But if holding a job is a positive factor in a discrimination claim, then discharge claims should also have been more successful than other types of cases. An allegation of an unlawful discharge, however, was not a significant factor in predicting a proplaintiff result. In fact, although the results are not statistically significant, the coefficient for the discharge factor was *negative*. Were I to combine discharge and demotion into a single factor, the new factor—loss of job status—would not be significant.

It is possible that plaintiffs who allege a demotion rather than an outright discharge are viewed more favorably by the courts because they appear to be more qualified for employment. Alternatively, it is possible that my demotion result is a spurious result in the data set that will disappear over time.

4. Defenses

No statistical significance was found for the defenses that were raised by the defendant.

5. Type of Impairment

The type of physical or mental impairment was found to be statistically significant. Plaintiffs who alleged that they had an impairment due to diabetes or extremities impairments[28] were more likely to prevail than other plaintiffs.

The plaintiffs with extremities impairments had a wide variety of problems ranging from arthritis to amputated limbs. Those cases, however, did not include mere back injuries and may therefore have seemed like more sympathetic cases to judges on appeal. (Back impairments are the most commonly alleged impairment under the ADA and are subject to the common questions about unverifiable soft tissue injuries that one sees in tort and worker compensation cases.) These data preceded the Supreme Court's recent decisions narrowing the definition of disability. Those cases are likely to have an influence on diabetes cases, so it will be interesting to see if this trend continues over time.

6. Circuit

The circuit in which the plaintiff litigated was also a highly significant factor. The D.C., Second, and Third Circuits were significantly more likely to produce proplaintiff results than the Sixth Circuit. The Fourth Circuit was significantly more likely to produce prodefendant results than the Sixth Circuit. The Third Circuit results, however, may have been affected by its notoriously low publication rate.[29]

Not only does the Third Circuit not make its unpublished decisions available to the public but it publishes relatively few opinions. Published decisions tend to be more proplaintiff than unpublished decisions. Because the Third Circuit does not make its unpublished decisions available to electronic services and publishes a comparatively small percentage of its decisions, its appellate results are skewed in a proplaintiff direction as compared to the other circuits.

7. PLAINTIFF'S OCCUPATION

Plaintiff's occupation was not a significant factor in predicting appellate outcome. I also coded whether the defendant was a public or private entity; that factor was not significant in predicting appellate outcome.

8. EEOC PARTICIPATION AS AMICUS

The EEOC participation as amicus was a significant factor predicting plaintiff success on appeal. It is possible that EEOC participation did not *cause* the proplaintiff outcome; the EEOC may simply have happened to choose to participate in cases that were already likely to yield proplaintiff results. Nonetheless, EEOC participation as a *party* did not significantly correlate with a proplaintiff outcome. That result may be due to the fact that there were only eight cases in the database in which the EEOC participated as a party, thereby making it difficult to find statistical significance. (The EEOC's own data, discussed earlier, suggest that its participation as a party does correlate with a successful outcome, at least at the trial court level.) By contrast, there were 42 cases in which the EEOC participated as an amicus. With more data, I may find that EEOC's status as a party is a significant factor. Alternatively, the prejudice against the EEOC limits the degree to which it can be effective in a lawsuit. Thus, EEOC participation as an amicus may be more acceptable to some judges than EEOC participation as a party.

My analysis of appellate decisions under the ADA suggests that defendants are much more likely than plaintiffs to prevail in appellate litigation. Although defendant success rates are generally higher than plaintiff success rates in other comparable areas of the law, the results under the ADA are more prodefendant than has been found by other researchers. When Age Discrimination (ADEA) and Title VII issues are part of ADA litigation, however, these other causes of action also fare quite poorly. It is only when Title VII cases are brought independently from ADA cases that they fare better than ADA cases. These comparative results suggest that there is something distinctive about ADA litigation that accounts for these disparate prodefendant results.

It is possible to account for judicial outcomes by saying that plaintiffs are making poor decisions about which cases to litigate and appeal. (The EEOC, however, appears to be using its resources effectively in deciding in which cases to participate as an amicus.) Over time, however, one would expect the plaintiff bar to respond to the statistical reality of the unlikeliness of prevailing. With contingency fee awards the predominant method of compensation, plaintiff lawyers have a very strong incentive to make conservative judgments about litigation.

One factor that may be causing the plaintiff bar to overpredict judicial outcomes is that ADA cases appear to be faring much worse than Title VII litigation. Appellate outcomes under the ADA are also much more prodefendant than were appellate outcomes under the Rehabilitation Act on the eve of the effective date of the ADA. The litigation assumptions that these lawyers may be making based on their Title VII experience may not be applicable to the ADA.

It is also possible that plaintiff lawyers simply do not yet fully understand the legal requirements of the ADA. To the extent that cases lose because of the distinctive features of the ADA—like the reasonable accommodation requirement and the definition of disability—that hypothesis may make sense. But my data do not support that hypothesis because reasonable accommodation cases do not fare worse than other kinds of ADA cases.

I also tried to determine which factors in litigation may predict judicial outcome. The significant factors included EEOC participation as amicus, *pro se* status, trial court outcome, D.C. Circuit, Second Circuit, and Third Circuit. There was a trend toward significance in the First and Ninth Circuits. The Third Circuit result may reflect a narrow decision about which kinds of cases to make available to the public rather than an overall proplaintiff bias. There was a trend toward diabetes and extremities disabilities predicting proplaintiff outcomes on appeal. EEOC participation as an amicus was a very strong factor in predicting a proplaintiff outcome on appeal. In general, however, it is very difficult to paint a precise picture of which factors are significant in predicting winning or losing ADA litigation because many decisions are per curiam and provide researchers with few facts about the case or outcome.

4

The Face of Judicial Backlash

In chapter 3, we saw that there is empirical evidence to support the claim that the appellate courts have been hostile to ADA claims. Complete and accurate trial court data do not exist; however, it appears that plaintiffs may be faring better before juries than judges. Anecdotal evidence suggests that plaintiffs are facing two major and interrelated hurdles at the trial court level. First, trial court judges are concluding too readily that plaintiffs do not meet the statutory definition of "disability." Second, trial court judges are too eager to grant defendants' motions for summary judgment, thereby resolving cases at a preliminary stage, and precluding them from even going to a jury. These problems are interrelated because judges are often concluding that summary judgment for the defendant is appropriate because the plaintiff is not disabled. Nonetheless, this is not the only issue being resolved adversely to plaintiffs at the summary judgment stage. Other issues include the reasonable accommodation requirement and the direct threat defense. These two inquiries, along with the definition of disability inquiry, are supposed to be resolved through individualized inquiries that are jury questions. It is typically inappropriate for a judge to decide these questions himself or herself in granting a defendant's motion for summary judgment.

When judges make errors at the trial court level, the appeals process is supposed to help correct the errors. But, as we saw in chapter 3, plaintiffs are rarely successful when they appeal an adverse trial court decision. In fact, one might argue that trial court judges have relatively free rein to abuse the summary judgment device because they have little cause for concern that they will be reversed on appeal. Thus, the prodefendant appellate data may be influencing judicial behavior at the trial court level.

This chapter seeks to put a face on many of the statistics in chapter 3. In part I, I will describe the kinds of plaintiffs who the courts have found to be not "disabled." Many of these individuals were exactly the kind of people that Congress thought it was protecting when it enacted the ADA. In part II, I will examine cases in which I contend that the courts have abused the summary judgment device. Some of these cases involve the definition of disability; others involve issues such as reasonable accommodation or the direct threat defense. The common thread, however, is that trial court judges have resolved some factual inquiries themselves, rather than sending them to the jury. And these decisions are overwhelmingly prodefendant.

I. Definition of Disability

Although the ADA was built, in part, on the Civil Rights Act of 1964, its conception of statutory coverage is radically different from that of the Civil Rights Act of 1964. The ADA is built on an "antisubordination"[1] notion for protected classes under which Congress sought to assist a historically disadvantaged class: individuals with disabilities. By contrast, the Supreme Court has generally interpreted the Civil Rights Act of 1964 to reflect an "antidifferentiation" notion of protected classes under which Congress sought to eliminate all discrimination (or different treatment) on the basis of race, sex, national origin, or religion—irrespective of whether the individuals who faced that discrimination were members of a historically disadvantaged class. Hence, under the antidifferentiation model, whites and men, as well as African Americans and women, can bring claims of race and gender discrimination. By contrast, under the antisubordination model, only individuals with disabilities can bring claims of discrimination under the ADA.

The difference between an antisubordination and an antidifferentiation model can be readily seen by examining the basic language of the ADA and the Civil Rights Act of 1964. Under the ADA, one can bring a claim of discrimination only if one qualifies as an "individual with a disability." The statute provides rights to a group that Congress understood to have faced a history of discrimination.

The Civil Rights Act, by contrast, creates a cause of action to anyone who believes that he or she has faced discrimination on the basis of race, gender, national origin, or religion. The Supreme Court has held that Caucasians, as well as African Americans, may bring a charge of race discrimination. The history of racism and slavery in the United States is usually irrelevant under the antidifferentiation model created by the courts to resolve Civil Rights Act complaints. Hence, Title VII of the Civil Rights Act has generated "reverse discrimination" suits brought by whites alleging employment discrimination. Further, it is difficult (although not impossible) for employers to create voluntary affirmative action policies without fear of reverse discrimination litigation.[2] Affirmative action stands in tension with the antidifferentiation model, so the courts have tolerated voluntary affirmative action for racial minorities and women only on a narrow basis.

The language of the Civil Rights Act supports an antidifferentiation model because Congress did not single out suspect classes for protection under the act. It provided protection against all "race" discrimination, not merely race discrimination visited upon African Americans or other racial minorities. Similarly, the act provided protection against all "sex" discrimination, not merely sex discrimination visited upon women. That language laid the foundation for the Supreme Court to rule that whites, as well as men, could bring race and sex discrimination claims, respectively, under Title VII.

The ADA, by contrast, does not provide protection against disability discrimination for all persons; it provides protection against disability discrimination only for individuals who meet the statutory definition of being disabled. It does not countenance reverse discrimination lawsuits because only members of the protected class—individuals with disabilities—can bring lawsuits. Moreover, the ADA embeds the concept of "reasonable accommodation" within the core statutory structure, so that, in theory, there should be little question that the statute permits, and even requires, affirmative steps to assist individuals with disabilities. In other words, a form of affirmative action is explicitly permitted by the ADA. In the findings section, Congress described individuals with disabilities as a "discrete and insular class" and made clear that it sought to assist such individuals in all areas of daily living. In particular, Congress specified in its fourth finding that the ADA was intended to provide necessary legal recourse to individuals with disabilities.[3] It estimated in its first finding that more than 43 million Americans are disabled and would benefit from the ADA's broad protections.[4]

Because of this explicit antisubordination framework,[5] nondisabled individuals cannot seek the protections afforded by the statute, nor can they challenge favorable treatment to individuals with disabilities. Accordingly, if an employer accommodates an employee who has cancer by allowing him or her to leave early on Fridays for chemotherapy treatment, a nondisabled employee cannot challenge that favorable treatment as "disability" discrimination. This antisubordination framework offers employers and other entities the opportunity to provide reasonable accommodations without fear of reverse discrimination lawsuits. It also limits the statute's coverage to those who have disabilities, as defined by the ADA.

The antisubordination framework has been very difficult for the courts to countenance after three decades of moving the Civil Rights Act of 1964 toward an antidifferentiation model. In the early days of the enforcement of the act, the courts did not have to consider whether it reflected an antisubordination or antidifferentiation perspective because the plaintiffs were racial minorities or women who had claims of discrimination under either legal theory. The courts soon concluded, however, that the act did not embody a pure antidifferentiation perspective and allowed whites and men to bring race and gender discrimination claims. At first, however, the courts also tolerated affirmative action for racial minorities and women, even though those programs conflicted with a pure antidifferentiation perspective. Over time, however, the courts have more and more narrowly construed the ability of employers to institute affirmative action programs and hence have moved the Civil Rights Act to a more pure antidifferentiation model.[6] During the same time period, the courts have been asked to interpret the ADA's antisubordination language. As I will argue below, they have not interpreted this language to achieve Congress's antisubordination objectives. Their reluctance to employ a strong antisubordination model under the ADA may stem, in part, from their discomfort with using such a model under the Civil Rights Act even though the statutory language is very different in the two statutes.

In theory, the courts could have chosen two avenues to limit the scope of the ADA's protections if the courts disagreed with the antisubordination rationale. First, they could have entirely resisted the antisubordination approach by allowing nondisabled individuals to bring suit under the ADA. If that approach were followed, reverse discrimination cases would be permitted under the ADA. Second, the courts could have rendered the antisubordination approach ineffective by narrowly construing the group protected by the statute.[7] This step might technically leave the statute in an antisubordination framework, but the framework would protect far fewer than the 43 million Americans with disabilities who, Congress claimed, it sought to protect.

The first approach is not plausible, given the statutory language of the ADA. The text of the ADA requires that individuals must be disabled to bring suit and authorizes the use of reasonable accommodations. The first approach was possible under Title VII of the Civil Rights Act because it did not require an individual to be a member of a minority group to bring suit. Further, the Civil Rights Act is silent as to whether affirmative action is permissible. The act also specifies that affirmative action is never *required*. Thus, although an antisubordination approach may have been possible under the act, courts that were hostile to that approach had statutory language to support an antidifferentiation approach, under which anyone can bring suit and affirmative action is impermissible.

The second approach has been more possible under the ADA because of the vagueness of the statutory definition of disability. Borrowing from Section 504 of the Rehabilitation Act, the ADA states that an individual is disabled if he or she has a physical or mental impairment that substantially limits one or more major life activities. (An individual can also be considered disabled if he or she is "regarded as" disabled or has a "record of" a disability, but those legal theories have not played a major role under the ADA.) Under Section 504, the courts had applied the definition of disability broadly to include people with psychiatric impairments, diabetes, epilepsy, and heart conditions, as well as the more traditional disabilities such as blindness, deafness, and mobility impairments. By using the same well-accepted and workable definition in the ADA as in Section 504, the drafters thought they were achieving legal clarity. The "deal" that was struck when the ADA was enacted was that the definition of disability would not change except for certain minor exclusions. The ADA would use the definition that had existed for nearly thirty years under Section 504. Congress recited its intention to maintain this broad definition of disability when it stated in the first finding of the ADA that "some 43,000,000 Americans have one or more physical or mental disabilities, and this number is increasing as the population as a whole is growing older." By this calculation roughly one in five Americans was considered disabled, and the number would grow over time.

Despite Congress's attempt to craft a statute with broad disability protection, the courts have narrowly construed the definition of disability under the ADA so that far fewer than 43 million Americans can take advantage of its protection. Although Justice Sandra Day O'Connor has said that Congress "undoubtedly would have cited a much higher number of disabled persons in the findings" if it had intended a broad definition of disability,[8] the opposite conclusion is appropriate upon a fuller examination of the statute. Congress was undoubtedly seeking to create expansive judicial protection for individuals with disabilities, and its base figure was serving as a floor rather than a ceiling.

But this conclusion gets us ahead of ourselves. We need to understand how the definition of disability is used in the statute to understand how the courts have created a narrow interpretation of the term.

To bring suit under the ADA, an individual must establish that he or she is an "individual with a disability." The ADA defines "disability" as

(A) a physical or mental impairment that substantially limits one or more of the major life activities of such individual;

(B) a record of such an impairment; or

(C) being regarded as having such an impairment.[9]

This definition has three prongs: (A) an actually disabled prong, (B) a record of disability prong, and (C) a regarded as disabled prong. At first glance, the coverage of all three is wide ranging in scope. Even if one is not actually disabled at the time of discrimination (and thereby not covered by the first prong), one might be covered under the second or third prong. Hence, an individual who has had a history of cancer but whose cancer is in remission could receive protection under the second prong if an employer failed to hire her or him out of a concern that the cancer would recur. Similarly, an individual who is entirely healthy but who is falsely regarded as having AIDS, and therefore was not hired, could receive protection under the third prong.

Despite this seemingly broad definition, the Supreme Court and the lower courts have consistently ruled that individuals with impairments that have been the basis of their exclusion from employment do not come within this definition. Twin sisters—Karin Sutton and Kimberly Hinton—who sought employment as airline pilots were excluded from consideration for employment because they could not pass the employer's vision test without the use of corrective lenses.[10] (Without corrective lenses, their vision was 20/200; with corrective lenses, it was 20/20.) The district court dismissed their case because it found they were not disabled;[11] the appellate court[12] and Supreme Court agreed with this conclusion. Because their case was dismissed at a pretrial stage, the twins were never able to present evidence that the employer had unlawfully discriminated against them on the basis of disability. The employer did not have to demonstrate that the vision requirement was justifiable under the ADA.

Hallie Kirkingburg sought employment as a truck driver.[13] He was denied employment consideration because he could not meet the employer's vision requirement. He has amblyopia, an uncorrectable condition that leaves him with 20/200 vision in his left eye, that is, monocular vision. The defendant argued that Kirkingburg's visual impairment did not constitute a disability under the ADA although it disqualified him from employment (despite his safe driving record). The trial court granted summary judgment for the defendant-employer, concluding that Kirkingburg was not disabled.[14] The court of appeals reversed[15] but the Supreme Court reversed the appellate court, ruling in favor of the defendant-employer. Like United Airlines in the *Sutton* case, the defendant-employer in the *Kirkingburg* case did not have to demonstrate the validity of its vision requirement in order to prevail under the ADA; it could stand on the position that the plaintiff was not covered by the statute.

In another case, Vaughn Murphy sought employment as a mechanic with UPS but was denied employment because of his high blood pressure.[16] Unmedicated, Murphy's blood pressure is 250/160, but, with medication, it is around 160/100. UPS failed to hire him as a mechanic because, it argued, he could not safely drive trucks that he was repairing (due to his high blood pressure). Nonetheless, UPS argued that Murphy was not so disabled as to be covered by the ADA. The trial court granted summary judgment for the defendant-employer, concluding that Murphy was not disabled.[17] That decision was affirmed by both the court of appeals[18] and the Supreme Court.

Not everyone, however, loses under the ADA on the threshold question of whether he or she is disabled. In a highly publicized case, Casey Martin was successfully able to invoke statutory protection to argue that the Professional Golf Association should be required to permit him to use a golf cart to compete professionally.[19] It does seem ironic that Martin, a gifted athlete, was found to be covered by the statute, but individuals with poor vision who sought to be airline pilots or truckers, or an individual with high blood pressure who sought to be a mechanic, are not found to be covered by the ADA. Senators Robert Dole (R-Kans.) and Tom Harkin (D-Iowa) held a news conference in support of Martin,[20] yet there was little public support from members of Congress for the other ADA plaintiffs described here. Does the ADA protect only those who can provide good photo opportunities for members of Congress? Few athletes will benefit from the Martin decision because few gifted athletes are also disabled. Yet many Americans would benefit from the ADA's extending its protection to individuals with 20/200 vision or high blood pressure. The Court's attempt to limit coverage of the ADA to 43 million Americans has created an odd scope of coverage. Although the ADA's legislative history and agency regulations[21] indicate that the ADA was intended to assist ordinary Americans, rather than gifted athletes, the intentions have not been realized.

In each of the cases discussed above in which the plaintiff lost, the employer unquestionably treated the plaintiff adversely because of the plaintiff's physical impairment in its uncorrected or unmitigated state. Had the courts concluded that these plaintiffs were disabled, then they would have had their day in court to prove that the discrimination that they faced was *unlawful* discrimination. Is it important for airline pilots to have vision that is better than 20/100 in its uncorrected state? Is it important for truck drivers to have bifocal vision? Is it important for mechanics who repair trucks to have normal blood pressure? By dismissing these cases at an early stage, the courts did not have to wrestle with these important questions.[22]

The ADA is unlike most other civil rights statutes in that it requires an individual to demonstrate that he or she is in a protected class in order for a lawsuit to go forward. Under Title VII of the Civil Rights Act of 1964, an individual can bring a gender discrimination lawsuit irrespective of whether the individual is a man or a woman. Similarly, one can bring a race discrimination lawsuit irrespective of whether one is black or white. The question is whether the employer considered an impermissible factor—race or gender—not whether the individual is a member of a protected class.

By contrast, under the ADA, one can bring suit only if one establishes that he or she is an individual with a disability. Section 504 of the Rehabilitation Act of 1973 had used that framework since 1973 when it was imported into the ADA. An early version of the ADA tried to broaden the Section 504 rule by not imposing a substantial limitation or major life activity requirement. Under that bill, an individual had only to demonstrate that he or she was treated differently "because of a physical or mental impairment, perceived impairment, or record of impairment."[23] At no time did anyone suggest that the physical or mental impairment requirement be dropped altogether.

It is interesting to inquire why Congress always assumed that the protected class model was appropriate for the ADA but not for the Civil Rights Act of 1964. Some commentators might argue that this framework was chosen out of a sense of paternalism for individuals with disabilities—that Congress wanted to offer a helping hand only to those it considered the "truly disabled." There is not much evidence of this paternalism, however, in the legislative record. The legislative history suggests the drafters of the ADA were seeking a very strong civil rights bill.

The protected class model made sense, because it would allow the ADA to contain accommodation principles. The Title VII model would have created the problem of reverse discrimination litigation. It is also clear that the drafters of the ADA were borrowing from Section 504's protected class model and saw the ADA as enhancing Section 504's basic framework. In President Bush's signing statement, he deflected concerns that the ADA was "too vague or too costly and will lead to an explosion of litigation." He noted that "the Administration and the Congress have carefully crafted the ADA to give the business community the flexibility to meet the requirements of the Act without incurring undue costs." He also mentioned that the statute was carefully modeled on Section 504 of the Rehabilitation Act so that the standards under the act would be familiar and workable.[24] As we saw in chapter 2, no member of Congress tried to weaken what was understood to be a broad definition of disability.

One would therefore have expected that Congress envisioned consistent treatment of the term "disability" under Section 504 and the ADA. If individuals with poor vision or high blood pressure were considered disabled under Section 504, then they would be considered disabled under the ADA. If the definition of disability was not a substantial hurdle under Section 504, then it would not be a substantial hurdle under the ADA.

Although Congress may not have intended the definition-of-disability requirement to be a substantial hurdle, it has become one. A plaintiff frequently loses at the summary judgment stage at trial because the employer successfully argues that he or she is not an individual with a disability. In that instance, the court never considers whether the plaintiff faced discrimination on the basis of a physical or mental characteristic that is irrelevant to his or her ability to perform the job. This chapter will examine those narrow interpretations of the definition of the term "disability."

A. Prong One

Judicial decisions have undercut the ability of plaintiffs to use each of the three prongs of the disability definition. The Supreme Court has interpreted the meaning of the term in conjunction with the congressional finding that approximately 43 million Americans have disabilities.[25] It has tried to find a definition of disability that is broad enough to cover approximately 43 million Americans but not so broad as to cover 150 million Americans. Under the first prong of this definition, it has ruled that Congress intended the definition of disability to include only individuals who are substantially limited in one or more major life activities even after they take advantage of mitigating measures such as eyeglasses, hearing aids, or prosthetic limbs.

This rule of law emerged from the Court's decision in *Sutton v. United Airlines*, 523 U.S. 437 (1999). The facts in *Sutton* involved twin sisters who were excluded from consideration for employment as airline pilots for United Airlines because they could not pass the vision test. Although their corrected visual acuity was 20/20, the employer's rules required them to take the vision test without the use of corrective lenses. Their uncorrected vision of 20/200 in one eye and 20/400 in the other eye could not meet the employer's requirement. When they brought suit under the ADA, the Supreme Court ruled on appeal that a court should determine whether the plaintiffs were disabled in their *corrected* state, despite the fact that the employer insisted that they take the test in their uncorrected state. By concluding at the preliminary stage of the case that the plaintiffs did not qualify as "disabled" under the ADA, the Court avoided the harder question of whether the employer could reasonably require visual acuity of 20/100 without the use of corrective lenses.

One might try to limit the consequences of this case by noting that it involved individuals who used a very common corrective measure, corrective lenses. Possibly, it makes sense to exclude people with suboptimal vision from the coverage of the ADA in order not to have the act cover nearly every adult American. Under Great Britain's disability discrimination statute, a court determines whether an individual is disabled by reference to his or her impairment in its uncorrected state *unless* the individual uses corrective lenses.[26]

Under an antisubordination model, one might conclude that the British model is correct, i.e., that individuals who use corrective lenses are not likely to have faced a history of discrimination on the basis of disability. Corrective lenses are so commonplace in our society, one might argue, that it makes little sense for the ADA to cover an individual merely because his or her vision is suboptimal.

If the Supreme Court had gone down that policy path, then one would have to determine where to draw the line in figuring out which people with visual impairments should be covered by the statute. Certainly, one would expect that Congress intended individuals who are *blind* to be covered by the ADA, given the hardships that such individuals have historically faced in a world that emphasizes visual reading and learning. But are there people whose vision is so weak that they, too, should qualify for protection under the ADA, even though they are not technically blind? Under the Individuals with Disabilities Education Act, courts typically inquire if a child's physical or cognitive abilities are two standard deviations below the mean to determine if the child qualifies for services under the statute. Arguably, that kind of approach would be appropriate in ADA cases involving visual acuity. If that approach were to be applied, then we would inquire whether 20/200 vision is two standard deviations below the mean for the American population. If that is so, we might conclude that Congress intended the Sutton twins to receive statutory protection.

That antisubordination approach, however, is not the approach that the Court took in *Sutton*. Instead, the Court developed a rule that broadly excluded from statutory coverage many individuals who Congress certainly understood would be covered by the ADA. The Court concluded that we should determine whether an individual has a physical or mental impairment that substantially limits him or her in a major life activity after the individual utilizes corrective measures. Courts have interpreted that rule to disallow claims of discrimination by individuals with all types of physical or mental impairments, not merely suboptimal vision. In fact, lower courts have used that narrow definition to conclude that individuals with hearing impairments, mental illness, diabetes, high blood pressure, and monocular vision are not disabled.[27] Defense lawyers have even tried to argue that individuals born with a deformed limb are not disabled under the ADA's definition.[28]

Derek Matlock's experience exemplifies application of the Court's approach. Matlock suffered partial hearing loss while serving in Operation Desert Storm and wore hearing aids to improve his hearing.[29] When he applied for a position with the Dallas Police Department, he was required to take the test without use of the hearing aids and failed the test. Because Matlock's hearing in its corrected state did not constitute a "disability," the employer did not have to justify excluding him based on his hearing in its *uncorrected* state. Although the employer treated him adversely because of his hearing in its uncorrected state, the court considered Matlock's hearing in its *corrected* state for the purpose of determining whether he was disabled. Had Matlock attained statutory coverage, he might have been able to demonstrate that when using hearing aids,[30] he was a *qualified* individual with disabilities. In fact, Matlock was successfully employed as a police officer for the Metropolitan Water Regulation District of Greater Chicago. As Justice Stevens argued in dissent in *Sutton*, the narrow definition of disability "may have the perverse effect of denying coverage for a sizeable portion of the core group of 43 million."[31] Matlock is clearly one among such people. The definition of disability precluded having his case heard before a jury, under an actually disabled theory of disability, to determine if he had faced illegal discrimination.

The Court has given too much weight to trying to mesh the findings section and the definition of disability. The original version of the ADA, which was introduced as H.R. 4498 by Representative Tony Coelho (D-Calif.) and as S. 2345 by Senator Lowell Weicker (R-Conn.) in 1988, contained both a broader definition of disability and a smaller estimate of the number of Americans with disabilities.[32] It estimated the number of individuals with disabilities to be only 36 million Americans. Yet, the definition of disability (which was then termed "on the basis of handicap") was much broader than the definition quoted above. In the initial bills, an individual had to demonstrate only that he or she was treated differently "because of a physical or mental impairment, perceived impairment, or record of impairment."[33] There was no requirement that the impairment substantially limit one or more major life activities, as is required under the ADA. The term "physical or mental impairment" was also much broader, requiring only proof of a "physiological disorder or condition, cosmetic disfigurement, or anatomical loss affecting one or more systems of the body" or "any mental or psychological disorder, such as mental retardation, organic brain syndrome, emotional or mental illness, and specific learning disabilities."[34]

Ironically, Congress employed the exceptionally broad definition of disability (which would probably cover nearly all Americans) while estimating the number of individuals covered by the statute at 36 million. Congress then amended the ADA so that the definition was *narrowed* to be the same as the one used under Section 504 while it also *expanded* the estimate of the numbers of individuals covered by the statute from 36 million to 43 million. Congress's inconsistence suggests that Congress, itself, did not take seriously its attempt to estimate the number of individuals covered by the statute.

Although most of the decisions construing the definition of disability have occurred under ADA Title I—the employment title—the definition of disability crosscuts the entire act. Hence, Matlock, the police officer applicant with a hearing impairment who was found not to be disabled for the purposes of bringing an employment discrimination claim, is also not disabled for purpose of requesting reasonable accommodations at a hotel or restaurant, or in accessing a public service. At night, when he sleeps at a hotel, he may want to know that the hotel has a system of blinking lights to alert people to an emergency, rather than merely an auditory alarm. But, in deciding whether he is disabled for the purposes of bringing a lawsuit under ADA Title III (the public accommodations provision), a court would have to consider him in his corrected state, despite the fact that he is unlikely to sleep while wearing hearing aids.

Judicial interpretation of the first prong of the definition of disability does a disservice to the rich legislative history underlying the ADA and to the broad antisubordination purpose embodied in the statute. It is ridiculous to think that Congress expected that individuals with substantial hearing loss, visual impairment, or seizure disorders would not be covered by the ADA. But the courts have interpreted prong one of the ADA to reach that nonsensical result.

B. Prong Two

The "record of" impairment prong of the statute has not been an important tool for plaintiffs in the first decade of ADA enforcement but could become important in response to the mitigating-measures ruling narrowing the usefulness of the actually disabled prong. The courts have offered little guidance on the scope of the second prong, leaving confusion about the potential reach of the "record of" prong.

The ADA's legislative history suggests that the "record of" prong is intended to benefit the plaintiff who is no longer disabled but was formerly disabled. In other words, if an individual at one time had cancer and the cancer, itself, is a disability under the statute (because it "substantially limits one or more major life activities"), then the individual can qualify under prong two if the cancer is currently in remission but is the basis for a discriminatory action.

The mitigating-measures ruling under prong one, however, creates an enormous conceptual problem with the application of prong two, because a "mitigating measure" may be the reason that an individual is no longer currently disabled. Can we then consider the person in her unmitigated state to determine whether she meets the "record of" prong of the statute? Consider Vaughn Murphy, the mechanic who was fired because of his high blood pressure.[35] Murphy takes medication to keep his blood pressure at a relatively safe level. Before he was diagnosed with high blood pressure, he presumably had readings that would have been high enough to qualify him as an individual with a disability. Unmedicated, his blood pressure is 250/160, which is probably so high as to preclude him from engaging in most activities of daily living.

Murphy brought his case under the first prong of the statute (as well as the "regarded as" prong) and lost. The Court ruled that his blood pressure, while under medication, was not so high as to qualify him as an individual with a disability. But what if he had brought his lawsuit under the "record of" prong. Could he have argued that he was disabled at the age of 10, when his high blood pressure was first detected, but he currently has only a "record of" disability because mediation corrects his condition? It seems unlikely that the courts will allow the "record of" prong to essentially overturn the mitigating-measures ruling, but the mitigating-measures decisions do leave much confusion about the interplay between the first two prongs of the statute.

In *Sutton*, Justice John Paul Stevens, in dissent, hinted at the confusion created by the Court in considering the interplay between the first and second prongs of the statute: "Still, if I correctly understand the Court's opinion, it holds that one who *continues to wear* a hearing aid that she has worn all her life might not be covered—fully cured impairments are covered, but merely treatable ones are not. The text of the Act surely does not require such a bizarre result."[36] And what about a person who is born deaf but has a cochlear implant? Does that person have a "record of" deafness or, like the person who uses a hearing aid, is he or she simply someone who is using a mitigating measure and thereby not covered by the statute? What does it mean to be "fully cured"? So far, the courts have offered little useful guidance on these questions.

In 1987, in interpreting Section 504 of the Rehabilitation Act, the Supreme Court actually suggested that the "record of" prong could be used rather easily in *School Board of Nassau County v. Arline*, 480 U.S. 273 (1987). Gene Arline was hospitalized for tuberculosis in 1957. For the next twenty years, her disease was in remission. Then, in 1977, a culture revealed that tuberculosis was again active in her system; cultures taken in March 1978 and November 1978 were also positive.

Arline had taught elementary school from 1966 until the school district discharged her in 1979 because of her history of tuberculosis. Arline brought suit challenging her discharge as violating Section 504 because her tuberculosis had been in remission at the time of her discharge. She argued that she could perform her job safely and was discharged only because of her prior history of tuberculosis. The district court found that she was not a qualified individual with a disability and the court of appeals reversed. It remanded the case for further findings as to whether the risks of infection precluded Arline from being qualified for the job with or without reasonable accommodation. The Supreme Court affirmed.

A key aspect of the Court's decision was its conclusion that Arline was an individual with a "record of" a disability under Section 504 (which uses the same definition of disability as the ADA). This is the evidence that the Court found sufficient to conclude she met the "record of" definition of disability:

> This impairment [tuberculosis] was serious enough to require hospitalization, a fact more than sufficient to establish that one or more major life activities were substantially limited by her impairment. Thus, Arline's hospitalization for tuberculosis in 1957 suffices to establish that she has a "record of . . . impairment" within the meaning of 29 U.S.C. § 706(7)(B)(ii), and is therefore a handicapped individual.

But did the Court really mean to imply that one is clearly disabled if one has ever been hospitalized due to a medical condition? What if Vaughn Murphy had been hospitalized when his high blood pressure was first detected at age 10? Or what if he had been hospitalized at a later age to adjust his medications so that his high blood pressure would be controllable? Could he qualify as disabled even though the Court considered his current condition not to be disabling?

The lower courts have not interpreted *Arline* broadly. Mere evidence of hospitalization for a condition does not suffice to demonstrate a record of disability.

Sergeant Charles R. Ellinger suffered a cerebral hemorrhage in 1984, after which he was hospitalized for approximately thirty days and remained at home for an additional six months. His only remaining symptom is that he sometimes experiences a sensation in his head that feels like the onset of another cerebral hemorrhage. Through the use of biofeedback, Ellinger is able to ease his fears. He was assigned to light-duty status upon his return to work, under which he worked days to avoid stress and confrontation, and was able to avoid extreme elements such as cold and heat. When Ellinger was denied a promotion, he brought suit under the ADA, arguing that he was discriminated against because of his record of disability. To support his argument, he cited *Arline*.

Ellinger's case went to trial and the jury awarded him more than $200,000 in compensatory damages.[37] The county appealed the jury verdict, arguing that there was not sufficient evidence for the jury to find that he was disabled within the meaning of the ADA. On appeal, the Second Circuit reversed the jury verdict, finding that Ellinger was not disabled.[38] Although the court agreed that Ellinger's hospitalization was a *record* of an impairment and that the hemorrhage was an impairment, it found that there was insufficient evidence that the impairment for which he was hospitalized was imposing a substantial limitation on one or more major life activities. "[A] seven-month impairment of his ability to work, with the non-particularized and unspecific residual limitations described on his police work, is of too short a duration and too vague an extent to be substantially limiting."[39]

Laura Sorensen was diagnosed with multiple sclerosis on October 30, 1993. She was then hospitalized for five days. The University of Utah Hospital employed Sorensen as a nurse from August 1990 through March 1994. At the time of her allegedly constructive discharge, she was an AirMed Flight Nurse. Sorenson quit her job after the hospital questioned her medical condition for five months and did not permit her to return to her former duties. She then brought suit against the hospital, alleging that she was discriminated against because of her disability. The district court granted summary judgment for the defendant, finding as a matter of law that Sorenson was not an individual with a disability.[40] The Tenth Circuit Court of Appeals affirmed the trial court decision.[41] The

Tenth Circuit found that Sorenson presented insufficient evidence of a substantial limitation of a major life activity because her "MS symptoms affected her for only a brief period of time and do not presently impact her ability to perform her job."[42]

The Second Circuit and Tenth Circuit are not alone in failing to follow the reasoning in *Arline* with regard to evidence of a hospitalization. The Eighth Circuit rejected the argument that proof of hospitalization for thyroid cancer established a disability.[43] The Sixth Circuit, in a case involving a back impairment, also agreed that *Arline* should not be read "as establishing the nonsensical proposition that any hospital stay is sufficient evidence of 'record of impairment.'"[44]

Possibly, the *Arline* Court spoke sloppily when it suggested that the mere evidence of a hospital stay was sufficient to establish a disability. But it seems equally absurd for plaintiffs with muscular dystrophy or a cerebral hemorrhage not to be "disabled" for the purposes of the ADA. The courts of appeals have created no meaningful standards by which to assess when a period of hospitalization helps establish the severity of a condition for the purposes of the ADA. In not wanting the "record of" prong to eliminate the mitigating-measures rule, the courts of appeals have gone too far in narrowing the usefulness of that method of establishing discrimination.

C. Prong Three

The "regarded as" disabled prong of the ADA has been relatively ineffective in protecting individuals with disabilities. The Supreme Court has narrowly construed this prong of the definition, and the lower courts have used it sparingly.

According to the EEOC regulations, the "regarded as" prong should be available in the following three situations:

> 1. When an individual has a physical or mental impairment that does not substantially limit major life activities but is treated by a covered entity as constituting such limitation,
> 2. When an individual has a physical or mental impairment that substantially limits major life activities only as a result of the attitudes of others toward such impairment; or
> 3. When an individual does not have an impairment but is treated by a covered entity as having a substantially limiting impairment.

In the first example, an individual actually has an impairment—such as high blood pressure—but the impairment does not actually limit him or her. The covered entity, however, acts on the basis of stereotype, misinformation, or prejudice and treats the individual as if the impairment is limiting. The second example is similar to the first, but it is the outside public rather than the covered entity that acts on the basis of stereotype, misinformation, or prejudice. An individual might have a cosmetic disfigurement that does not actually limit him or her. The public, however, could shun the individual if she or he works as a receptionist or in some other public capacity. If an employer refused to hire the individual due to such negative reactions, the situation fits the second example. The third example occurs when a covered entity acts on the basis of stereotype by assuming, for example, that a gay man is HIV-positive.

The courts, however, have rarely found that an individual is disabled through the application of prong three. Vaughn Murphy should have had a strong case under prong three.[45] He acknowledged that he had high blood pressure but argued that, with medication, it was under control and did not interfere with his mechanic duties. UPS, though, considered him too disabled to be a mechanic who would also have to drive a commercial motor vehicle as part of his job duties. In fact, Murphy had worked in the mechanic position for more than a month before UPS learned of his hypertension.

The legal hurdle for Murphy was that he had to demonstrate that UPS regarded him as having a physical impairment that substantially limited him in one or more major life activities. The impairment prong was easy to establish because everyone agreed that UPS regarded him as having high blood pressure. The substantial limitation prong, however, proved more difficult because Murphy had to show a nexus to a major life activity. He chose to argue that he was erroneously regarded as unable to work. The argument seemed pretty straightforward because UPS acknowledged that it terminated him because of his high blood pressure, and Murphy maintained that he was qualified to work.

Nonetheless, Murphy lost his case because the Supreme Court found that he had to establish that UPS regarded him as unable to work in a "class of jobs utilizing his skills." The Court found: "At most, petitioner has shown that he is regarded as unable to perform the job of mechanic only when the job requires driving a commercial motor vehicle."[46] Further, in the *Sutton* case, the Court hinted that it did not even believe that "working" should be on the list of major life activities. In dicta, the Court stated: "We note, however, that there may be some conceptual difficulty in defining 'major life activities' to include work, for it seems 'to argue in a circle to say that if one is excluded, for instance, by reason of [an impairment, from working with others] . . . then that exclusion itself is by reason of handicap.'"[47] Thus, even if UPS erroneously regarded Murphy as unqualified for *any* mechanic job because of his high blood pressure, the Court might have been unprepared to conclude that Murphy fit the third prong of the definition of disability.

In the employment context (ADA Title I), however, it is hard to imagine that one could construct a "regarded as" case that did *not* involve the major life activity of working. An employer is not likely to have an opinion of an employee with regard to other major life activities like eating, sleeping, walking, and so on. Those activities would simply not be of concern to it. By narrowly construing—or even throwing out—the major life activity of work, the Court has effectively taken the "regarded as" prong out of the ADA.

Congress took an innovative approach when it defined who was covered by the ADA. Rather than risk "reverse" discrimination cases by allowing anyone to bring suit under the ADA, it limited coverage to "individuals with disabilities." This approach has backfired, however, because the Supreme Court has narrowly construed each of the three prongs of the definition of disability. The Court has taken Congress's expansive approach to defining who is protected by the statute and turned it into a restrictive approach.

II. Misuse of the Summary Judgment Device

Procedurally, the plaintiffs who have been found not to be "disabled" have typically lost through the use of a summary judgment motion by a defendant. A summary judgment motion is a pretrial device whereby the defendant asks the trial court judge to rule in his or her favor because no reasonable jury could find for the plaintiff, or because the plaintiff must lose as a matter of law. When a court rules on a defendant's motion for summary judgment, it is supposed to consider the evidence in the light most favorable to the plaintiff. In theory, if a case presents close factual questions, the judge should deny the motion for summary judgment and send the case to trial, where the jury would decide the factual questions.

In practice, however, trial court judges seem too eager to rule in favor of defendants at the summary judgment phase of a proceeding, thereby precluding the jury from resolving the factual disputes.

Although trial court judges are supposed to give plaintiffs the benefit of the doubt in disposing of defendants' motions for summary judgment, the exact opposite has often occurred in practice and appellate courts rarely reverse the error. The narrow definition of disability coupled with misuse of the summary judgment device is a powerful one-two punch against plaintiffs. The empirical evidence suggests that plaintiffs have a reasonable chance of prevailing if their cases go all the way to the jury but also face a strong possibility of losing on the basis of an adverse summary judgment decision at the pretrial stage. It is possible that trial court judges are abusing the summary judgment device because they do not trust juries to resolve the factual disputes in these cases. Hence, the judges take the factual disputes away from the juries and decide the cases themselves. Nonetheless, that is not how the judicial process is supposed to work. Plaintiffs have a right to their "day in court," where juries resolve close factual disputes.

District courts have abused the summary judgment process in two ways and the courts of appeals have typically failed to correct these errors on appeal. First, district courts are refusing to send normative factual questions to the jury, such as issues of whether an individual has a disability, whether an individual is qualified to perform what are considered to be the essential functions of the job, whether a requested accommodation is reasonable, whether the risk that an individual poses at the workplace is significant enough to constitute a direct threat, and whether the hardship imposed by an accommodation is undue. Instead, trial courts are substituting their own normative judgments for that of the jury.

Courts are also abusing the summary judgment device by creating an impossibly high threshold of proof for defeating a summary judgment motion. In particular, courts are often ignoring elementary principles of who bears the burden of proof on issues in which a defendant seeks summary judgment. On issues such as whether a plaintiff poses a direct threat to the health or safety of others, the ADA clearly requires the defendant to bear the burden of proof in employment discrimination cases.[48] Yet courts are often granting summary judgment for the defendant on that issue, despite what appear to be genuine issues of fact raised by the plaintiff.

In 2000, the Supreme Court reiterated these principles. In reviewing a defendant's motion for summary judgment or judgment as a matter of

law, the Court found that the trial court "must draw all reasonable inferences in favor of the [plaintiff], and it may not make credibility determinations or weigh the evidence."[49] Quoting from a previous case, the
Court emphasized: "Credibility determinations, the weighing of the evidence, and the drawing of legitimate inferences from the facts are jury
functions, not those of a judge."[50]

Many of the cases in my appellate database—which reflect the time period shortly before the 2000 Supreme Court decision—do not reflect application of those summary judgment principles. Representative cases
from the Sixth and Fourth Circuits exemplify this problem. The Fourth
Circuit examples are not surprising because my data reflected that plaintiffs fared particularly poorly in the Fourth Circuit. The Sixth Court,
however, was a moderate circuit and, in fact, the circuit I used as my
"control" in evaluating trends across circuits. If a "typical" circuit is
abusing the summary judgment standard, then there does appear to be a
pervasive problem with that procedural device in ADA cases.

A. Fourth Circuit

The Fourth Circuit has characterized factual questions as matters of law
in order to avoid sending them to the jury. Yet the Fourth Circuit has also
created one of the highest thresholds of proof for establishing that there
is a genuine issue of material fact. This threshold standard deserves close
scrutiny.

The Fourth Circuit's inappropriately high threshold standard can be
seen in *Ennis v. National Association of Business & Educational Radio,
Inc.*,[51] one of its early ADA cases. The plaintiff, Joan Ennis, was a book-
keeping clerk at the National Association of Business and Educational
Radio (NABER) when she decided to adopt a boy who was infected with
HIV. She argued that she was discharged because of her relationship with
a disabled person, in violation of 42 U.S.C. § 12112(b)(4). In support of
this theory, she offered evidence that the director of human resources had
circulated a memo to all employees one month before she was suspended
and six months before she was fired stating that "if we have a couple of
very expensive cases, our rates could be more dramatically affected than
they currently are."[52] Ennis also offered evidence that the company recently had "the first of the 'couple of very expensive cases.'"[53] Based on
these statements, Ennis asked the court to find that her association with
her son was the basis for her discharge.

The district court granted summary judgment for the defendant, concluding that the evidence was too insubstantial to permit an inference of discrimination. By granting the motion for summary judgment, it precluded the plaintiff's taking the case to the jury. The Fourth Circuit affirmed, concluding that the plaintiff had offered only "unsupported speculation" that should not go to the jury on the defendant's state of mind.[54] One must wonder, however, what better evidence a plaintiff could have in a case concerning a decision maker's state of mind. Because meetings are rarely recorded, office memoranda are often the best indicators of state of mind. Given that the plaintiff usually is not in attendance at management meetings where the company's rationale might be explained, one might argue that a memo can function as useful inferential data. Yet the Fourth Circuit held otherwise, giving lower courts room to grant summary judgment even on cases involving state-of-mind evidence, so long as they conclude that the evidence requires too much inference.

The *Ennis* holding was extended in *Runnebaum v. Nationsbank*.[55] This case further seems to embolden district court judges who prefer to decide contested factual issues themselves rather than send them to the jury. The plaintiff, William Runnebaum, an asymptomatic individual infected with HIV, brought suit against NationsBank of Maryland after being discharged from his position in the bank's trust department.

Runnebaum filed suit in federal court to challenge his discharge as violating the ADA. The trial court judge, for the purpose of defendant's summary judgment motion, assumed that Runnebaum was disabled under the ADA's definition of disability. Nonetheless, the district court granted summary judgment for the defendant, concluding that he had not made out a prima facie case of disability discrimination.

A three-judge panel of the Fourth Circuit then heard Runnebaum's case on appeal. With one dissent, it reversed the district court's grant of summary judgment, holding that Runnebaum established a prima facie case of discrimination and forecast enough evidence to create a genuine issue of material fact as to whether he was fired because he was regarded as having a disability.[56]

The plaintiff then sought a rehiring before the entire Fourth Circuit (i.e., en banc). The Fourth Circuit granted his motion for rehearing and heard the case en banc. A divided en banc panel reversed the trial court judge with respect to the possibility of Runnebaum's being disabled. It held, as a matter of law, that Runnebaum was not disabled because he had not presented sufficient evidence to meet the ADA's definition of disability. With respect to the district court's grant of summary judgment to the defendant on the second issue, the en banc panel affirmed. Because meeting the statutory definition of disability is a prerequisite to filing suit, the en banc panel essentially held that the district court should have granted summary judgment for the defendant on the disability definition issue without even reaching the question of whether the plaintiff was a victim of discrimination.

The *Runnebaum* case is an example of an appellate court that was very eager to embrace summary judgment principles to the detriment of a plaintiff in an ADA lawsuit. At trial, no one contested that Runnebaum's HIV infection was a disability for the purposes of the ADA. The dissent interpreted the majority's decision as creating a "per se rule excluding those with asymptomatic HIV from the protections of the ADA."[57] A year later, the Supreme Court appears to have reached exactly the opposite conclusion about the status of HIV infection under the ADA. In *Bragdon v. Abbott*, 118 S. Ct. 2196 (1998), the Court concluded that the plaintiff, Sidney Abbott, was entitled to summary judgment on the question of whether she was an individual with a disability. Like Runnebaum, she was asymptomatic and alleged that her reproductive capacity was significantly limited by her HIV status. The mere evidence that Abbott was HIV-positive was sufficient for the Court to conclude that she suffered from a physical impairment. Moreover, her deposition testimony that she would refrain from reproductive activity was sufficient to demonstrate that she was substantially limited in the major life activity of reproduction.

Contrary to the *Bragdon* decision, the en banc Fourth Circuit panel concluded that "asymptomatic HIV does not substantially limit procreation or intimate sexual relations for purposes of the ADA."[58] Even if HIV infection could constitute a physical impairment under the ADA, the en banc panel also held that "there is no evidence in the record that Runnebaum, because of his infection, forewent having children or engaging in intimate sexual relations. Nothing in the record indicates that Runnebaum refrained from having children out of fear that he would pass the virus on to his child. Indeed, nothing in the record so much as suggests that Runnebaum was at all interested in fathering a child."[59]

Of course, the procedural posture of the case virtually precluded Runnebaum's presenting such evidence. His disability status was conceded by the defendants, so he had no reason to offer such specific evidence in the summary judgment proceeding. In *Bragdon*, the Supreme Court accepted a minor assertion concerning the plaintiff's interest in reproduction in a deposition as sufficient evidence to grant summary judgment *for* the plaintiff. Certainly, Runnebaum had offered sufficient evidence to get the case to the jury.

Unfortunately, this aspect of the en banc decision can be explained only as an example of homophobia. Earlier in the opinion, the en banc panel gratuitously mentioned that Runnebaum was a "homosexual."[60] It also contended that "Runnebaum's complaint may also be read to allege that he is disabled because of his homosexuality. As the district court correctly noted, and as Runnebaum conceded at oral argument, the ADA specifically excludes homosexuality as a disability."[61] Although the en banc panel was clearly troubled by Runnebaum's "homosexuality," the record suggests that Runnebaum was comfortable with his sexual orientation and openly shared that aspect of his private life with coworkers.

It appears that the en banc panel held against the plaintiff out of its disbelief that a gay man could be interested in fathering a child. It was not willing to entertain the possibility that a gay man, like others in our society, might be interested in engaging in procreation. The procreative status of a man who is HIV-positive is actually more limited than that of a woman who is HIV-positive. A woman who is HIV-positive could safely procreate through sperm donation. She would not have to share bodily fluids with another adult and risk infecting her partner. A man who is HIV-positive, however, can procreate only by donating bodily fluid—sperm—to a woman. Whether he does so through a test tube or vaginal intercourse produces the same risk of infection for the woman. The *Bradgon* Court did not even consider the possibility that Sidney Abbott might still safely procreate through sperm donation. It seemed to proceed on the assumption that procreation is possible only through heterosexual intercourse. Similarly, the en banc Fourth Circuit seemed to proceed on the assumption that procreation is possible only through heterosexual intercourse. It therefore found, as a matter of law, that a gay man who was HIV-positive could not be substantially limited in his desire to procreate. One must wonder how the Supreme Court would have ruled in *Bragdon* had the plaintiff been a gay man. Would it have understood the health risks associated with an HIV-positive man's seeking to procreate, and also understood that a gay man may desire to procreate?

Reaching the second issue presented in the case, the en banc panel also affirmed the trial court on the question of whether Runnebaum alleged a cognizable claim of discrimination. Here, the en banc panel, as well as the trial court, overlooked evidence that could have caused a reasonable juror to conclude that Runnebaum was fired because of his HIV status. Runnebaum introduced evidence that he informed a supervisor, Michael Brown, that he was HIV-positive. Brown described his reaction in a deposition as

> being in a state of panic, panic because I was thinking how am I going to work, you know and be a friend to somebody who is HIV positive. . . . But, you know, suppose he dies on me. Should I tell [the supervisor, Pettit] at this point, should I tell [the employer]? I remember feeling panicky, uncontrolled.[62]

At her deposition, Pettit acknowledged that Brown did tell her of Runnebaum's HIV status two months before Runnebaum was terminated. Runnebaum also introduced evidence that the bank knew he was HIV-positive because packages containing AZT, which were addressed to Runnebaum, were twice inadvertently opened by bank personnel. Although Pettit testified at her deposition that she had decided to fire Runnebaum before she learned of his HIV status, there were no complaints in his file about his work performance until after she learned of his HIV status. In addition, Runnebaum offered evidence that his work performance greatly exceeded that of a coemployee who was retained. These facts should have been sufficient to get the case to the jury so that it could determine whether Runnebaum's work performance or his HIV status were the cause of his termination. The en banc panel characterized Runnebaum's case as being founded on "mere unsupported speculation." By contrast, the dissent characterized the majority decision as not following elementary rules of civil procedure in not viewing the evidence in the light most favorable to the plaintiff when deciding a defendant's motion for summary judgment. I agree with the dissent that the decision represents a flagrant disregard for the general principles of the summary judgment standard.

B. Sixth Circuit

Possibly, one might explain the Fourth Circuit's cases as being reflective of the commonly acknowledged conservatism in the Fourth Circuit. But what about the Sixth Circuit, a circuit that is considered more mainstream? Why is it also disregarding basic principles of civil procedure in granting motions for summary judgment by defendants in ADA cases, particularly cases involving HIV infection?

In February 1998, the Sixth Circuit decided two ADA cases adversely to the plaintiff in what appears to be a flagrant abuse of the summary judgment standard. The decision in the first of these two cases, in particular, can only be described as ridiculous.

The first case involved Steven Sharp,[63] a part-time produce clerk at a Prevo's Market in Traverse City, Michigan. After working at the store for several months, Sharp told his employers that he had tested positively for HIV. He also told his employer that he was planning to participate in an AIDS awareness and education program and would be speaking at the local high school. Dan Prevo, president of the grocery chain, decided to reassign Sharp to a part-time position in the receiving area, with comparable hours and pay. Sharp was not happy with the new assignment and Prevo placed Sharp on a leave of absence "to give Prevo's a chance to get the information they needed to properly handle the situation."[64] When Sharp refused to provide additional medical information, his employer scheduled an appointment for him to see an infectious disease specialist. Sharp missed that appointment but did provide his employer with a letter from his own physician stating that he tested negatively for hepatitis and tuberculosis. (Prevo had expressed concern that Sharp would be susceptible to other infectious diseases, including hepatitis and tuberculosis.) After Sharp continued to refuse to see a company physician, he was terminated.

Sharp filed a charge of discrimination with the EEOC. The EEOC found reasonable cause to believe that unlawful discrimination had occurred and brought suit on behalf of Sharp in federal court. The EEOC alleged that Prevo's Market had violated the ADA's medical examination rule.[65] That rule precludes requiring an employee to take a medical examination "unless such examination is shown to be job-related and consistent with business necessity." Upon advice from legal counsel, Sharp refused to consent to a medical examination because it was hard to imagine how further information about his medical status could be relevant to his ability to work as a produce clerk.

The district court ruled for Sharp, concluding that a medical examination was not necessary, given the low risk of transmission and the fact that the low risk of transmission could be further reduced by proper hygiene procedures. The judge then submitted the matter of damages to a jury, and issued an order of reinstatement. The jury awarded Sharp

$10,000 in compensatory damages and $45,000 in punitive damages. On appeal, the Sixth Circuit reversed, finding the medical examination request to be job-related and consistent with business necessity.

In reversing the district court, the Sixth Circuit interpreted the statute as if a proposed amendment had passed (when, in fact, that amendment had failed). Two months before passage of the ADA, Representative Jim Chapman (D-Tex.) had offered a food handling amendment to the ADA. Under the proposed amendment, an employer could reassign a food handling employee with an "infectious or communicable disease of public health significance."[66] In supporting this amendment, Senator Jesse Helms (R-N.C.) argued that restaurants needed to be protected from hiring individuals who are HIV-positive because, otherwise, patronage would decrease.[67] Even Helms recognized, however, that the available evidence is that AIDS cannot be transmitted in the process of handling food.

Senator Orrin Hatch (R-Utah) brokered a compromise to deal with this problem; he suggested an amendment, which was adopted, that would give the secretary of health and human services the responsibility of preparing a list of infectious and communicable diseases that could be transmitted through food handling.[68] The Centers for Disease Control (CDC) has maintained such a list and has never placed HIV or AIDS on it. The Sixth Circuit's opinion, however, interprets the ADA as if the Chapman amendment had succeeded, or as if the CDC had placed HIV on its list of diseases that could be transmitted through food handling.

The Sixth Circuit strikes an apologetic tone in its opinion, which implies that it was aware that it employed the wrong legal standard. The court says, sympathetically, "Prevo's is simply a grocery store chain. . . . As Prevo's contends, the EEOC's argument would impose upon Prevo's a duty to become an expert in the field of HIV transmission and control. We do not believe the statute and regulation impose such a burden."[69]

The Hatch amendment, however, did not require Prevo's Market to become a medical expert. Instead, it allowed an employer to defer to the judgment of the CDC on the question of whether a particular condition could pose a danger to the food supply. The CDC is well aware that produce clerks may cut themselves while preparing food but has apparently decided that such a fact pattern does not pose a risk to the food supply.

The real problem in this fact pattern is that the employer offered no explanation for singling out Sharp for a medical examination. Poor hygiene practices (such as the sharing of bloodied knives) can present risk of infection to everyone in the workplace. Such practices would particularly increase the risk of infection of hepatitis B or C, both of which are more readily spread than HIV. The EEOC's expert therefore testified that Prevo's Market should have modified its general practice of sharing bloodied knives "on general infection control grounds rather than due to anything unique to HIV."[70]

As the dissenting Judge Moore said in this case: "[T]he majority opinion allows employers to elevate fear over facts, ignorance over information, and mythology over medicine."[71] The Sixth Circuit's sympathy for "simply a grocery store chain" allowed it to interpret the ADA contrary to Congress's stated intentions. The opinion was rooted in AIDS hysteria rather than the ADA.

Unfortunately, the Sixth Circuit repeated its error a couple of weeks later in *The Estate of William C. Mauro v. Borgess Medical Center*, 137 F.3d 398 (6th Cir. 1998). Admittedly, the fact pattern in this case was more difficult for the plaintiff than the fact pattern in *Prevo's Market*. Nonetheless, the Sixth Circuit failed to follow standard rules for motions for summary judgment in resolving this case.

William C. Mauro was an operating-room technician. He was not a surgeon, nor was he an operating-room assistant. Upon receiving an anonymous tip that Mauro had "full blown AIDS" the medical center transferred him to a position that would not involve patient contact. When Mauro refused to accept the new position, he was fired. Mauro filed suit to contest his discharge and the medical center moved for summary judgment, arguing that it was entitled to remove Mauro from his operating-room position because his HIV-status posed a direct threat to the health and safety of others.

The ADA does have a "direct threat" defense under which an employer is entitled to insist that an employee not pose a direct threat of harm to others through his employment. The courts have emphasized that this defense involves an individualized inquiry under a four-factor test outlined in *School Board v. Arline*, 480 U.S. 273 (1987). These factors include the nature, duration, severity of the risk, and the probability that the disease will be transmitted. The CDC has issued guidance to assist health care entities to evaluate this risk. The CDC cautions that there is a somewhat heightened risk of infection if the health care worker performs a limited category of "exposure-prone" invasive procedures. "Characteristics of exposure-prone procedures include digital palpation of a needle tip in a body cavity or the simultaneous presence of the [health care worker's] fingers and a needle or other sharp instrument or object in a poorly visualized or highly confined anatomic site."[72]

There was a factual dispute as to whether Mauro performed such procedures. Mauro testified in his deposition that he was a surgical technician, not a surgical assistant. He handed instruments to the surgeon and would, at times, hold a retractor with one hand in the wound area. But Mauro testified that he would not have his hands in the wound area but that he never had his hand in a body cavity "because the small size of the surgical incision prevented too many hands from being placed inside the body cavity."[73] A registered nurse, Sharon Hickman, testified that a surgical technician was sometimes, although infrequently, asked to assist in the performance of a surgical procedure in a way that could cause the technician's hands to be placed in the body cavity. Based on this, and other deposition testimony, the trial court granted summary judgment for the medical center, thereby precluding the case from going to the jury. The court of appeals affirmed, concluding that there was no genuine issue of material fact for the jury's consideration.

As the dissent argues, the court of appeals should have reversed the trial court judge, thereby sending the case to the jury for determination. The trial court was supposed to evaluate the record in the light most favorable to the plaintiff in deciding how to rule on the motion for summary judgment. As noted by the dissenting judge: "[T]he exact nature of Mauro's duties are a matter of considerable dispute, especially when the record is read, as we must read it, in a light most favorable to him."[74] Viewing the record in that light, the dissenting judge concluded that Mauro did no more than retract tissue at the edge of an incision in a way that could hardly be called a dangerous "entry into a wound." The purpose of Mauro's work with a retractor "was to expand the wound to help the surgeon see inside; but that does not mean that it was hard to see *Mauro's* fingers, out at the edge, or that his own fingers were in confined space."[75]

In *Prevo's Market*, the trial court judge did send the case to the jury, and the jury returned an award for both compensatory and punitive damages. That award was overturned on appeal. In *Mauro*, the trial court judge never sent the case to the jury, so we have no way of knowing how the jury would have evaluated the conflicting testimony. One must wonder if the trial court judge refused to send the case to the jury out of the fear that the jury, unlike the judge, would respond fairly rather than out of AIDS hysteria.

III. Conclusion

A narrow definition of disability coupled with abuse of the summary judgment process is very problematic for plaintiffs. Anecdotal evidence from some cases involving plaintiffs who are HIV-positive suggest that judges are sometimes abusing the summary judgment process to avoid having these cases go to juries that might be sympathetic to the plight of the plaintiff.

This problem may be particularly rampant in certain circuits. Empirical evidence suggests that plaintiffs have a much weaker chance of prevailing in the Fourth Circuit than in other circuits. The anecdotal evidence of abuse of the summary judgment process includes some flagrant examples from the Fourth Circuit. Justice should not depend upon geographical location. The empirical data, supported by anecdotal accounts, suggest that ADA Title I is not being fairly administered by the judiciary throughout the fifty states. The ADA is a federal statute and plaintiffs are entitled to uniform consideration around the country. At this point, however, the judicial system is being undermined by flagrant abuse of the summary judgment device in some circuits. That is not an easy problem to correct. Nonetheless, plaintiffs need to be forceful in insisting on their right to have their cases be decided by juries. Judges, not juries, may be the problem for plaintiffs in ADA cases.

5

ADA Title II

*The Supreme Court, The Courts
of Appeals, and the States:
A Swinging Pendulum*

Although the employment title of the ADA has received the most attention in the media and the courts, ADA Title II is of equal importance to individuals with disabilities. With the unemployment rate for individuals with disabilities hovering around 70 percent, many of these individuals are dependent upon state programs and services for their very survival. ADA Title II directly prohibits discrimination on the basis of disability by the state and local government and provides for a broad array of relief, including retrospective damages.

It should assist individuals like L.C. and E.W., women with mental retardation. L.C. has also been diagnosed with schizophrenia, and E.W. with a personality disorder. Both women have a history of treatment in institutional settings. In May 1992, L.C. was voluntarily admitted to Georgia Regional Hospital at Atlanta (GRH), where she was confined for treatment in a psychiatric unit. By May 1993, her psychiatric condition had stabilized and her treatment team at GRH agreed that her needs could be met appropriately in one of the community-based programs the state supported. Despite this recommendation, she remained in an institutionalized setting for three more years.

E.W. was voluntarily admitted to GRH in February 1995. She, too, was confined for treatment in the psychiatric unit. In March 1995, GRH sought to discharge her to a homeless shelter, but abandoned that plan after her attorney filed an administrative complaint. She remained institutionalized until a suit was filed on her behalf, and she prevailed.

L.C. filed a legal action against the Georgia Department of Human Resources in May 1995, when she was still institutionalized.[1] She argued that her continued confinement in a segregated environment violated ADA Title II. She requested that the state place her in a community-care residential program, and that she receive treatment with the ultimate goal of integrating her into the mainstream of society. E.W. intervened in the action, stating an identical claim.

The state responded that E.W. and L.C. had not faced discrimination "by reason of" their disabilities but, instead, had been treated appropriately, given the state's financial situation. Further, the state argued that requiring immediate transfer of these women to community-based treatment programs would "fundamentally alter" the state's activity.

The district court judge rejected both of these arguments and ruled for the plaintiffs. Because ADA Title II does not explicitly permit a cost-based defense, the district court judge rejected that argument by the state. On appeal, the Eleventh Circuit affirmed the district court's consideration of the "fundamental alteration" argument but remanded for assessment of the state's cost-based defense.[2] It concluded that a cost-based defense was appropriate in limited circumstances.

In what many viewed as a landmark decision for individuals with disabilities, the U.S. Supreme Court ruled in *Olmstead v. L.C.*, 527 U.S. 581 (1999) that unjustified isolation is discrimination on the basis of disability under ADA Title II. The media favorably compared that part of the ruling to *Brown v. Board of Education* because it emphasized the importance of integration to the disability-based civil rights model.

In a less noticed aspect of the Court's ruling, however, the Court also held that the Court of Appeals was unduly restrictive in considering the state's cost defense. In an opinion written by Justice Ruth Bader Ginsburg, the Court held: "In evaluating a State's fundamental-alteration defense, the District Court must consider, in view of the resources available to the State, not only the cost of providing community-based care to the litigants, but also the range of services the State provides others with mental disabilities, and the State's obligation to mete out those services equitably."[3]

Although the Court's handling of the unjustified isolation problem was certainly important for individuals with disabilities, its handling of the cost issue has foreshadowed the larger trend in litigation under ADA Title II in the hands of the Supreme Court. The Court has utilized various devices to make it difficult, if not impossible, for individuals to obtain effective remedies against the state. If L.C. and E.W. remain institutionalized for many years due to cost arguments by the state, then ADA Title

II's promise that they should not be subjected to unnecessary isolation becomes little more than an ineffective symbol.

The Supreme Court has used a series of devices to make it difficult for plaintiffs to obtain effective relief against the state and, in some cases, local governments as well. First, in *Olmstead*, as discussed above, it created a cost defense, although the statute does not explicitly provide for such a defense. Second, in *Board of Trustees of the University of Alabama v. Garrett*, 531 U.S. 356 (2001), it found that principles of sovereign immunity preclude suits by individuals for damage actions against state officials in cases of employment discrimination. Finally, in *Alexander v. Sandoval*, 523 U.S. 275 (2001), it was suggested that plaintiffs may not use the courts to attain relief for many of the regulations underlying ADA Title II.

The story of ADA Title II involves a fascinating dance between the Supreme Court and the courts of appeals. Chapter 3 demonstrated that under ADA Title I, the courts of appeals are complicit with the district courts in abusing the summary judgment standard to the disservice of plaintiffs. Under ADA Title II, however, the courts of appeals have tried to *resist* the Supreme Court's attempts to protect the states from damage actions. They have narrowly interpreted *Olmstead, Garrett*, and *Sandoval* to the benefit of plaintiffs. Of course, the Supreme Court has the ultimate word in interpreting the ADA, so it may overrule these recalcitrant attempts by the courts of appeals. On the other hand, the Court, itself, may learn from the lower courts and swing the pendulum further back toward the middle. Most recently, it reflected such pendulum swinging when it held in *Tennessee v. Lane*, 124 S. Ct. 1978 (2004) that ADA Title II is constitutional to the extent that it permits private individuals to bring damage actions against the state for barriers to access to the courthouse. The holding in this case borrowed heavily from the Sixth Circuit's decision in *Popovich v. Cuyahoga County Court*, 276 F.3d 808 (6th Cir. 2002). But, unfortunately, as we will see, it left open as many questions as it answered—leaving the pendulum to continue to swing.

Irrespective of what steps the Supreme Court takes to protect the states, the states, themselves, have an opportunity to offer nondiscrimination protection to individuals with disabilities under state law. As we will see, however, the states have been very lax in this area. They have generally not provided antidiscrimination protection that would apply to the state, itself, that parallels ADA Title II. To the extent that the Court's decisions under ADA Title II are embedded in constitutional law, they cannot be overruled by Congress. Hence, the enforcement problems discussed in this chapter are some of the most important problems found under the ADA. Absent a sharp change in Court membership, these problems are likely to be long lasting.

In part I, I will trace the devices created by the Supreme Court to protect the states from actions under ADA Title II. In part II, I will discuss the response to the Court's decisions by the courts of appeals. In part III, I will discuss the Court's most recent opinion interpreting ADA Title II and speculate whether it really reflects the swinging of the pendulum back in a proplaintiff direction. In part IV, I will discuss developments at the state level. In Part V, I will conclude with consideration of how to reverse this troubling trend of ineffective enforcement of ADA Title II.

I. The Supreme Court

The Supreme Court has decided three cases that undercut the ability of private parties to attain effective relief under ADA Title II: *Olmstead*, *Garrett*, and *Sandoval*. Nonetheless, its recent decision in *Lane* provides a modest opportunity for plaintiffs to continue to use ADA Title II to redress discrimination by state actors. I will discuss the *Lane* decision in part III.

A. *Olmstead*

When Congress drafted the ADA, it put explicit cost defenses into certain parts of the statute. In ADA Title I (the employment title), it provided that an employer must provide reasonable accommodation unless the accommodation would impose "an undue hardship on the operation of the business or such covered entity."[4] The term "undue hardship" was then defined to mean "an action requiring significant difficulty or expense."[5] Similarly, in ADA Title III (the public accommodations title), the ADA provides that covered entities must remove "readily achievable" barriers. The term "readily achievable" is defined in 42 U.S.C. § 12181(9) as "easily accomplishable and able to be carried out without much difficulty or expense."

ADA Title II, by contrast, contains no explicit cost defenses. Hence, in 1993, the Third Circuit interpreted ADA Title II as permitting a cost defense only in very limited circumstances. At issue was whether the City of

Philadelphia could raise a cost defense to its failure to abide by ADA regulations that clearly specified that entities were to install curb cuts when they repaved roads.[6] The Third Circuit held that in the context of new construction or alterations (like the repaving of a road) that Congress intended no cost defense. For existing facilities, it recognized that the ADA regulations excuse a public entity from taking "any action that it can demonstrate would result in a fundamental alteration in the nature of a service, program, or activity or in undue financial and administrative burdens."[7]

Like the Third Circuit, the Eleventh Circuit in *Olmstead* recognized that ADA Title II provides states with only a limited cost defense in a suit charging the state with discriminatory provision of services. The regulation that the plaintiffs cited in *Olmstead* as the foundation of their lawsuit was the "integration" regulation. It requires a public entity to administer programs "in the most integrated setting appropriate to the needs of qualified individuals with disabilities.[8] It provides no explicit cost defense, although it does provide that the state need not take measures that would "fundamentally alter" the nature of the entity's program.[9] In *Olmstead*, the lower courts interpreted this fundamental-alteration defense quite narrowly. The trial court found that this regulation permitted no cost defense. The Eleventh Circuit found that "[u]nless the State can prove that requiring it to make these additional expenditures would be so unreasonable given the demands of the State's mental health budget that it would fundamentally alter the service it provides, the ADA requires the State to make these additional expenditures."[10]

To justify its narrow interpretation of the cost defense, the Eleventh Circuit quoted from the legislative history. The House Committee on the Judiciary report explained: "The fact that it is more convenient, either administratively or fiscally, to provide services in a segregated manner, does not constitute a valid justification for separate or different services under Section 504 of the Rehabilitation Act, or under this title. . . . The existence of such programs can never be used as a basis to . . . refuse to provide an accommodation in a regular setting."[11] Congress therefore considered, and rejected, a cost defense for the integration requirement. By failing to provide a cost defense, the regulations are consistent with Congress's intentions.

Despite the fact that the language of the statute, the regulations promulgated to enforce the integration requirement, and the legislative history all reject a cost defense, the Supreme Court interpreted ADA Title II to contain a cost defense to the integration requirement. Specifically, the Court said it would be all right for the state to have "a waiting list that moved at a reasonable pace."[12] Thinking back to the failed attempt by the Court in the school desegregation context to instruct school districts to end segregation "at all deliberate speed,"[13] one must wonder why the Court would attempt a "reasonable pace" rule in the disability-segregation setting. The Court offered no guidance as to what pace would be "reasonable." It effectively amended the statute to create a cost defense that had been rejected by Congress. As hindsight now reflects, the Court was signaling that it was very protective of sovereign immunity principles under the ADA.

B. *Garrett*

The next backpedaling by the Supreme Court to protect state interests arose in an ADA Title I case: *Board of Trustees of the University of Alabama v. Garrett*, 531 U.S. 356 (2001). Unlike *Olmstead*, this case involved constitutional issues rather than an interpretation of the statutory language.

Patricia Garrett, a registered nurse, was employed as the director of nursing, OB/Gyn/Neonatal Services, for the University of Alabama in Birmingham Hospital. In 1994, she was diagnosed with breast cancer and subsequently underwent a lumpectomy, radiation treatment, and chemotherapy. The medical treatments required her to take substantial leave from work. Upon returning to work in July 1995, Garrett's supervisor informed her that she would have to give up her director position. She then applied for and received a transfer to another, lower-paying position as a nurse manager.

Milton Ash worked as a security officer for the Alabama Department of Youth Services. Upon commencing this employment, Ash informed the department that he suffered from chronic asthma and that his doctor recommended he avoid carbon monoxide and cigarette smoke. He requested that his job duties be modified to minimize his exposure to these substances. After he was also diagnosed with sleep apnea, he requested reassignment to a day-shift position. Both requests were denied, and his performance evaluations were lower subsequent to his filing a charge of discrimination with the EEOC.

Garrett and Ash filed separate lawsuits in district court, both seeking monetary damages under the ADA. In theory, their lawsuits could have been filed under ADA Title I or II, because the definition of "employer" under ADA Title I includes public entities. The Supreme Court treated the lawsuits as if they had been filed under ADA Title I, and considered the question of whether Congress exceeded its constitutional authority in providing a cause of action for money damages against the state.

The constitutional issue before the Supreme Court is rather complicated but can be simplified for our purposes. Essentially, the Court was trying to determine if Congress had the authority to provide for a remedy against the states under its authority pursuant to Section 5 of the Fourteenth Amendment. The U.S. Constitution establishes a system of limited government whereby Congress can enact legislation pursuant only to one of its enumerated powers. Specifically, Congress has limited authority to regulate the states because of a "sovereign immunity" principle that has been broadly construed by the Rehnquist Court.[14] One source that Congress may use when it wishes to regulate the states is Section 5 of the Fourteenth Amendment. Section 5 provides that Congress may enact legislation to enforce the Fourteenth Amendment. Section 1 of the amendment provides that states may not infringe individuals' right to "equal protection." Hence, Congress may enact civil rights laws pursuant to its Section 5 authority when such laws seek to protect individuals from equal protection violations at the hands of the state.

The story, however, has another layer of complication. The scope of Congress's Section 5 authority depends, in part, on *whose* civil rights it is seeking to protect. Congress has the most latitude when it seeks to protect race-based equal protection rights, somewhat less latitude when it seeks to protect gender-based equal protection rights, and little latitude when it seeks to protect age-based equal protection rights.

When Congress enacted the ADA in 1990, the courts were more generous in defining the scope of Congress's authority. At that time, it was understood that Congress could use its commerce clause authority to regulate the states. Hence, the legislative history reflects that Congress thought it had authority to regulate the states pursuant to its authority under both the Commerce Clause *and* Section 5 of the Fourteenth Amendment. Six years after Congress enacted the ADA, however, the Supreme Court declared that Congress could not regulate the states under the Commerce Clause and its powers under Section 5 were more limited than had been previously understood.[15] Congress could no longer provide more remedies against states than were constitutionally required under Section 1 of the Fourteenth Amendment. It could enforce existing rights but could not create new rights. It could not use the Commerce Clause at all as a basis to regulate the states.

This change in the law left the validity of ADA Title II, particularly its creation of remedies against the states, in a context of confusion. In order to know whether ADA Title II constitutionally created a private right of action against the states, one would have to know what constitutional guarantees existed for individuals with disabilities. Are individuals with disabilities like racial minorities and therefore can be protected broadly by Congress? Or, are they more like older Americans who can be only minimally protected by Congress from discrimination? In an ambiguous decision, the Supreme Court had ruled in 1985, in *City of Cleburne v. Cleburne Living Center,* that a Texas city violated Section 1 of the Fourteenth Amendment when it denied a special use permit for the operation of a group home for individuals with mental retardation.[16] The Constitution was violated, the Court ruled, because the denial of the special use permit had been grounded in "irrational prejudice against the mentally retarded." This decision led some people to believe that Congress could protect individuals with disabilities.

Nonetheless, the Court also ruled in *City of Cleburne* that individuals with mental retardation (and presumably other groups of individuals with disabilities) should not be accorded the strong constitutional protection that is provided to African Americans or women when they are treated differently on the basis of race or gender, respectively. The court of appeals had accorded the plaintiffs such protection.[17] And three members of the Supreme Court—Justices Thurgood Marshall, William J. Brennan, and Harry A. Blackmun—were willing to accord them such protection. But a majority of the Court refused to take that step. The Court explained: "Because mental retardation is a characteristic that the government may legitimately take into account in a wide range of decisions, and because both State and Federal Governments have recently committed themselves to assisting the retarded, we will not presume that any given legislative action, even one that disadvantages retarded individuals, is rooted in considerations that the Constitution will not tolerate."[18] However, "invidious" discrimination was unconstitutional.

These decisions thus raised the question: In banning employment discrimination by the state in ADA Title I and banning discrimination in the provision of public programs and services by the state in ADA Title II, did Congress exceed its constitutional authority?

Before looking at the Supreme Court's partial response to that question in *Garrett*, I should note that any decision by the Court in this area does not affect all of ADA Title I or Title II. The principle of sovereign immunity protects only the *state*, itself, from suit by *private individuals* for *monetary relief*. Local government does not get the protection of sovereign immunity. (And private defendants, of course, receive no protection.) In addition, the federal government has the authority to enforce ADA Title II and is not limited by principles of sovereign immunity in its enforcement attempts. Finally, individuals may still sue states for *injunctive relief*. Hence, irrespective of the Court's holding in *Garrett*, the federal government could bring a suit on the plaintiff's behalf for monetary damages, or the plaintiff could seek injunctive relief to receive, for example, Garrett's previous employment position or the accommodations desired by Ash. It was only because each of the plaintiffs sought monetary relief in a suit filed on her and his own behalf, respectively, that the principle of sovereign immunity was implicated.

The *Garrett* decision only partially resolved the sovereign immunity question but sent strong hints that the Court was willing to protect the states broadly from private suits under the ADA. The Court interpreted the *Garrett* case as involving only the constitutionality of ADA Title I's coverage of the state in suits by private individuals. It refrained from broadly considering the constitutionality of ADA Title II.

The plaintiffs in *Garrett* tried to defend the constitutionality of ADA Title I by asking the Court to reconsider its holding in *City of Cleburne* that individuals with disabilities are not a "quasi-suspect" or "suspect class" deserving of "heightened scrutiny." The Court rejected that invitation and ruled that the Constitution does not require states to make "special accommodations for the disabled, so long as their actions towards such individuals are rational."[19] Because it found that ADA Title I requires employers to make accommodations even when their conduct would be fiscally rational, the Court ruled that Congress exceeded its authority under ADA Title I.[20]

In reversing the court of appeals, and finding ADA Title I unconstitutional to the extent that it provides a private right of action against state government, the Court entirely ignored the facts of Garrett's and Ash's complaints. Was it rational for the state to demote Garrett after she returned from chemotherapy treatment? Was it rational for the state to fail to provide Ash with accommodations that would permit him to maintain gainful employment?

Ironically, the Supreme Court ruled two years later that the Family and Medical Leave Act (FMLA) was constitutional as applied to state actors in *Nevada Department of Human Resources v. Hibbs*, 123 S. Ct. 1972 (2000). The remedy provided by the FMLA is retention of one's job after the return from a medical leave of absence. Garrett had actually brought suit under both the ADA and FMLA. The district court in *Garrett* had found both statutes unconstitutional to the extent that they provided a cause of action against the state.[21] The court of appeals had reversed the district court with respect to the ADA but not the FMLA.[22] The Supreme Court then heard only the ADA issue on appeal in *Garrett*. The FMLA issue was not pressed by the plaintiff. With hindsight, it appears that the court of appeals (and the plaintiff) made exactly the wrong judgment. The court of appeals thought that it was *harder* to justify the FMLA than the ADA, with respect to a request for a leave and retention of one's job upon return. Plaintiff Garrett did not seek to have the FMLA part of the appellate court's decision reversed. Yet *Hibbs* leaves open that cause of action.

The misjudgments of the appellate court and plaintiff Garrett reflect the confusion that underlies the Supreme Court's decisions in this area. *Garrett* invalidated ADA Title I as applied to the states, and *Hibbs* validated the FMLA as applied to the states, yet both statutes offer a remedy to an individual such as Garrett, who needed job security while she took a medical leave of absence. There is no rational way to explain why Garrett was entitled to twelve weeks of unpaid leave, with a guarantee of the return of her original position, under the FMLA but not under the ADA. The Supreme Court justified the FMLA in *Hibbs* under *gender-based* equality principles because women often need to take leaves of absences to recover from a pregnancy. But when women, like Garrett, need to take leaves of absence for medical reasons, there is no inherent gender-based norm implicated. If any equality norm is implicated, it might be a disability-based norm. Certainly, individuals with disabilities are at least as likely as women to need medical leaves of absence. Yet, the combination of the Supreme Court's ADA and FMLA decisions results in workers entitled to leave under the FMLA but not the ADA if they work for state government.

The *Garrett* decision only applied to ADA Title I, but the Court hinted broadly in the FMLA case that it was limiting the constitutional scope of ADA Title II. Recognizing that it had invalidated the ADA while validating the FMLA, the Court repeated its comment from *Garrett*: "States are not required by the Fourteenth Amendment to make special accommodations for the disabled, so long as their actions toward such individuals are rational."[23] It then repeated its conclusion from *Garrett*, that Congress had not sufficiently identified a "widespread pattern" of irrational reliance on disability-based criteria to justify ADA Title I.[24]

Thus, *Hibbs* upheld the FMLA while hinting broadly that the Court would ultimately invalidate some aspects of ADA Title II, as applied to the states. In her speech at Georgetown Law School, Justice O'Connor observed that Supreme Court decisions often reflect a pendulum, that the Court takes what may seem like an extreme position in one direction and then swings back toward the center in one of its next decisions. *Hibbs* was an attempt by the Court to deflect arguments that it had been too protective of states' rights when it struck down ADA Title I as applied to the states in *Garrett* and struck down the Age Discrimination Act as applied to states in *Kimel v. Florida Bd. of Regents*, 528 U.S. 62 (2000). By upholding the FMLA, it swung the pendulum back toward the middle. The Court's most recent decision, in *Lane*, reflects a continuation of the pendulum swinging in a proplaintiff direction while also suggesting that the Court is prepared to strike down large aspects of ADA Title II as applied to the states.

Abstractly, *Hibbs* and *Lane* reflect a moderation of the Court's sovereign immunity jurisprudence but, for individuals with disabilities, they foreshadow that the Court is prepared to strike down many aspects of ADA Title II. Justice O'Connor's perception of the Court's moderation may be ultimately misplaced.

C. *Alexander v. Sandoval*

The final potential blow that the Supreme Court gave to ADA Title II came through a somewhat circuitous route. In *Alexander v. Sandoval*, 532 U.S. 275 (2001), the Court was asked to consider the somewhat obscure question of whether individuals may sue to enforce disparate-impact regulations promulgated under Title VI of the Civil Rights Act of 1964. The Court answered no in a decision that could affect its interpretations of ADA Title II. Like the *Olmstead* decision, this ruling was primarily based on principles of statutory interpretation rather than constitutional law. Hence, Congress could, in theory, overturn the decision. But looking over its shoulder at a conservative Congress, the Rehnquist Court does not fear that possibility. Hence, it confidently offers technical opinions that can have a big impact on the interpretation of various civil rights laws that are patterned on Title VI of the Civil Rights Act of 1964.

Title VI provides that no person shall "on the ground of race, color, or national origin, be excluded from participation in, be denied the benefits of, or be subjected to discrimination under any program or activity" covered by Title VI.[25] Congress patterned Section 504 of the Rehabilitation Act of 1973 on the language found in Title VI. Section 504 therefore provides that no person shall be excluded from participation in, be denied the benefits of, or be subjected to discrimination under any program or activity on the basis of disability. ADA Title II uses virtually the same language as Section 504. ADA Title II covers all "public entities," whereas Section 504 and Title VI cover all entities receiving federal financial assistance.

Each of these three statutes—Title VI, Section 504, and ADA Title II—also provides that federal agencies enforce these requirements by issuing rules, regulations, or orders of general applicability. The statutes share a similar enforcement scheme.

To comply with its enforcement obligations under Title VI, the U.S. Department of Justice promulgated a regulation forbidding recipients to "utilize criteria or methods of administration which have the effect of subjecting individuals to discrimination because of their race, color, or national origin."[26]

In 1990, the state of Alabama amended its Constitution to declare English to be the "official language of the state of Alabama." To comply with this rule, the Alabama Department of Public Safety began to administer its state driver's license examinations only in English. Martha Sandoval, a non-English-speaking resident of the state, brought suit against the state challenging the English-only rule as violating the Title VI regulation because it had the effect of subjecting non-English speakers to discrimination on the basis of their national origin. In response, the state of Alabama contended that private individuals had no authority to enforce the Title VI regulation.

The Court agreed with the state of Alabama. Although it found that the Alabama Department of Justice had the authority to promulgate (and enforce) regulations, it did not have the authority to grant a private right of action to individuals to enforce those regulations. Only Congress, it found, could define the scope of that private right of action, and it found that Congress intended private rights of actions under Title VI to be limited to cases of intentional discrimination. Because the regulation at issue did not require a showing of intent, it could not be enforced by a private party. Only the DOJ, itself, could enforce the regulation.

So what does this ruling have to do with Section 504 and ADA Title II? Because Section 504 and ADA Title II use nearly identical language and enforcement mechanisms as Title VI, the Supreme Court's holding in *Sandoval* could potentially extend to those other statutes. The Court implied that result by discussing Section 504 cases along with Title VI cases in its opinion.

What, then, could be the impact of *Sandoval* on ADA Title II? *Sandoval's* impact could be much broader than *Olmstead's* or *Garrett's* because it is not limited to cases brought against the state itself. Nor is it limited to cases seeking monetary relief. Sandoval sought an injunction to force the state of Alabama to offer the driver's license examination in languages other than English.

The impact of the *Sandoval* decision could be broad under the ADA, because few cases under ADA Title II involve examples of *intentional* discrimination. Moreover, it is hard to know what the concept of intentional discrimination even means in the disability context. ADA Title II cases involve fact patterns like a failure to build curb cuts, inaccessible courthouses, unnecessary segregation of individuals with disabilities, or a failure to offer sign language interpreters by law enforcement authorities. These fact patterns typically reflect "business as usual," with individuals with disabilities being entirely ignored. That is not the intentional discrimination model that the courts have used under the civil rights acts. Broad application of *Sandoval* to ADA Title II could therefore undermine nearly all the cases proceeding under that title.

In sum, the combined impact of *Olmstead, Garrett,* and *Sandoval* on ADA Title II could be fatal to that title. So far, however, resistance by the courts of appeals has helped avoid that fate. The story of resistance follows.

II. Response by the Courts of Appeals and Trial Courts

Although the Supreme Court has given the lower courts much opportunity to limit the effectiveness of ADA Title II, the courts of appeals, and some trial courts, have resisted such overtures. Here are some stories of resistance.

Joseph Popovich is hearing impaired. He was involved in a child custody dispute concerning whether he (or his wife) should have custody of their daughter. Popovich requested closed-captioning or real-time transcription so that he could meaningfully participate in the child custody case. The trial court judge told Popovich that he would have to delay the trial considerably in order to grant this request. When Popovich insisted on receiving the requested accommodation, the trial was delayed for eighteen months, and Popovich ultimately lost the custody of his child to the child's mother. Popovich was repeatedly requested to waive his right to sue the state court under ADA Title II, but refused. He ultimately sued the state court pursuant to ADA Title II. After a four-day trial, a jury rendered a verdict of $400,000 in compensatory damages. The state appealed the adverse ruling, arguing that it was immune from suit pursuant to sovereign immunity principles. A three-judge panel agreed with the state's argument, but the plaintiff then successfully petitioned the Sixth Circuit to hear the case en banc. The Sixth Circuit agreed to hear the case en banc and ruled that a plaintiff could constitutionally bring a claim under ADA Title II if he or she had been arguably denied due process of law.[27]

Unfortunately, however, the Sixth Circuit had to remand for a new trial because the original jury had been erroneously instructed that it could find an ADA Title II violation if the plaintiff's *equal protection* or due process rights were violated. The Sixth Circuit interpreted *Garrett* to mean that one cannot use ADA Title II to pursue an equal protection violation. But the court concluded that a due process theory was nonetheless still available.

The Sixth Circuit's response to *Garrett* was very creative because it left open the door for some ADA Title II cases to proceed notwithstanding the *Garrett* decision. The Second Circuit has taken a similar approach, holding that Title II actions for monetary damages may be brought by plaintiffs who can "establish that the Title II violation was motivated by discriminatory animus or ill will based on the plaintiff's disability."[28] The Ninth Circuit has taken the most liberal approach, holding that ADA Title II is constitutional in its entirety.[29] The courts of appeals are split on this issue. The Fourth, Fifth, and Tenth Circuits have found that ADA Title II is unconstitutional to the extent that it permits monetary damages in private actions against the state.[30] As we will see in part III, the Supreme Court ultimately adopted the Sixth Circuit's approach.

Another mechanism being employed by courts of appeals to permit ADA Title II lawsuits to go forward against the state is an *Ex Parte Young* theory of liability.[31] Under the *Ex Parte Young* doctrine, a private plaintiff can sue a *state official* rather than the state itself for *injunctive relief*. Most of the courts of appeals have embraced this theory for relief under ADA Title II.[32]

Some courts are also narrowly interpreting *Olmstead* in order to require the states to avoid segregation of individuals with disabilities. Levi Townsend was told by the state of Washington that he would have to move to a nursing home within thirty days or lose his Medicaid benefits. Townsend preferred to receive services in a community-based setting so that he could be close to his community, friends, and family. He was in his eighties, had diabetic peripheral vascular disease, and was a bilateral amputee. He required medical treatment, assistance preparing meals, performing housework, bathing, dressing, and attending to other personal hygiene needs.

Townsend filed a class action lawsuit against the state, seeking to enjoin the requirement that he move to a nursing home as a condition of receiving needed, available Medicaid services.[33] He filed suit under ADA Title II, arguing that the state contravened the principles expressed in *Olmstead*. The trial court ruled against the plaintiffs, granting summary judgment to the state. On appeal, the Ninth Circuit reversed the district court and remanded the case to determine whether the modifications requested by the plaintiffs would fundamentally alter the state's program by requiring it to cut back services to other Medicaid recipients in order to provide the requested relief. The trial court had found that the plaintiffs' request was a fundamental alteration; the court of appeals required further fact-finding on that issue.

Finally, some trial courts are resisting the Court's decision in *Sandoval* by finding that it does not apply to the regulations promulgated under ADA Title II. The City of Sandusky has failed to install curb ramps on sidewalks in violation of an ADA regulation that requires the installation of curb cuts and ramps when resurfacing city streets.[34] A nonprofit organization that represents individuals with disabilities brought suit challenging the city's failure to comply with ADA Title II. The city defended the lawsuit by arguing that there was no private right of action to enforce the curb ramp regulation because the statutory language of ADA Title II did not explicitly provide for that rule. The trial court disagreed. It noted that the findings section of the ADA specifically refers to the importance of removing architectural barriers so that the curb-cut regulation was clearly contemplated by Congress when it enacted ADA Title II.[35] This and other cases may, of course, be appealed and there is no way to predict the reaction from the appellate courts.

In sum, some lower courts are trying to swing the pendulum back to moderation with respect to sovereign immunity doctrine. They are trying to distinguish Supreme Court precedent and find creative ways to permit ADA Title II to be fully enforced by private individuals. It is too early to know whether these efforts will be successful, but it is encouraging to see this attempt at moderation.

III. Tennessee v. Lane

In September 1996, George Lane was compelled to appear at the Polk County, Tennessee, courthouse to answer a set of criminal charges that the state had filed against him.[36] Lane used a wheelchair to ambulate and could neither walk nor climb stairs. The courthouse had no elevator, and all proceedings were held on the second floor. Lane crawled up the stairs to appear in court that day. In October, Lane was again summoned to appear in the same courtroom. He sent word to the judge, after arriving on time, that he was not willing to crawl up the stairs to appear in court. The judge offered to have court employees carry Lane to the courtroom. Lane refused that request, arguing that it would not be safe. Lane was then arrested and jailed for his failure to appear in court. When the court continued not to make an accessible courtroom available to him, the judge suggested that Lane bring an independent civil suit under the ADA to make the courtroom accessible, but held that the inaccessibility of the courthouse was no basis for delaying or dismissing the pending criminal case.

Lane and other Tennessee residents who had been denied access to accessible courthouses, filed suit on August 10, 1998, against the State of Tennessee and a number of counties. They sought both damages and injunctive relief.

The state moved to dismiss the lawsuit on Eleventh Amendment grounds, but the district court denied the motion. Relying on its holding in *Popovich*, the Sixth Circuit affirmed the denial of the motion to dismiss and remanded for further proceedings.

The State of Tennessee appealed the case to the U.S. Supreme Court. In a 5-4 decision, the Court narrowly ruled in favor of the plaintiffs.

What is interesting about the case is *not* that the Court ruled for the plaintiffs. What is interesting is that *four dissenters* thought that Lane had no constitutionally protected right that could be enforced by ADA Title II to have access to the courthouse.

The majority opinion narrowly framed the issue before the Court: "[T]his case is not [about] whether Congress can validly subject the States to private suits for money damages for failing to provide reasonable access to hockey rinks, or even to voting booths, but whether Congress had the power under section five to enforce the constitutional right of access to the courts." The majority opinion concluded, "Title II is unquestionably valid section five legislation as it applies to the class of cases implicating the accessibility of judicial services."

The *Lane* decision probably has few implications for other ADA Title II cases other than cases involving voting rights. In a footnote, it mentions evidence about the inaccessibility of voting to some individuals with disabilities. And its phrase "even to voting booths" suggests that voting, like access to courthouses, is a fundamental right that is properly protected by ADA Title II. What else is protected, however, is unclear. Other important state services include higher education, health care, and incarceration. It is not clear that individuals with disabilities who have arguably faced discriminatory treatment in those areas could bring a claim for monetary damages against the state. It is not clear that the *Olmstead* decision, itself, withstands the *Lane* decision.

The narrowness of the Court's holding is highlighted by the fact that the four dissenters were not even willing to conclude that Congress had the power under ADA Title II to mandate access to courthouses. Speaking for the dissenters, Chief Justice Rehnquist said:

> Even if the anecdotal evidence and conclusory statements relied on by the majority could be properly considered, the mere existence of an architecturally "inaccessible" courthouse—*i.e.*, one a disabled person cannot utilize without assistance—does not state a constitutional violation. A violation of due process occurs only when a person is actually denied the constitutional right to access a given judicial proceeding. We have never held that a person has a *constitutional* right to make his way into a courtroom without any external assistance.

The dissenters' reasoning is troubling on two levels. First, they do not understand why it is fundamentally disrespectful for an individual to be expected to crawl or be carried to the courtroom. Second, the dissenters confuse the remedy with the question of whether the plaintiff has standing. In this case, Lane alleges that he could not safely travel to the courtroom. The state alleges that it made a reasonable offer to carry him to the courtroom. Under the dissenters' theory of the case, the court does not have jurisdiction because the court knows on the basis of the pleadings that Lane has been offered constitutional access to the courtroom.

But how can the court make such a judgment on the basis of the pleadings? Whether the offer was reasonable (and therefore arguably permissible and lawful under the ADA) would depend on whether it was effective. Lane argues that the offer was not a safe alternative. How does the trial court judge (or the Supreme Court) know otherwise without fact-finding? The record does not apparently disclose how much Lane weighed, how many stairs needed to be climbed, the precise nature of Lane's disability, and the physical skill and ability of the individuals who would be carrying him to the courtroom. Even if one did not accept that Lane had legitimate personal-integrity reasons for wanting to arrive at the courtroom independently, the court would still have to resolve whether the state's offer was reasonable and effective. The Supreme Court dissenters anointed themselves experts on this basic question in ruling for the state. As in so many of the other decisions by the courts, the dissenters' opinion reflects no sensitivity to what it means to be an individual with a disability who, in this case, uses a wheelchair. Their decision is also consistent with the abuse of the summary judgment device (see chapter 4). Once again, judges are deciding factual issues for themselves rather than sending them to the jury.

The *Lane* decision was generally heralded in the media as a success for the disability rights movement. As a technical matter, it is true that the plaintiffs prevailed in that their case will now be remanded to the trial court to determine if the state had made reasonable steps to accommodate them. But the larger question is what we can expect in the future. Will many claims against states be permitted to be heard in the future under ADA Title II? Other than voting rights cases, it is hard to imagine a broad class of cases going forward against states under ADA Title II. And disability plaintiffs are only one vote away from not even having a judicially enforceable access to the courthouse.

The *Garrett* and *Lane* decisions, therefore, place a great deal of weight on the importance of state law. Can individuals with disabilities obtain ample recourse under state law if their cases cannot be brought against the states in federal court under ADA Title II? That is the next topic under consideration.

IV. State Protection

Even if ADA Title II were found not to be constitutional with respect to providing a cause of action against the state, there could, in theory, still be state law that could be used as a basis for a cause of action. In the first sentence of the "Statement" section of its brief before the Supreme Court in *Garrett*, the State of Alabama said that "all 50 States prohibit government-based discrimination against the disabled and, more, affirmatively require all manner of employment and public-access accommodations designed to provide the disabled with the kind of equal opportunity and dignity that all individuals deserve."[37] The brief later elaborated that "[t]hese [state] laws and administrative regulations predate passage of the ADA, far exceed the rational-basis requirements of equal-protection review, all permit monetary relief against the sovereign, and in the end markedly overprotect rather than underprotect the constitutional rights of the disabled."[38]

Each statement was followed by a citation to Appendix A of the brief, which listed state disability discrimination statutes and regulations. Although the appendix listed specific statutes and regulations that allow for "[e]quitable and monetary remedies" for employment discrimination, it merely identifies state statutes with "policies requiring accessibility and accommodation."[39] There was no mention of the scope of the policies nor of the types of remedies they provide, if any. Nonetheless, the Supreme Court in *Garrett* echoed Alabama's brief and declared that "state laws protecting the rights of persons with disabilities in employment and other aspects of life provide independent avenues of redress."[40] The Court offered no support for the "other aspects of life" statement.

Are there state statutes barring state governments from discriminating in public access and services and, if so, do they offer remedies similar to those found in ADA Title II? To answer these questions, one has to define the scope of protections afforded by ADA Title II. The protections include

—prohibition of discrimination in access to "facilities";
—prohibition of discrimination in access to "services";

—a private right of action to enforce these protections, including compensatory damages; and

—availability of attorney's fees.

Collaborating with Professor Adam Milani, I researched the law in each of the fifty states. Our research shows that the statements in the State of Alabama's brief that "50 States" have "laws and administrative regulations" that "permit monetary relief against the sovereign" are simply not true with regard to access to state facilities and services. In fact, the statements are not even true for a majority of the states—including Alabama. We found that only twenty-four of fifty-one states provide clear statutory language with protection comparable to ADA Title II.

A. Prohibition of Discrimination in Access to Facilities

The ADA Title II regulations provide broad protection against discrimination at facilities, and we found that all states have laws specifically requiring government-owned buildings to be accessible. Nonetheless, we found ambiguities regarding the statutes' coverage and problems with their enforcement. First, although every state appears to require that public "buildings" be accessible to individuals with disabilities, it is unclear in some states whether this rule applies more broadly to all government-owned entities. Second, fifteen states do not have clear, effective, private enforcement mechanisms for their accessibility policies.

ADA Title II covers state property that encompasses far more than the buildings themselves. Under ADA Title II, streets and sidewalks as well as parks and recreational facilities must be accessible. Accessible sidewalks are a particularly important right guaranteed by ADA Title II. Without accessible sidewalks, a person with a disability might never get to the front door of a public building. Indeed, one of the earliest appellate court decisions on ADA Title II was a successful class action suit against the secretary of the Pennsylvania Department of Transportation and the commissioner of the Philadelphia Streets Department that sought to compel the city to install curb ramps on streets that had been resurfaced since the effective date of the ADA.[41]

Most state statutes specifically cover both "buildings" and "facilities," which indicates that their scope is equivalent to the coverage found in

ADA Title II. Many states also adopt the Americans with Disabilities Act Accessibility Guidelines for Buildings and Facilities (ADAAG) or accessibility standards promulgated by the American National Standards Institute (ANSI), which cover a broad range of facilities. Still others have state statutes that specifically include sidewalks and curb ramps.

Determining whether sidewalks and other facilities such as state parks are covered is problematic, however, in three states that limit their accessibility rules to state "buildings." For example, Ohio has a state statute requiring "all buildings" to be accessible to individuals with disabilities,[42] and presumably this statute covers state-owned buildings, but it does not have a public accommodations statute that clearly applies to the state and would cover all state facilities. Similarly, Tennessee has a state policy to make all "public buildings" accessible; the definition of "public buildings" does not mention state parks or sidewalks.[43] Wisconsin has a state statute requiring public "building(s)" to be accessible to individuals with disabilities;[44] it does not appear to have a public accommodation statute that would be broadly applicable to all state facilities. Although these states adopt ADAAG or ANSI standards, it is hard to know if the standards would apply to sidewalks because sidewalks might not come within the scope of the state statute.

Table 5.1 shows whether there is a state statute requiring government-owned facilities to be accessible as well as any ambiguities or problems with respect to coverage or enforcement. For states with ineffective private enforcement mechanisms, the coverage of streets and sidewalks may be of little consolation to a person with a disability who has no remedy if the state does not follow its own law.

B. Prohibition of Discrimination in Services

ADA Title II covers far more than physical access; it bars discrimination in the "services, programs, or activities of a public entity." Some states have statutes barring disability discrimination in state "services," but many do not. Therefore, we looked to statutes barring disability discrimination by "public accommodations" to see if they provided such protection. We found two problems in assessing state coverage in this area: (1) whether the state public accommodation statute barred "services" discrimination, and (2) whether public accommodations statutes that specifically bar services discrimination applied to the state. The sparse case law in this area indicates that these ambiguities can be significant. Accordingly, we have concluded that only twenty-four of fifty-one statutes clearly cover services discrimination by the states.

The first problem with state public accommodations laws is that twenty-four states do not have statutes that explicitly cover "services" discrimination. This lack may not be a significant issue in four of the states, however, because they have adopted language clearly modeled after section 504 of the Rehabilitation Act, which states that people with disabilities shall not "be excluded from the participation in, be denied the benefits of, or be subjected to discrimination under any program or activity receiving Federal financial assistance." The language does not explicitly list "services" discrimination, but it is reasonable to assume that a state court would interpret it broadly and thereby imply such coverage.

Three states, however, do not have a broad public accommodation statute that applies to discrimination on the basis of disability. Hence, it is not possible for a court to find a nondiscrimination policy in the provision of state services in those states.

The remaining seventeen states have public accommodation statutes that do not clearly state whether they apply to services. In eight, the public accommodation statute does not apply to the state, so whether it applies to services discrimination is not relevant to the present inquiry.

Of the remaining nine states where coverage of services was ambiguous, courts have interpreted two of the statutes to apply only to "places" or "physical structures." Specifically, in *Fell v. Spokane Transit Authority*,[45] the Washington Supreme Court held that the state's public accommodations statute did not apply to paratransit services. The statute at issue prohibited any person from committing an act that "directly or indirectly results in any distinction, restriction, or discrimination, . . . in any place of public resort, accommodation, assemblage, or amusement" because of an individual's disability.[46]

The parties agreed that public transit was a "public accommodation," and the plaintiffs argued that the relevant "place" of public accommodation was the transit authority's entire service area. The court rejected this argument, saying that the statutory language "ma[de] it very clear that the reach of the statute extends to places and facilities, not services."[47] It noted that "Titles II and III of the ADA . . . distinguish services from places of public accommodation," and further declared:

> What must be very clear . . . is that the [state] statutory mandate to provide access to places of public accommodation is not a mandate to pro-

TABLE 5.1.
Scope of Nondiscrimination Statutes: Facilities

State	Clearly Covers State Facilities Title II for Facility Accessibility	Enforcement Comparable to ADA	Comments
Alabama	Yes	No	One statute covers "all buildings and facilities" constructed with state funds, but only enforcement mechanism is state fire marshal's power to order that the building conform with accessibility standards. Another statute covers "places of public accommodation," but only remedy is misdemeanor, which would not apply to the state.
Alaska	Yes	Yes	Covers public "facilities."
Arizona	Yes	Yes	Covers "buildings and facilities" "used or funded by public entities."
Arkansas	Yes	No	Only remedy is misdemeanor, which would not apply to the state; definition of disability limited to "visually handicapped, hearing impaired, and ... physically handicapped."
California	Yes	Possibly	One statute requires facilities and sidewalks to be accessible, but no private remedies. Separate statute requires accessibility at "business establishments"; not clear whether state could be sued under this provision. See *Black v. Dept. of Mental Health*, 100 Cal. Rptr. 2d 39, 42 n.4 (2000) (declining to rule whether the statute applies to the state).
Colorado	Yes	No	Covers public "facilities"; relief appears limited to equitable relief.
Connecticut	Yes	Yes	Covers public "facilities."
Delaware	Yes	Yes	Covers public "facilities."
D.C.	Yes	Yes	Covers public "facilities."
Florida	Yes	Unclear	One statute requires state buildings and facilities to be accessible, but there is no private enforcement. Separate statute requires accessibility at public accommodations, but only remedy is misdemeanor, which would not apply to the state. Another statute provides private cause of action for "public accommodations" discrimination but does not specify scope of the nondiscrimination policy.
Georgia	Yes	No	Covers "public buildings," but only remedy is misdemeanor, which would not apply to the state.
Hawaii	Yes	Yes	Covers any program or activity receiving state financial assistance; building code rule requires accessibility.
Idaho	Yes	No	Statute covers state buildings and facilities; only remedy is misdemeanor, which would not apply to the state.
Illinois	Yes	Yes	Covers public "facilities."
Indiana	Yes	Yes	Covers "public conveniences and accommodations."
Iowa	Yes	Yes	Covers public "facilities."
Kansas	Yes	No	Covers public "facilities"; $2,000 limit for pain, suffering, and humiliation award before Civil Rights Commission.
Kentucky	Yes	Yes	Covers public facilities; state building code.
Louisiana	Yes	Yes	Covers programs or activities that receive financial assistance from the state or any of its political subdivisions.
Maine	Yes	Yes	Covers public facilities.
Maryland	Yes	No	Covers public facilities bur enforcement limited to state civil rights commission.

State			
Massachusetts	Yes	Yes	Covers public facilities.
Michigan	Yes	Yes	Covers public facilities.
Minnesota	Yes	Yes	Covers public facilities.
Mississippi	Yes	No	Covers public facilities, only remedy is misdemeanor, which would not apply to the state; definition of disability limited to "blind persons, visually handicapped persons, deaf persons and other physically disabled persons."
Missouri	Yes	Yes	Covers public "facilities."
Montana	Yes	Yes	Covers public "facilities."
Nebraska	Yes	No	Covers public "facilities"; only remedy is misdemeanor, which would not apply to the state; protects only the "partially blind, hearing-impaired, or physically disabled."
Nevada	Yes	Yes	State facility rule; enforcement for public accommodation statute that is reasonably interpreted to cover state.
New Hampshire	Yes	Yes	Covers places of "public accommodation"; state explicitly covered.
New Jersey	Yes	Yes	Covers places of "public accommodation"; state not explicitly covered, but some state entities explicitly exempted.
New Mexico	Yes	Yes	Covers public "facilities."
New York	Yes	Yes	Covers public "buildings and facilities."
North Carolina	Yes	No	Covers state "facilities." Only declaratory and injunctive relief available.
North Dakota	Yes	Yes	Covers places of "public accommodation"; explicitly covers state.
Ohio	No	Unclear	General building code statute covers "all buildings" and presumably applies to the state, but enforcement mechanism against the state unclear. Public accommodation statute does not explicitly cover the state.
Oklahoma	Yes	Yes	Covers public "facilities."
Oregon	Yes	Yes	Covers places of "public accommodation"; case law suggests coverage of the state; public facilities rules; specific reference to curb cuts.
Pennsylvania	Yes	Yes	Covers "public accommodation"; explicitly covers state.
Rhode Island	Yes	Yes	Covers public "facilities."
South Carolina	Yes	Yes	Covers "public accommodations" and "public services"; building code rules require accessibility.
South Dakota	Yes	Yes	Covers "public accommodations"; explicitly covers state; explicitly covers curb ramps.
Tennessee	No	No	Has a state policy that all "public buildings" are accessible, but no penalty or fine may be assessed against the state for noncompliance.
Texas	Yes	Yes	Covers public "building or facility."
Utah	Yes	No	Covers "all buildings and facilities"; only remedy is misdemeanor, which would not apply to the state.
Vermont	Yes	Yes	Covers "public accommodations"; explicitly covers state; building code rules.
Virginia	Yes	Yes	Covers any program or activity receiving state financial assistance or any program or activity conducted by or on behalf of any state agency.
Washington	Yes	Yes	Covers access to places of public accommodation; definition of disability appears limited to "the blind, the visually handicapped, the hearing impaired, and the otherwise physically disabled"; specifically mentions "walkways."
West Virginia	Yes	Yes	Covers place of "public accommodation"; explicitly includes state.
Wisconsin	No	Yes	Requires public "buildings" to be accessible.
Wyoming	Yes	No	Requires public "buildings" to be accessible; no enforcement mechanism specified; public accommodation statute provides a misdemeanor remedy, which would not apply to the state; coverage of sidewalks explicit.

vide services. While entitlement to services may be in the ADA, the Legislature has not enacted a counterpart to the ADA in Washington creating such entitlements.[48]

A federal court interpreting an Ohio statute reached a similar conclusion.[49] The Ohio statute forbids discrimination in "the full enjoyment of the accommodations, advantages, facilities, or privileges of the place of public accommodation."[50] A patient sued a medical clinic under this statute when it refused to provide a sign language interpreter during marital counseling services. The clinic argued that the Ohio Civil Rights Commission's regulations interpreting this section "prohibit[] a facility that is a place of public accommodation from engaging in affirmative acts discrimination against the handicapped, but does not require such facilities to 'accommodate' a handicap beyond making modifications to physical structures." The court agreed:

> Unlike the implementing regulations for the ADA and the Rehabilitation Act, nothing in (the state regulations) requires a place of public accommodation to provide auxiliary aids. . . . Rather, . . . the regulation requires, as an accommodation, some modification of the relevant facilities and identifies various structural considerations.[51]

Nonetheless, a federal district court in New Jersey interpreted New Jersey's state law (which is similar to Ohio's) to include services discrimination.[52]

A second problem with state public accommodation statutes is determining whether they apply to the state itself. Of the twenty-seven states that specifically ban discrimination in services to individuals with disabilities, three have statutes that do not clearly indicate that the rule against discrimination applies to the state. In California, the only legal authority was contrary to implied coverage of the state. California's public accommodation statute—the Unruh Civil Rights Act—states that people with disabilities are "entitled to the full and equal accommodations, advantages, facilities, privileges, or services in all business establishments of every kind whatsoever."[53] In *Black v. Department of Mental Health*, the trial court held that the state was not covered under the Unruh act because it was not a "business establishment."[54] Black, the administrator of the estate of a long-term mental patient, argued on appeal that "the [Unruh] Act did away with any such limitation by incorporating the ADA in its entirety, including provisions which applied to public entities."[55] The appellate court, however, said that it need not resolve this issue because it could affirm on a different ground. Accordingly, it is still an open question whether the State of California is covered under the Unruh act.

In other states, however, the absence of specific mention of the state in a public accommodation statute might be interpreted narrowly by a court. Indeed, the Delaware State Attorney General's Office took the position that the state is not covered under the Delaware Equal Accommodations Law because it was not specifically included as a covered entity.[56] The statute's prohibition of discrimination provides:

> No person being the owner, lessee, proprietor, manager, superintendent, agent or employee of any place of public accommodation, shall directly or indirectly refuse, withhold from or deny to any person, on account of race, age, marital status, creed, color, sex, handicap or national origin, any of the accommodations, facilities, advantages or privileges thereof.[57]

The term "person" is not defined in the chapter, but another statute declares that it includes "corporations, companies, associations, firms, partnerships, societies and joint-stock companies, as well as individuals."[58] The attorney general concluded that because the state was not mentioned in the equal accommodations law's definitions or other provisions "there is no manifest intent that the General Assembly intended to include the State" in its definition of "person." Although this opinion letter is not binding legal authority, it is instructive for our present inquiry because the statutory ambiguity problem in the Delaware statute is similar to the ambiguity we found in Ohio, Oregon, Vermont, and Wisconsin. These states also have public accommodation statutes that do not specifically identify whether the state is covered.

Table 5.2 is informative on each state's stance on prohibiting services discrimination by the state government. We found that twenty-nine states had coverage equivalent to ADA Title 5.2 by virtue of express language, implied statutory language, or case law. If a state had adopted Section 504's language, we concluded that services discrimination could reasonably be expected to be covered. In light of the negative precedent found in California, and the narrow interpretation offered by the Delaware attorney general, however, we have indicated that it is "unclear" if a state is covered under a "public accommodation" law unless it is specifically identified in the statute. Similarly, if a state statute failed to say explicitly

TABLE 5.2.

Scope of Nondiscrimination Statutes: Services Discrimination

State	Services Covered	State Covered	Comments
Alabama	Unclear	No	Public accommodation statute does not mention "services" discrimination, and only remedy is misdemeanor, which would not be applicable to the state.
Alaska	Yes	Yes	Statute updated after passage of ADA to parallel its protections, but no specific reference to "services."
Arizona	Unclear	Yes	Public accommodation statute does not mention "services" discrimination, which would not be applicable to the state; state civil rights act does not mention "services" discrimination and bars recovery against state.
Arkansas	Unclear	No	
California	Yes	Unclear	Provides for nondiscrimination in services at "business establishments"; court declined to rule whether the statute applies to the state; *Black v. Dept. of Mental Health*, 100 Cal. Rptr. 2d 39, 42 n.4 (2000).
Colorado	Yes	Yes	
Connecticut	Yes	Yes	
Delaware	Unclear	No	Attorney general opinion states that state and political subdivisions not covered under Delaware Equal Accommodations Law; a separate "public accommodation" statute does not mention "services" discrimination, and only remedy is misdemeanor, which would not be applicable to the state.
D.C.	Yes	Yes	Prohibits discrimination at place of "public accommodation" but does not specifically mention "services" discrimination.
Florida	Unclear	Yes	Public accommodation statute does not mention "services" discrimination, and only remedy is misdemeanor, which would not be applicable to the state.
Georgia	Unclear	No	Adopts language based on Section 504: "No otherwise qualified individual in the state shall, solely by reason of his or her disability, be excluded from the participation in, be denied the benefits of, or be subjected to discrimination by State agencies, or under any program or activity receiving State financial assistance." No mention of "services" discrimination but reasonably implied.
Hawaii	Yes (by reasonable implication)	Yes	Public accommodation statute does not mention "services" discrimination, and only remedy is misdemeanor, which would not be applicable to the state.
Idaho	Unclear	No	
Illinois	Yes	Yes	
Indiana	No	Yes	"It is the public policy of the state to provide all of its citizens equal opportunity for education, employment, access to public conveniences and accommodations . . . and to eliminate segregation and separation based solely on . . . disability." Some services specified as covered but no general services language.
Iowa	Yes	Yes	
Kansas	Yes	Yes	
Kentucky	Yes	Yes	
Louisiana	Yes (by reasonable implication)	Yes	Adopts language based on Section 504: person with a disability cannot be "excluded from participating in, or denied the benefits of, any program or activity which receives financial assistance from the state or any of its political subdivisions"; no explicit mention of "services" discrimination but reasonably implied.
Maine	Yes	Yes	
Maryland	Unclear	Yes	Unlawful to deny any person "the accommodations, advantages, facilities or privileges" of any place of public accommodation; "public accommodation" defined as "a public or private entity"; no mention of "services" discrimination; only the state Civil Rights Commission can seek relief; no private right of action; separate statute bars discrimination in public accommodations against "blind or the visually handicapped and the deaf or hearing impaired," but it is not clear if this covers state and enforcement is misdemeanor or action for injunctive relief.
Massachusetts	Yes (by reasonable implication)	Yes	Adopts language based on Section 504: state Constitution states that "No otherwise qualified handicapped individual shall, solely by reason of his handicap, be excluded from the participation in, denied the benefits of, or be subject to discrimination under any program or activity within the commonwealth." Mass. Const. Amend. Art. 114. Chapter 272, section 98, creates the right to a public accommodation as a civil right. No explicit mention of "services" discrimination but reasonably implied under state Constitution.
Michigan	Yes	Yes	
Minnesota	Yes	Yes	
Mississippi	Unclear	No	Public accommodation statute does not mention "services" discrimination, and only remedy is misdemeanor, which would not be applicable to the state.

State			Notes
Missouri	Yes	Yes	
Montana	Yes	Yes	
Nebraska	Unclear	No	
Nevada	Yes	Yes	
New Hampshire	Yes	Yes	Services discrimination not specified in public accommodation statute; only misdemeanor penalty, which is not applicable against the state.
New Jersey	Yes (by case law)	Yes (by law)	Public entities not specifically listed as a type of public accommodation but seem to be covered by implication; statute does not specifically cover services; instead it mentions "advantages, facilities and privileges of any place of public accommodation"; case law interprets statutes to include services. *D.B. v. Bloom*, 896 F. Supp. 166 (D.N.J. 1995).
New Mexico	Yes	Yes	Public accommodation statute does not explicitly cover "services" discrimination; exempts educational institutions and public libraries.
New York	Unclear	Yes, but incomplete	
North Carolina	Yes	Yes	
North Dakota	Yes	Yes	
Ohio	No (by case law)	Unclear	Unlawful to deny any person "the accommodations, advantages, facilities or privileges" of any place of public accommodation; not clear whether definition of public accommodation includes the state; statute has been interpreted not to include provision of services. *Davis v. Flexman*, 109 F. Supp. 2d 776, 797 (S.D. Ohio 1999); state law does prohibit disability discrimination at places of higher education.
Oklahoma	Yes	Yes	
Oregon	Yes	Unclear	
Pennsylvania	Yes	Yes	Public accommodation covers "services" but does not specifically list public entities as a type of public accommodation.
Rhode Island	Yes	Yes	
South Carolina	Yes, but narrow definition of disability	Yes	Definition of disability does not include mental illness and includes only impairments that appear "reasonably certain to continue throughout the lifetime of the individual without substantial improvement."
South Dakota	Yes	Yes	Public accommodation statute does not include disability.
Tennessee	No	No	Persons with disabilities have the same right as the able-bodied to the full use and enjoyment of any public facility in the state; no mention of services.
Texas	Unclear	Yes	General public accommodation statute does not include disability; separate statute on disability rights does not mention "services" and provides only misdemeanor penalty, which is not applicable against the state.
Utah	Unclear	No	Covers "services" discrimination at place of public accommodation; not clear whether state is covered under the definition of public accommodation but reference to schools as being covered suggests coverage of public entities.
Vermont	Yes	Unclear	Adopts language based on Section 504: "No otherwise qualified person with a disability shall, on the basis of disability, be excluded from participation in, be denied the benefits of, or be subjected to discrimination under any program or activity receiving state financial assistance or under any program or activity conducted by or on behalf of any state agency."
Virginia	Yes (by reasonable implication)	Yes	
Washington	No (by case law)	Yes	"What must be very clear . . . is that the statutory mandate to provide access to places of public accommodation is not a mandate to provide services." *Fell v. Spokane Transit Authority*, 911 P.2d 1319, 1329 (Wash. 1996).
West Virginia	Yes	Yes	
Wisconsin	Unclear	Unclear	Unlawful for a place of public accommodation to "[d]eny to another or charge another a higher price than the regular rate for the full and equal enjoyment of any public place of accommodation or amusement because of . . . disability"; the definition of "public accommodation" does not specify that it covers state facilities.
Wyoming	No	No	State has only a public facilities statute; does not have a public services statute, and general public accommodation statute does not apply to disability.

that "services" are covered, we have described the status of that state as "unclear" in light of the adverse precedent interpreting the Ohio and Washington statutes.

C. Relief

No matter how broad the coverage of state statutes prohibiting disability discrimination, their effectiveness may be limited if they cannot be enforced by those with the greatest incentive to do so: individuals with disabilities who have been harmed by discrimination. In enacting the ADA, Congress was aware that "[c]ivil right laws depend heavily on private enforcement" and that the "inclusion of penalties and damages is the driving force that facilitates voluntary compliance."[59] Two enforcement problems exist with the state statutes: (1) nine states have no enforcement mechanism at all against the state; and (2) seven other states provide for enforcement against the state but limit remedies that would be available under ADA Title II. Hence, relief is equivalent to ADA Title II in thirty-five of fifty-one states.

The nine states with no private enforcement mechanism against the state have antiquated disability laws. These states allow no more than a misdemeanor remedy or enforcement by the state fire marshal for public accommodation or public facility discrimination, thereby making no private remedy available against the state.

Alabama is a prime example of a state that has an antiquated statutory scheme and needs to strengthen its state laws on disability discrimination by allowing for private enforcement. The Alabama statute mandating accessibility in state buildings and facilities charges the state fire marshal with enforcing the standards. The fire marshal has the power to order that the building conform with the accessibility standards and "(s)uch order may be appealed and enforced in the same manner prescribed for appealing and enforcing the Fire Marshal's orders relative to the elimination of fire hazards."[60] The right to appeal, however, applies only to the "owner or occupant of such building or premises."[61]

Alabama's public accommodation statute states a general policy "to encourage and enable" full participation "in the social and economic life of the state and to engage in remunerative employment," which is limited to the "blind, visually handicapped and the otherwise physically disabled."[62] More specifically, the statute then provides the right of the "blind, the visually handicapped and the otherwise physically disabled" to have the "full and free use of the streets, highways, sidewalks, walkways, public buildings, public facilities and other public places."[63] It also provides the right of the "blind, the visually handicapped and the otherwise physically disabled" to the "full and equal accommodations, advantages, facilities and privileges of . . . public conveyances or modes of transportation, and hotels, lodging places, places of public accommodation, amusement or resort and other places to which the general public is invited."[64] Finally, it provides the right of a person who is "totally or partially blind" to use an assistive animal without being required to pay an extra charge.[65]

The penalty for violating these rules is a misdemeanor conviction. Enforcement through a misdemeanor penalty, however, would not apply to the state because neither the state attorney general nor a local prosecutor can charge a fellow state agency with a criminal violation. Thus, under Alabama law there is no private cause of action for compensatory damages stemming from disability discrimination outside the employment arena. Accordingly, although Patricia Garrett could have brought her claim for employment discrimination under state law, she could not have brought a claim of discrimination against the state for a discriminatory denial of services or access to facilities.

The Alabama public accommodation statute's limitation to "physical disabilities" also appears to preclude coverage of many individuals who are covered under federal disability laws. Discrimination based on psychiatric and learning disabilities now make up more than 13 percent of EEOC charges. Neither of these disabilities appears to be covered under Alabama law.

Maryland permits no private enforcement actions; only the state civil rights commission can enforce its public accommodation statute. Limited protection also exists in Colorado and North Carolina because no compensatory damages are permitted against the state.[66] Four states cap damages in some way. Florida limits damages to $100,000 per plaintiff.[67] Nevada's limit is $50,000.[68] Kansas limits damages for pain, suffering, and humiliation to $2,000 in orders by the Civil Rights Commission.[69] South Carolina allows injured persons to seek injunctive relief or civil damages but caps damages at $5,000. Courts interpreting ADA Title II, however, have required a showing of intentional discrimination to recover such damages, so these damage caps may not be a significant limit on private enforcement.[70] Nonetheless, sixteen states offer less relief than is provided under the language of ADA Title II.

TABLE 5.3.
Private Right of Action against State

State	Private Right of Action	No Limit on Compensatory Damages	Comments
Alabama	No	No	
Alaska	Yes	Yes	
Arizona	Yes	Yes	
Arkansas	No	No	
California	Yes	Yes	
Colorado	Yes	No	Probably only injunctive relief; no compensatory damages available.
Connecticut	Yes	Yes	
D.C.	Yes	Yes	
Delaware	Yes	Yes	Private right of action for facilities discrimination but not for public accommodation discrimination.
Florida	Yes	Yes, but $100,000 limit	$100,000 limit per plaintiff in actions against state.
Georgia	No	No	
Hawaii	Yes	Yes	
Idaho	No	No	
Illinois	Yes	Yes	
Indiana	Yes	Yes	
Iowa	Yes	Yes	
Kansas	Yes	Yes, but limit on pain and suffering.	$2,000 limit for pain, suffering, and humiliation award before Civil Rights Commission.
Kentucky	Yes	Yes	
Louisiana	Yes	Yes	
Maine	Yes	Yes	$10,000 fine also available.
Maryland	No	No	Only Civil Rights Commission can enforce; *Dillon v. Great Atlantic Pacific Tea Co.*, 1978 WL 3435 (Md. Cir. Ct. 1978).
Massachusetts	Yes	Yes	
Michigan	Yes	Yes	
Minnesota	Yes	Yes	Punitive damages limited to $8,500.
Mississippi	No	No	Misdemeanor conviction, which would not apply to the state.
Missouri	Yes	Yes	

Table 5.3 records whether state statutes provide a private right of action for victims of discrimination by a state actor. It does not distinguish between states based on the scope of the nondiscrimination protection. If a state prohibits only facility discrimination, but not services discrimination, and provides a private right of action, then it is listed as a "Yes" in the private right of action column.

TABLE 5.3.
Private Right of Action against State

State	Private Right of Action	No Limit on Compensatory Damages	Comments
Montana	Yes	Yes	
Nebraska	No	No	
Nevada	Yes	Yes, but limited to $50,000	$50,000 limit on damages in tort actions against the state.
New Hampshire	Yes	Yes	$10,000 civil penalty also available.
New Jersey	Yes	Yes	
New Mexico	Yes	Yes	
New York	Yes	Yes	
North Carolina	Yes	No	Relief limited to declaratory and injunctive relief.
North Dakota	Yes	Yes	Injunctive and equitable relief available.
Ohio	Yes	Yes	Private right of action may be available if state is covered, but it is not clear that state is even covered.
Oklahoma	Yes	Yes	
Oregon	Yes	Yes	
Pennsylvania	Yes	Yes	
Rhode Island	Yes	Yes	
South Carolina	Yes	No	Relief limited to $5,000.
South Dakota	Yes	Yes	
Tennessee	No	No	Public accommodation statute does not even apply to the state.
Texas	Yes	Yes	Cause of action limited to "full use or enjoyment of any public facility or conveyance."
Utah	No	No	Only remedy is misdemeanor remedy that would not apply to the state.
Vermont	Yes	Yes	
Virginia	Yes	Yes	
Washington	Yes	Yes	
West Virginia	Yes	Yes	
Wisconsin	Yes	Yes	State statute requiring "public buildings" to be accessible includes private right of action.
Wyoming	No	No	No private right of action; statutes pertaining to public accommodations do not apply to individuals with disabilities.

D. Attorney's Fees

Even if a state allows a private right of action, the ability to assert that right may be limited if a person who has been discriminated against is unable to find an attorney to file an action. The availability of representation may depend in part on whether attorney's fees are available for a successful suit against the state. Moreover, the prospect of having to pay a prevailing plaintiff's attorney's fees often acts as an incentive for complying with a law. Attorney's fees are expressly provided for by statute in only thirty-four of fifty-one states.

The importance of an attorney's fees provision was demonstrated in *Sutherland v. Nationwide General Insurance Co.*,[71] where the court refused to award fees to a plaintiff who sued under an Ohio law that created a private right of action for discrimination in the workplace. The statute provided that "[w]hoever violates this chapter is subject to a civil action for damages, injunctive relief, or any other appropriate relief."[72] The plaintiff contended that the language "any other appropriate relief" included attorney fee awards. The court disagreed, citing *Sorin v. Warrensville Heights School District Board of Education*[73] wherein the Ohio Supreme Court rejected the argument that a statute's broad remedial language "impliedly permits a court to exercise its equitable powers in awarding attorney fees." Instead, the *Sorin* court deferred to the legislature on the statutory authorization for recovery of attorney fees and "rejected the argument that public policy would be subverted if recovery of attorney fees were not permitted."[74]

The *Sutherland* court also deferred to the legislature. It noted that the legislature was "certainly aware of the method, means and procedure for legislating attorney fee shifting" because several antidiscrimination statutes expressly authorized recovery of attorney fees. The court also rejected the plaintiff's attempt to use the "'private attorney general' doctrine because she constructively acted as a private attorney general by helping to end discrimination."[75] It noted that the U.S. Supreme Court had expressly rejected this doctrine in *Alyeska Pipeline Services Co. v. Wilderness Society.*[76]

Nonetheless, one might argue that courts sometimes have general equitable discretion to award attorney's fees. Not only is relying on such discretion problematic for an attorney who depends on fees to support herself but it can be eliminated at the whim of the legislature. In Ohio, for example, plaintiffs' attorneys had a short-lived era in which they could obtain discretionary attorney's fees, but that court-made result was quickly overturned by the legislature.[77] Table 5.4 summarizes our results with respect to the availability of attorney's fees under state law.

TABLE 5.4.
Attorney's Fees Available

State	Attorney's Fees Clearly Available	Comments
Alabama	No	
Alaska	Yes	
Arizona	Yes	
Arkansas	No	
California	Yes	
Colorado	No	
Connecticut	Yes	
Delaware	Yes	State statute requiring public facilities to be accessible permits attorney's fees.
D.C	Yes	
Florida	Yes	
Georgia	No	
Hawaii	Yes	Limited to 25 percent of the damages award.
Idaho	No	
Illinois	Yes	
Indiana	Yes	
Iowa	Yes	
Kansas	No	No express provision for attorney's fees, although other state civil rights provisions do contain such language. *See, e.g.*, Kan. St. Ann. 44–1021(4) (housing discrimination).
Kentucky	Yes	
Louisiana	Yes	
Maine	Yes	
Maryland	No	
Massachusetts	Yes	
Michigan	Yes	
Minnesota	Yes	
Mississippi	No	
Missouri	Yes	
Montana	Yes	
Nebraska	No	
Nevada	Yes	
New Hampshire	Yes	
New Jersey	Yes	
New Mexico	Yes	
New York	No	Case law interprets statute as not permitting attorney's fees. *New York City Bd. of Educ. v. Sears*, 443 N.Y.S.2d 23, 25 (App. Div. 1981).
North Carolina	Yes	
North Dakota	Yes	
Ohio	No	Court found lack of an attorney's fees provision to preclude award of fees to a plaintiff who sued under an Ohio law that created a private right of action for discrimination in the workplace. *Sutherland v. Nationwide Gen. Ins. Co.*, 657 N.E.2d 281 (Ohio Ct. App. 1995).
Oklahoma	Yes	
Oregon	Yes	
Pennsylvania	Yes	
Rhode Island	Yes	
South Carolina	Yes	
South Dakota	Yes	
Tennessee	No	
Texas	No	
Utah	No	
Vermont	Yes	
Virginia	Yes	
Washington	Yes	
West Virginia	Yes	
Wisconsin	Yes	State statute requiring "public buildings" to be accessible allows for attorney's fees.
Wyoming	No	

E. Comparison to ADA Title II

As noted above, the Supreme Court suggested in *Garrett* that its holding that ADA Title I claims against the states for monetary damages were barred in federal courts would have little effect because "state laws protecting the rights of persons with disabilities in employment and other aspects of life provide independent avenues of redress."[78] However, the Court also acknowledged that "[a] number of these provisions . . . did not go as far as the ADA did in requiring accommodation."[79] Our study confirms the accuracy of the second statement—only a minority of states actually have statutory protection against disability discrimination in "other aspects of life" similar to that found in ADA Title II.

1. Coverage Equivalent to ADA Title II

Only twenty-four of fifty-one states have disability discrimination statutes that appear comparable to ADA Title II (see table 5.1). Thus, about half of the states provide less protection than ADA Title II. If *Garrett* were extended to ADA Title II, the effect would be profound.

Although Connecticut is listed as providing full protection against disability discrimination, its definition of disability is actually more narrow than the one found in the ADA.[80] Hence, Connecticut should amend its statute to provide broader coverage of individuals with disabilities.

2. Moderate Protection from State Disability Discrimination

Sixteen states offer moderate protection from state disability discrimination. These states clearly allow for a private right of action to enforce their disability laws, but there is (1) ambiguity in the scope of those statutes' coverage or (2) a limit on compensatory damages or attorney's fees.

Eight states have public accommodation statutes that might be interpreted to cover the state and provide adequate enforcement but do not explicitly state that they cover all "services" discrimination. Because these states already have a public accommodations statute, they could amend it by specifically covering services without major legislative overhaul. In addition, three states have statutes that might ban services discrimination but do not explicitly cover the state. One state has both problems. These statutes could be amended by making explicit reference to the state.

Seven states might cover services discrimination by the state but have some limitations on compensatory damages or attorney's fees. (Three of the seven had some of the problems mentioned in the previous paragraph.) The relevant statutes could be amended by removing the limit on compensatory damages and by enacting an explicit attorney's fees provision.

3. Limited Protection from State Disability Discrimination

Eleven states have very limited protection against disability discrimination because there are few enforcement mechanisms available for what is often a narrowly drafted disability discrimination statute. Nine states have no enforcement mechanism at all against the state for public access discrimination. Maryland permits no private enforcement actions; only the state civil rights commission can enforce its public accommodation statute. Finally, Ohio has case law that specifically holds that "services" are not covered under its public accommodation statute and that suggests that attorney's fees are not available to enforce the public accommodations rule.[81] These states need a major legislative overhaul. They could use the Michigan statute as a model for new legislation. Table 5.5 summarizes our comparison of ADA Title II coverage and the level of protection in each state.

F. Proposal for Reform

There are a number of ways to remedy this lack of protection at the state level if *Garrett* were extended to ADA Title II. A simple remedy would be for states to waive their sovereign immunity under Title II. Legislation to do so has passed in three states (Illinois, Minnesota, and North Carolina) and been introduced in several others. Some of these bills, however, are limited solely to the employment discrimination provisions of the ADA and other statutes.

If states are not willing to waive sovereign immunity under Title II, they can take action to strengthen their state laws. Alabama took a step toward this end when the Alabamians with Disabilities Act was passed by the state Senate in 2001. This statute would cover both facilities and services, but remedies appear to be limited to injunctive relief: "[i]n any civil action brought under this act that includes a claim against one or more state defendants, the court may award any equitable relief it deems appropriate, including attorney's fees and costs, as are recognized and

Table 5.5.

Summary and Comparison to ADA Title II Coverage

State	Clearly Covers State "Facilities"	Clearly Covers Discrimination	Clearly Covers "State" in Services Discrimination Statute	Clear Private Right of Action	No Limit on Compensatory Damages	Clearly Provides Attorney's Fees	Overall Category
Alabama	Yes	Unclear	No	No	No	No	Limited
Alaska	Yes	Yes	Yes	Yes	Yes	Yes	Full
Arizona	Yes	Unclear	Yes	Yes	Yes	Yes	Moderate
Arkansas	Yes	Unclear	No	No	No	No	Limited
California	Yes	Yes	Unclear	Yes	Yes	Yes	Moderate
Colorado	Yes	Yes	Yes	Yes	No	No	Moderate
Connecticut	Yes	Yes	Yes	Yes	Yes	Yes	Full, but limited definition of disability.
Delaware	Yes	Unclear	No	Yes	Yes	Yes	Moderate
District of Columbia	Yes	Yes	Yes	Yes	Yes	Yes	Full
Florida	Yes	Unclear	Yes	Yes	Yes with limit of $100,000	Yes	Moderate
Georgia	Yes	Unclear	No	No	No	No	Limited
Hawaii	Yes	Yes (by reasonable implication)	Yes	Yes	Yes	Yes, with limits.	Full but limit on attorney's fees.
Idaho	Yes	Unclear	No	No	No	No	Limited
Illinois	Yes	Yes	Yes	Yes	Yes	Yes	Full
Indiana	Yes	Unclear	Yes	Yes	Yes	Yes	Moderate
Iowa	Yes	Yes	Yes	Yes	Yes	Yes	Full
Kansas	Yes	Yes	Yes	Yes	Yes, with limits on pain and suffering to $10,000.	No	Moderate
Kentucky	Yes	Yes implication).	Yes	Yes	Yes	Yes	Full
Louisiana	Yes	Yes (by reasonable	Yes	Yes	Yes	Yes	Full
Maine	Yes	Yes	Yes	Yes	Yes	Yes	Full
Maryland	Yes	Unclear	Yes	No	No	No	Limited
Massachusetts	Yes	Yes (by reasonable implication).	Yes	Yes	Yes	Yes	Full

Michigan	Yes	Yes	Yes	Yes	Yes	Full
Minnesota	Yes	Yes	Yes	Yes	Yes	Full
Mississippi	Yes	Unclear	No	No	No	Limited
Missouri	Yes	Yes	Yes	Yes	Yes	Full
Montana	Yes	Yes	Yes	Yes	Yes	Full
Nebraska	Yes	Unclear	No	No	No	Limited
Nevada	Yes	Yes	Yes	Yes, but limited to $50,000.	Yes	Moderate to full
New Hampshire	Yes	Yes	Yes	Yes	Yes	Full
New Jersey	Yes (by case law)	Yes (by case law)	Yes	Yes	Yes	Full
New Mexico	Yes	Yes	Yes	Yes	Yes	Full
New York	Yes	Unclear	Yes	Yes	No (case law)	Moderate
North Carolina	Yes	Yes	Yes	No	Yes	Moderate
North Dakota	Yes	Yes	Yes	Yes	Yes	Full
Ohio	No (by case law)	No (by case law)	Unclear	Yes	No	Limited
Oklahoma	Yes	Yes	Yes	Yes	Yes	Full
Oregon	Yes	Yes	Unclear	Yes	Yes	Moderate
Pennsylvania	Yes	Yes	Yes	Yes	Yes	Full
Rhode Island	Yes	Yes	Yes	Yes	Yes	Full
South Carolina	Yes	Yes	Yes	No	Yes	Moderate
South Dakota	Yes	Yes	Yes	Yes	Yes	Full
Tennessee	No	No	No	No	No	Limited
Texas	Yes	Unclear	Yes	Yes	No	Moderate
Utah	Yes	Unclear	No	No	No	Limited
Vermont	Yes	Yes	Unclear	Yes	Yes	Moderate
Virginia	Yes (by reasonable implication).	Yes (by reasonable implication).	Yes	Yes	Yes	Full
Washington	Yes	No	Yes	Yes	Yes	Moderate
West Virginia	Yes	Yes	Yes	Yes	Yes	Full
Wisconsin	No	Unclear	Unclear	Yes	No	Moderate
Wyoming	Yes	No	No	No	No	Limited

authorized under Alabama law." Unfortunately, the legislative session ended before the House could act on the bill, and it did not carry over until the next session.

Other states have broad statutes on disability discrimination that parallel ADA Title II. For example, Michigan's Persons with Disabilities Civil Rights Act states:

> Except where permitted by law, a person shall not: Deny an individual the full and equal enjoyment of the goods, services, facilities, privileges, advantages, and accommodations of a place of . . . public service because of a disability that is unrelated to the individual's ability to utilize and benefit from the goods, services, facilities, privileges, advantages, or accommodations or because of the use by an individual of adaptive devices or aids.[82]

The enforcement mechanism underlying this rule is also quite broad. An individual can bring an action for injunctive relief or damages; damages includes reasonable attorney's fees. In addition, a civil rights commission exists that can enforce the disability laws.

If a state is not willing to waive sovereign immunity under the ADA, it should consider enacting legislation similar to the Michigan statute. That will ensure that people with disabilities have the same right to access state facilities and services as other citizens—and a way to enforce that right if they are denied access.

V. Conclusion

There is a range of state law protections in the area of disability discrimination, but few states offer protection as strong as that offered by ADA Title II. The U.S. Supreme Court recognized that fact in *Lane* when it cited this state law research and concluded that state law is "inadequate to address the pervasive problems of discrimination that people with disabilities are facing." This finding in *Lane* was in marked contrast to its suggestion in *Garrett* that state law was adequate in providing remedies against employment discrimination. Despite the finding in *Lane* about the inadequacy of state law, it is still possible that the Supreme Court will invalidate ADA Title II with respect to cases involving issues other than access to the courthouse. For example, it may be difficult to continue to apply ADA Title II to cases involving access to higher education or nonessential state programs and services. Many individuals with disabilities live in states with inadequate enforcement mechanisms to prevent state-sanctioned disability discrimination. An interesting political question is whether federalists and nonfederalists can come together to strengthen rights at the state level.

Broad national coverage is still needed in the disability area. It should not be acceptable for disability discrimination to go unremedied in Alabama but strongly enforced in Michigan. Unfortunately, there is little that can be done about this problem on the federal level because of the restrictions that the Supreme Court has imposed on Congress. Vigilance at the state level is crucial to the continuing protection of disability rights.

6

ADA Title III
A Fragile Compromise

Unlike ADA Titles I and II, the judiciary's interpretation of ADA Title III has not been the title's most significant impediment to an effective enforcement scheme. Instead, the primary problem with ADA Title III has been the enforcement scheme set up by Congress in 1990 when the ADA was adopted. The enforcement scheme—*which limits relief to injunctive relief*—provides little incentive for plaintiffs and their lawyers to seek legal remedies. Hence, the success of ADA Title III has largely been through voluntary compliance rather than court-ordered relief.

In two landmark cases, *Bragdon v. Abbott*, 524 U.S. 624 (1998) and *PGA Tour v. Martin*, 532 U.S. 661 (2001), plaintiffs fared well before the Supreme Court under ADA Title III. Although both victories are important, they do little for the typical accessibility problem faced by individuals with disabilities that should be redressed by ADA Title III.

Sidney Abbott's case was a test case to determine whether dentists could lawfully refuse to deny treatment to an individual who was HIV-positive. In the mid-1990's, Dr. Randon Bragdon, a dentist working in Maine, made public his views on not treating patients with HIV. He apparently welcomed a legal challenge to his position.[1] The Gay & Lesbian Advocates & Defenders AIDS Law Project decided to challenge this policy and recruited Sidney Abbott to be the plaintiff in a test case. Abbott, a woman who was HIV-positive and needed a cavity filled, visited Bragdon's office knowing that he would refuse to fill her cavity.

Abbott brought suit against Bragdon in federal court. Both parties moved for summary judgment. Abbott argued that she was clearly an individual with a disability who was entitled to medical treatment under the ADA. Bragdon argued that Abbott was not an individual with a disability and that he was entitled not to treat her in his office because she would pose a "direct threat" to his health.

The district court ruled for Abbott on both grounds, and the court of appeals affirmed. In a landmark decision, the U.S. Supreme Court ruled that the lower courts were correct to rule that Abbott was an individual with a disability under the ADA. Moreover, the Court rejected Bragdon's assertion that he could refuse to treat her under the "direct threat" defense. It remanded that issue to the court of appeals with instructions that would clearly permit Abbott to prevail on remand. Ultimately, the court of appeals, on remand, ruled that Abbott should prevail on the direct threat issue.[2]

Abbott needed no financial incentive to file suit because her suit was brought as a "test case" on principle. In truth, she could have readily obtained dental treatment elsewhere. She was entitled to $10,000 in damages under Maine law but decided not to pursue that relief because "the lawsuit was filed on principle." Although Bragdon could have challenged her standing to bring suit on justiciability grounds (because she hadn't suffered any genuine injury), he never did so, most likely because he desired a decision on the merits. Both parties therefore actually sought—and received—a decision on the merits. Because the case was primarily one of principle, injunctive relief rather than monetary damages was presumably satisfactory to Abbott. Hence, the problems with ADA Title III's enforcement scheme did not affect her.

Casey Martin was a professional golfer who suffered from a circulatory disorder that resulted in the malformation of his right leg. Walking a golf course, rather than riding in a cart, was not simply physically painful but could even be life threatening. He sued the PGA (a nonprofit professional golf association), alleging that its rule banning the use of golf carts in certain of its tournaments violated ADA Title III. He sought an injunction to require the PGA to allow him to use a golf cart in all of its tournaments. The PGA argued that it was not covered by ADA Title III and that the ADA does not require it to change its rules about the use of golf carts during certain tournaments because those rules are "fundamental" to the PGA tournaments.

Martin obtained injunctive relief at the trial court level, and the injunction was affirmed on appeal. In another landmark decision, the Supreme Court affirmed the lower courts, ruling that the PGA is covered by ADA Title III and that the rules regarding the use of golf carts are not fundamental to the game of golf. Hence, Martin was entitled to a modification in that policy under the ADA.

Because Martin had obtained an injunction at the trial court level, he did play with the use of a golf cart pending the outcome in the appellate courts. He therefore suffered no monetary harm and his problem could be readily solved with an injunction requiring a rule change.

Both Martin and Abbott sought policy or rule changes. They both were high-profile plaintiffs in major ADA lawsuits. And they both were victorious. The more typical persons who face discrimination at public accommodations cannot find legal relief so readily. When they find themselves unable to attend an event or visit a place of public accommodation because of accessibility problems, they do not have easy access to legal assistance. Lawyers have little incentive to take such cases because they cannot attain monetary awards under ADA Title III as part of the court-ordered relief. The lack of monetary awards makes a contingency agreement impossible.

When Congress enacted ADA Title III, it heard testimony from individuals who were excluded from restaurants because of their disfigurement or their inability to climb steps. It learned that simple tasks like food shopping or getting prescriptions filled can become impossible due to barriers like narrow aisles or heavy doors that impede access. Pervasive accessibility problems precluded many individuals with disabilities from traveling or even leaving their own homes.

ADA Title III protects individuals with disabilities from discrimination at places of public accommodation. The definition of "public accommodation" covers twelve categories of entities, ranging from laundromats to bowling alleys. The primary purpose of ADA Title III is to remove physical barriers that impede accessibility, although it also requires entities to modify policies and eligibility criteria that have the effect of excluding individuals with disabilities.

The definition of "public accommodation" under ADA Title III is broad. The title requires accessibility and nondiscrimination at entities that individuals visit on a frequent basis in order to obtain the basic essentials like food, lodging, and health care. The title also extends to entities that individuals visit to enhance the quality of their lives, such as restaurants, hotels, and places of amusement and recreation. ADA Title III therefore plays an enormously important role in the integration of individuals with disabilities into society in general.

However, the broad coverage of ADA Title III came at a price—what Senator Tom Harkin (D-Iowa) called a "fragile compromise" during its consideration in Congress.[3] In return for a broad list of covered entities, civil rights advocates agreed to a limited set of remedies under ADA Title III. When private parties bring suit under ADA Title III, they are able to obtain only injunctive relief and are not able to obtain monetary damages. This compromise was modeled after an agreement reached in 1964 when Title II of the Civil Rights Act of 1964 (CRA Title II) was enacted to prohibit racial discrimination at places of public accommodation. CRA Title II, like ADA Title III, permits private individuals to seek only injunctive relief. Unlike ADA Title III, however, CRA Title II covers only a few categories of public accommodations. Proponents of the ADA were therefore able to obtain broader coverage than previous civil rights activists had been able to obtain under CRA Title II, but they were not able to move beyond the limited set of remedies enacted under CRA Title II. In order to seek broader remedies under ADA Title III than under CRA Title II, disability rights advocates argued for Congress to consider a different legislative model, the Fair Housing Act (FHA),[4] which prohibits discrimination in the sale or rental of housing to any buyer or renter.

Enacted in 1968 to prohibit housing discrimination on the basis of race, the FHA has always contained compensatory and punitive damages as a potential source for relief. In 1988, when the act was amended to provide protection against discrimination for individuals with disabilities, it was also amended to remove the cap on punitive damages, as well as to provide for mandatory enforcement by the attorney general (AG) when the secretary of housing and urban development (HUD) "determines that reasonable cause exists to believe that a discriminatory housing practice has occurred or is about to occur" and a complainant chooses judicial rather than administrative relief.[5] Harkin argued that the FHA compensatory and punitive damages remedial scheme, rather than the CRA Title II injunctive remedial scheme, was appropriate for ADA Title III. In the end, however, the limited relief available under CRA Title II prevailed in a spirit of compromise.

When legislation is being considered by Congress, compromises are an essential ingredient of enactment. In this context, ADA proponents traded expanded coverage for limited relief. The compromise, however, was reached as part of a "one step at a time" approach, reserving for another day the question of whether this limited scheme of relief would be effective. Because CRA Title II has been relatively effective in vindicating the rights of racial minorities who are denied access to public accommodations, the compromise seemed like a reasonable one when the ADA was enacted in 1990. Proponents of ADA Title III could claim victory because they obtained broader coverage than that which exists under CRA Title II, with equivalent remedies.

Now that ten years have passed since enactment of ADA Title III, it is a good time to assess the success of the compromise. ADA Title III has been less successful than was originally hoped. Due in part to its limited avenue for relief, ADA Title III has spawned few lawsuits. In addition, courts have rendered exceedingly narrow interpretations of their already limited authority to grant injunctive relief. The second problem feeds into the first. By narrowly interpreting an already limited remedy, the courts have further reduced plaintiffs' incentives to bring a lawsuit under ADA Title III. Although state law can sometimes serve as a remedial gap filler in such situations, that has not occurred under ADA Title III. Many states passed their own civil rights laws with broader remedial provisions subsequent to the passage of CRA Title II, but few have used the passage of ADA Title III as impetus for expanding their state antidiscrimination remedies in the area of disability discrimination. Because it has been only ten years since passage of the ADA, additional state legislative action may be forthcoming, but there is little reason to believe that further "filling the gap" will occur under ADA Title III. State law remedies in this area are very limited and are sometimes contained in antiquated statutes in serious need of updating, yet little legislative activity is occurring in this area of the law on the state level.

Rather than respond to this enforcement problem in a way that would assist plaintiffs, the courts and Congress have actually taken steps that have worsened the problem. The one way that attorneys can afford to take these suits is if they represent the "prevailing party" and are awarded attorney's fees as part of a settlement or judgment. The Supreme Court, however, has recently rendered a very prodefendant decision regarding the circumstances in which one might obtain attorney's fees. In *Buckhannon Board and Care Home, Inc. v. West Virginia Dep't of Health and Human Resources*, 532 U.S. 598 (2001), the Court ruled that the ADA requires a party to secure either a judgment on the merits or a court-ordered consent decree in order to qualify as a "prevailing party" and thereby be entitled to attorney's fees. It is *not* sufficient for a party to be a "catalyst" for corrective action by the defendant in advance of trial.

That ruling has made it even more difficult for plaintiffs to find attorneys who will take their cases because there may be no attorney's fees if the defendant takes quick corrective action before trial.

Congress has taken no steps to correct these problems. In response to a complaint by Clint Eastwood and other owners of leisure facilities, Congress has actually considered making it more difficult to bring ADA Title III suits by imposing a ninety-day notice requirement. Somehow, the entertainment industry has tried to persuade Congress that it is *too easy* for plaintiffs to bring lawsuits when, in fact, the opposite is true. The combination of the *Buckhannon* case and the pending notice rule, however, could be deadly for plaintiffs' lawyers in ADA Title III actions. Under *Buckhannon*, the defendant is not required to pay attorney's fees to the plaintiff's lawyers if there is no court order requiring corrective action. In other words, if the defendant takes corrective action on the eve of litigation, the defendant does not need to pay attorney's fees. If the notice requirement rule were to become law, then defendants would have an additional ninety days to take corrective action and avoid being liable for attorney's fees. Ironically, Eastwood managed to escape legal liability at the hands of a highly sympathetic jury.[6] But that fact did not stop him from appearing on talk shows such as *Hardball* and *Crossfire*, arguing, "What happens is these lawyers, they come along and they end up driving off in a Mercedes and the disabled person ends up driving off in a wheelchair." In fact, plaintiff Diane Zum Brunnen was not able to enter the registration office and the guest room, or to find the toilet facility at Eastwood's facility, and her lawyer obtained no legal fees from the defendants for bringing this problem to their attention.

In part I of this chapter, I will discuss the relief available under ADA Title III, CRA Title II, and the FHA. In part II, I will examine the existing evidence of the effectiveness of ADA Title III. I will examine judicial outcomes (part A), verdict outcomes (part B), and settlement outcomes (part C). I will argue that this evidence indicates that Title III suffers from underenforcement due to the limited range of remedies that courts have construed are available. In part III, I will discuss the limited remedies currently available under state law to show that state law is not currently "filling the gaps" in remedies under ADA Title III, as has historically occurred under CRA Title II. In part IV, I will conclude that the current trend of underenforcement of ADA Title III should cause us to consider enhancing remedies at the state and federal levels.

I. Legislative History

A. The First Bill

The legislative history of the ADA was discussed extensively in chapter 2. This chapter will focus on the discussion relevant to the remedies under the ADA Title III. The ADA was introduced as H.R. 4498 by Representative Tony Coelho (D-Calif.) and as S. 2345 by Senator Lowell Weicker (R.-Conn.) in 1988. The enforcement section of the 1988 bill was much stronger than the enforcement provision in the finally enacted ADA. The original bill provided:

> Any person who believes that he or she or any specific class of individuals is being or is about to be subjected to discrimination on the basis of handicap in violation of this Act, shall have a right, by himself or herself, or by a representative, to file a civil action for injunctive relief, monetary damages, or both in a district court of the United States.[7]

The exhaustion of administrative enforcement procedures was required only for actions involving employment discrimination. Claims of discrimination involving barriers to access at public accommodations could be brought by private citizens for monetary damages. In contrast, the enacted bill permitted private parties to obtain only injunctive relief[8]—a weaker remedy.

B. Weakening of Legislation

Even on the day when the ADA was introduced, Senator Robert Dole (R-Kans.), a key sponsor of the ADA, spoke in favor of the need for such a bill but also stated that compromises were needed that would weaken the bill:

> I have reservations about many aspects of this bill including the elimination of the undue hardship criteria for reasonable accommodation, clarification on what constitutes a public accommodation and what such public accommodations would be required to do under the retrofitting provisions of this bill, what do we mean by transportation services and what is the scope of the provisions of this bill to intrastate transportation systems.[9]

Senate subcommittees held hearings nearly a year later (May 9, 1989) on Senate Bill 933, a modified version of the ADA that was introduced in the next Congress by Harkin. Harkin, the key sponsor of the ADA in the Senate, did not immediately acquiesce to Dole's views about the need to limit the provision on relief. The bill provided that the enforcement scheme for the FHA (which included both compensatory and punitive damages) should be available to redress discrimination at places of public accommodation.[10]

Attorney General Richard Thornburgh spoke in favor of the new bill, but made it clear that ADA Title III needed serious revision to limit its scope and protection. His objections were threefold: (1) businesses could not make accurate predictions of the types of modifications required because the "readily achievable" compliance standard was not well defined and did not exist under Section 504 of the Rehabilitation Act; (2) the remedies for violations of ADA Title III should parallel the remedies already present under CRA Title II, rather than the broader remedies existing in the FHA; and (3) the scope of businesses covered by ADA Title III should be narrowed so as not to impose undue hardship on small businesses.[11] Most of the suggested amendments were adopted before enactment of the final bill. The term "readily achievable" was retained, but it was defined as meaning "easily accomplishable and able to be carried out without much difficulty or expense."[12] Such factors as the size and financial resources of the covered entity were added to be considered when determining whether an accommodation was readily achievable, to make clear that the burden on small businesses would be minimal.

Despite his recognition of the need for strong remedies, Harkin capitulated on the remedies issue five months later, making it clear that this compromise was necessary to attain a bipartisan bill with a broad scope of coverage:

> Senator Kennedy and I are committed to this compromise. We will oppose all weakening amendments. We will also oppose any amendments that are intended to strengthen the substitute, if these amendments do not have the support of the administration and Senator Dole. We are pleased that the administration and Senator Dole share this commitment. We hope that other Senators will understand how fragile this compromise is and will support it.

The major component of the compromise was the agreement by the chief Senate sponsors to cutback the remedies included in the original bill in exchange for a broad scope of coverage under the public accommodations title of the bill; in other words to extend protections to most commercial establishments large and small open to the public. We would thus consider any amendment that pertains to either of these two aspects of the legislation an amendment designed to destroy this fragile compromise.[13]

In the name of a "fragile compromise," the remedies underlying ADA Title III were limited in exchange for an expansive list of commercial entities covered by the statute. The compromises accepted during passage of the ADA are not unusual. Enforcement was traded for scope of coverage. The participants in the compromise recognized, however, that the ADA would need to be reevaluated over time to see if it was effective. Attorney General Thornburgh recommended a "cautious" approach with continuing discussion and dialogue over time to see if a purely injunctive strategy would work.

Thus, the scope of coverage and strength of enforcement of ADA Title III were limited during the legislative process. The argument advanced for weakening the remedial scheme was that injunctive relief had proven effective under CRA Title II, hence there was no need for other relief, such as monetary relief. Nonetheless, proponents of the ADA were concerned about the effectiveness of injunctive relief. This chapter next examines the effectiveness of the ADA Title III remedies in light of our first decade of enforcement experience.

C. Limitations of Civil Rights Act Analogies

A fuller understanding of our experience under the civil rights laws should cause us to question the assumption that injunctive relief serves the objectives of ADA Title III. The scope of CRA Title II is narrower than the scope of ADA Title III. In addition, there is a broader array of state law remedies to supplement CRA Title II remedies than there are state law remedies to supplement ADA Title III remedies. Even assuming the effectiveness of the remedial scheme of CRA Title II, there are many reasons to doubt that a similar remedial scheme would be effective under ADA Title III.

A better analogy for ADA Title III is found by looking at the FHA. With the passage of time, Congress concluded that broad compensatory and punitive damages are required to provide effective remedies under the

FHA (along with an ambitious government enforcement scheme). The limited remedies passed under CRA Title II were part of a fragile compromise in order to enhance passage of the statute in a bipartisan atmosphere. To date, these remedies have not proven effective under ADA Title III.

1. TITLE II OF THE CIVIL RIGHTS ACT OF 1964

Although CRA Title VII has received the most legal attention in the past several decades, it was the need for CRA Title II that was most vividly in the public's imagination at the time the Civil Rights Act was passed. Four black students who had been refused cups of coffee in a Woolworth's store in Greensboro, North Carolina, on February 1, 1960, began a series of sit-ins and civil disobedience that formed the backdrop for passage of the Civil Rights Act.

Senator Weicker emphasized the analogy to those four black students in his opening remarks as sponsor of the ADA:

> People with cerebral palsy are turned away from restaurants because proprietors say their appearance will upset other patrons. People who use wheelchairs are blocked by curbs, steps, and narrow doorways from getting into many arenas, stadiums, theaters, and other public buildings. Many such facilities have done no planning for the use of their services by people with hearing or visual impairments.
>
> It has been over 30 years since some zoos and parks were closed to keep blacks from visiting them during the peak of civil rights demonstrations and boycotts. Yet it was only last month that the *Washington Post* reported the story of a New Jersey zoo keeper who refused to admit children with [Down] syndrome because he feared they would upset the chimpanzees. . . .
>
> [P]eople with disabilities still have to chain themselves to buses and to block their movement in order to focus the attention of the transit industry and the general public on the fact that most buses are inaccessible to them. "We aren't forced to the back of the bus," they say, "we can't get on the bus at all."[14]

Weicker could also have described the analogy to CRA Title II in another way, that ADA Title III, like its counterpart in the Civil Rights Act of 1964, was watered down during the legislative process to enhance its potential for enactment.

In the original civil rights bill proposed to Congress by President John F. Kennedy, the scope of protection under CRA Title II was somewhat broader than what was ultimately enacted. The original bill prohibited discrimination in public accommodations, including all places of lodging, eating, and amusement, and other retail or service establishments.[15] That bill was modified many times before passage. Most important, as a result of the McCulloch-Justice Department compromise, it specifically exempted private clubs and failed to explicitly cover "any retail shop, department store, market, drugstore, gasoline station, or other public places which keep goods for sale."[16] Like ADA Title III, the final CRA Title II listed specific entities covered, such as hotels, restaurants and places of entertainment, rather than including a more expansive generic definition of places open to the public. Although the rationale for limiting CRA Title II to those entities was never fully explained in the legislative history, one comment by Representative Howard "Judge" Smith (D-Va.) may have captured some of the sentiment at the time. Referring to the fact that a chiropodist whose office was in a hotel would be covered by CRA Title II, he is reported to have made a "shrill outburst": "If I were cutting corns . . . I would want to know whose feet I would have to be monkeying around with. I would want to know whether they smelled good or bad."[17]

Civil rights proponents, by contrast, saw no reason to exempt retail or service establishments from CRA Title II. For example, Representative Robert W. Kastenmeier (D-Wisc.) criticized the limited scope of CRA Title II in his additional views that he filed as part of the House Judiciary Committee report. Kastenmeier compared the strength of the original bill to the final bill. With respect to CRA Title II, he noted:

> [T]he bill would allow discrimination to continue in barber shops, beauty parlors, many other service establishments, retail stores, bowling alleys, and other places of recreation and participation sports, unless such places serve food. It is hard to follow a morality which allows one bowling alley to remain segregated, while another bowling alley down the street which serves sandwiches must allow Negroes to bowl. There may be constitutional limitations on what activities can be covered by Federal legislation, but the categories covered by title II of the reported bill are not based on constitutional limitations.[18]

Similarly, in one of the few constitutional cases to discuss the right of a property owner to have the state enforce his desire to exclude blacks from a restaurant, Justice William O. Douglas in a stinging concurrence argued in *Bell v. Maryland*[19] that the Constitution permits no discrimination of this sort in any place of public accommodation:

> Here [this case] it is a restaurant refusing service to a Negro. But so far as principle and law are concerned it might just as well be a hospital refusing admission to a sick or injured Negro . . . or a drugstore refusing antibiotics to a Negro, or a bus denying transportation to a Negro, or a telephone company refusing to install a telephone in a Negro's home. . . . Constitutionally speaking, why should Hooper Food Co., Inc., or Peoples Drug Stores—or any other establishment that dispenses food or medicines—stand on a higher, more sanctified level than Greyhound Bus when it comes to a constitutional right to pick and choose its customers?[20]

Ironically, the day that Justice Douglas issued the concurring opinion in *Bell v. Maryland* was also the day that the Civil Rights Act of 1964 was returned to the Senate for deliberation. By then, it was far too late to consider any amendments to expand the act's coverage to encompass the reach of what Justice Douglas considered constitutional. The bill was able to become law two weeks later only as a result of extraordinary political maneuvering. Political rather than constitutional concerns resulted in the limited scope of CRA Title II. Without the McCulloch-Justice Department compromise, the Civil Rights Act of 1964 would never have become law.

Not only did CRA Title II, as enacted in 1964, not cover retail and personal service establishments but it has never been amended to provide broader protection. Although state law prohibits discrimination in retail stores in most states, seven states (Alabama, Florida, Georgia, Mississippi, North Carolina, South Carolina, and Texas) have no such statute.[21]

Another issue that had to be confronted when the CRA was considered was the question of what kinds of remedies should be enacted. Civil rights activists had examined possible enforcement schemes. In a book published in 1959, civil rights activist Jack Greenberg observed that three enforcement schemes are generally possible: "criminal prosecution, private civil suit for damages or injunction by an aggrieved person, and administrative or injunctive implementation by public officials." He considered criminal enforcement to be problematic because of the high burden of proof, and the fact that "[t]rial has to be by jury, which may very likely be as prejudiced as the defendant." Similarly, he argued, civil suits for damages are problematic because they also involve juries, as well as the costs of engaging counsel. His preferred mechanism was use of an administrative agency or the attorney general to vigorously enforce antidiscrimination laws at public expense and without jury trials.[22] Other commentators argued that the token amounts awarded in actions for civil damages may not act as an effective deterrent; injunctive relief might be effective insofar as it would have a continuing effect, thereby permitting punishment for contempt if the injunctive order was violated. Based on the experience with states that used criminal penalties and private civil actions for damages, some commentators argued "that neither criminal prosecutions nor private civil actions for damages appreciably decrease the incidence of discrimination or give its victims an adequate legal remedy."[23] They emphasized the importance of injunctive relief with possible enforcement by an administrative agency, although other commentators suggested that there could be an option for a private civil action for damages.[24]

The Civil Rights Act generally reflected the approach recommended by Greenberg and other commentators, although each title of the Civil Rights Act utilized somewhat different enforcement schemes. CRA Title VII (the employment discrimination title) created a private right of action for make-whole relief and a modest administrative enforcement mechanism.[25] These two remedies were enhanced in 1972 to create a stronger administrative enforcement structure, and in 1991 to create the possibility of compensatory or punitive damages.[26] CRA Title II (the public accommodation title) created a private right of action for preventive or injunctive relief with the possibility of intervention by the attorney general if a complaining party could certify to the court that the case was of general public importance.[27] However, even when the attorney general intervened, CRA Title II did not provide for any kind of monetary damages. Moreover, unlike CRA Title VII, its remedies have not been enhanced since 1964. And unlike the FHA, the intervention on the part of the attorney general is entirely discretionary.

Nevertheless, CRA Title II has proven to be a relatively effective tool in eliminating discrimination in places of public accommodation. Its effect has been twofold. First, the availability of structural injunctions has led to large-scale changes in the way public accommodations conduct business. Second, state law has filled the remedial gap by providing compensatory damages and more expansive statutory coverage than CRA

Title II. Thus, an ability to enforce an antidiscrimination principle effectively in the area of public accommodations may be attributable to the partnership of state antidiscrimination laws and CRA Title II rather than attributable to CRA Title II alone.

The effectiveness of banning race discrimination at places of public accommodation may have also occurred through another important statutory vehicle: 42 U.S.C. § 1981. Several courts have concluded that private plaintiffs can sue for infringement of contract under section 1981 to obtain monetary damages when they are denied access to public accommodations, or discriminated against by entities that offer public accommodations. That cause of action is not available in the disability area, however, because section 1981 applies only to race discrimination.[28]

In assessing the performance of ADA Title III, one needs to ask whether structural injunctions and supplemental state or federal law remedies are likely in this area. Given the narrow way that many courts have interpreted their remedial powers under ADA Title III, structural injunctions appear unlikely. Moreover, the ten-year record of limited state law amendments suggests that enhanced relief at the state-law level is unlikely. It may be that an amendment to the ADA is the only possible way to improve the enforcement of ADA Title III because section 1981 is not available to enhance the penalties in the disability area.

2. FAIR HOUSING ACT AMENDMENTS OF 1988

Another analogy was also available when ADA Title III was being debated: the Fair Housing Act (FHA). As enacted in 1968, the FHA provided that plaintiffs could recover "actual damages and not more than $1,000 punitive damages, together with court costs and reasonable attorney fees in the case of a prevailing plaintiff"[29] to remedy race discrimination in the rental or sale of housing. The act was amended in 1988 to prohibit disability-based discrimination and to eliminate the cap on punitive damages.[30] As noted in the House Judiciary Committee report's section-by-section analysis, the limitation on punitive damages was eliminated because the committee concluded "that the limit on punitive damages served as a major impediment to imposing an effective deterrent on violators and a disincentive for private persons to bring suits under existing law."[31] Thus, although the FHA always contained a more ambitious range of remedies than ADA Title III, these remedies were broadened even further when disability discrimination in housing became unlawful.

During the debate over the ADA, Senator Harkin questioned the appropriateness of the FHA analogy for ADA Title III rather than CRA Title II. The FHA contains important parallels to ADA Title III, whereas the FHA covers the rental of apartments to individuals with disabilities, ADA Title III covers the rental of hotel rooms to people with disabilities. Yet, under current law, if a rental agent refuses to rent a house to an individual with a disability, he or she is subject to the full set of remedies provided under the FHA; if a motel owner refuses to rent a motel room to that same individual, the individual would be able to obtain only injunctive relief.

It is arguable that housing discrimination has longer-term consequences for individual tenants than does discrimination at a place of temporary lodging, and thus stiffer penalties are appropriate for the former. But the lack of accessibility at places of public accommodation serves to impede the mobility of many individuals with disabilities. Given the nature of our highly mobile society, such impediments have daily effects on the basic requirements of living (e.g., grocery stores), and broader effects on the ability of an individual to work and travel (e.g., hotels and restaurants). Being confined to one's home due to the inaccessibility of the outside community can be as significant as having difficulty obtaining housing itself. Moreover, even if housing discrimination is somewhat more significant than discrimination at places of public accommodation, it is questionable whether the degree of difference is sufficiently significant to justify such widely divergent relief.

In deciding which analogy makes more sense—CRA Title II or the FHA—we must consider the change in social consensus since passage of the Civil Rights Act in 1964. Passage followed what has been termed the "longest debate" due to a protracted filibuster in the Senate. CRA Title II was also passed at a time when civil rights advocates had serious reservations about jury trials for victims of race discrimination because southern juries were predominantly white. Such reservations are largely unfounded today and, in any event, are not particularly relevant to the law of disability discrimination. Jury trials are now commonplace under the Civil Rights Act of 1964 and state antidiscrimination laws.

By contrast, the Fair Housing Act Amendments of 1988 were passed by a bipartisan Congress. The remedies reflected the strong political and social commitment to making affordable housing available without discrimination on the basis of disability. The ADA was passed only two years later, again by a strongly bipartisan Congress. Although the scope of entities covered was narrowed during the legislative debate—as the scope had been narrowed during the legislative debate on CRA Title II— the list of entities ultimately covered under the ADA was much more comprehensive than the list covered by CRA Title II. Our emerging social consensus about the inappropriateness of discrimination was strong enough to justify a more stringent set of remedies for both race and disability discrimination than in 1964.

Nonetheless, the proponents of the ADA were never able to move the discussion of remedies beyond that of injunctive relief. They were stuck with the limited remedies that had been negotiated at another time— 1964—and in another context—race discrimination—where the fear of jury trials was particularly strong. Senator Harkin understood the importance of ensuring that the Fair Housing Act remedies rather than the CRA Title II remedies would be available under the ADA. The bill he introduced in the Senate Committee on Labor and Human Resources contained the FHA remedies for violations of the ADA's public accommodation section (what eventually was enacted as ADA Title III). At a Hearing held before the Committee on Labor and Human Resources and the Subcommittee on the Handicapped, Harkin stated that "without the existence of damages as a remedy, you would not get widespread voluntary compliance or negotiated settlements, short of litigation."[32]

Attorney General Thornburgh, however, did not agree that the FHA remedies were appropriate under the FHA. In response to Harkin's asking Thornburgh whether he thought the FHA remedies should be available under ADA Title III, he responded:

I think the view that the administration holds to is that this act should not be one designed to promote unnecessary litigation. The fair housing amendments of last year were adopted only after years of experience with the previous regimen of remedies, and I think that I can fairly express the view of the administration that those remedies are not necessarily appropriate for transport into a new piece of legislation without some similar experience in obtaining voluntary compliance and in securing the kinds of remedies that have been used in other civil rights areas, without particularly going to punitive damages and some of the more novel remedies proposed in this act, such as giving persons a right to enjoin action which is about to result in discrimination.

Again, before that kind of uncharted water is entered into in the remedial sense, some thought, I think, ought to be given to sticking with the remedial regimen that is contained in the present civil rights laws.

We are a litigious society, Senator Harkin, whether we like it or not, and there are a lot of people out there that the first thing they want to do is sue somebody, and particularly when you have provided punitive damages, which we learned from recent experience can be somewhat limitless in their reach. We are merely making a plea for the tried and true remedies under Titles II and VII of the Civil Rights Act of 1964, which not only provide for more voluntary compliance but limit the amount of litigation that is necessarily going to ensue, and the prospect of having that litigation, in fact, prove an obstacle to achieving the goals that we seek.[33]

Thornburgh's comments mischaracterized, in part, the experience under the FHA. Although the FHA's remedial scheme was strengthened in 1988, that remedial scheme has always been stronger than the one contained in the ADA. Since 1968, plaintiffs have been able to obtain actual damages and limited punitive damages under the FHA. The 1968 remedial scheme under the FHA would be far more effective than ADA Title III's purely injunctive scheme for relief.

Although Harkin compromised in order to attain bipartisan support of the ADA, he forecast that the limited remedial scheme of ADA Title III would lead to few lawsuits and underenforcement of the statute's mandate. Thornburgh seemingly agreed that there might be few lawsuits but predicted that there would be sufficient voluntary compliance to enforce the statute's mandate. The experience under the FHA, however, was that even a remedial scheme providing actual damages and limited punitive damages was insufficient to enforce the mandate of the act. Limited remedial schemes therefore need to be periodically revisited to see if they are effective.

D. Effectiveness of Remedies

Despite the limited scope of relief available under CRA Title II, there is far less discrimination on the basis of race at public accommodations today than there was in 1964. One no longer finds "Whites Only" signs on the doors of restaurants. The problems today are what we might call "second order" problems of discrimination—lesser service rather than a denial of entrance. In one of the most well-publicized public accommodation cases in recent years, a Denny's Restaurant in Maryland was alleged to have failed to serve six African American Secret Service agents while the white agents were served second and third helpings. Two class action lawsuits were filed on behalf of 294,537 plaintiffs under federal and state law, with a reported settlement two years later of $46 million and the discharge of more than one hundred employees for discriminatory behavior.[34] Denny's relatively prompt attempt to settle the lawsuit reflects the change in moral climate that has occurred since 1964. It is no longer good business, especially for a restaurant chain, to have the image of excluding African American customers.

The second-order problems in the area of race discrimination are being redressed through a combination of state and federal law. Federal law gave authority to the plaintiff to seek a structural injunction against Denny's; state law provided the opportunity to the plaintiffs to seek compensatory relief. The $46 million price tag in the Denny's case was the result of broader protection available under state than federal antidiscrimination law. In addition, 42 U.S.C. § 1981 can be used to enhance the penalty when individuals are denied service because of race.

By contrast, the injunctive relief remedial scheme of ADA Title III has not been sufficiently effective in eliminating barriers to access for individuals with disabilities. Physical barriers such as steps—which preclude entrance by people who use wheelchairs—and the lack of Telecommunication Devices for the Deaf (TDD) services at hotels—which impede the traveling opportunities of people who have hearing impairments—are only two commonplace examples of exclusion on the basis of disability by many places of public accommodation. Remedying violations of ADA Title III is different from remedying violations of CRA Title II. An apt analogy to CRA Title II would be a case in which a restaurant refuses service because of the physical appearance of an individual with a disability. That example fits the intentional discrimination model of CRA Title II. In the more typical case, however, the restaurant has effectively denied service by having a step at the front door. The step may have predated passage of the ADA and was probably not constructed with the intention of excluding a category of potential customers. In order to comply with the ADA, the restaurant must proactively remove the barrier, which, in turn, entails a cost for the restaurant. Under CRA Title II, it arguably makes economic sense to ban discrimination because a restaurant, for example, would ultimately increase its volume of business if it began to serve

African Americans. That fact may also be true under ADA Title III. A restaurant that can serve customers who use wheelchairs will also add to its patronage not only from individuals with disabilities but also from the friends and families of those individuals. But that outcome follows the restaurateur's initial expenditure. The threat of injunctive relief is not sufficient to create compliance because compliance requires a more substantial proactive step than merely removing a "whites only" sign and may entail what is perceived to be a significant expense.

Further, injunctive relief has been ineffective under ADA Title III because of courts' narrow interpretations of the judicial power to issue such relief. Courts have repeatedly concluded that they lacked jurisdiction to hear ADA Title III cases because plaintiffs' individual instances of discrimination did not create standing to seek injunctive relief. Many of the ADA Title III cases have involved a failure to provide medical services to individuals with disabilities, particularly individuals with HIV/AIDS. In such a situation, the plaintiff is likely to file suit against the doctor who did not provide treatment while also seeking treatment from another physician. Because the plaintiff obtained treatment from another physician, the courts reason that the case is moot because the injury is unlikely to recur and compensatory relief is not available. Accordingly, courts have concluded that they are powerless to order any relief even though a flagrant violation of the ADA may have occurred. When a court cannot order relief, it often cannot maintain jurisdiction over the case; it must dismiss the case or, if there is a supplemental state action, remand the case to state court.

The leading case governing this question of relief is *City of Los Angeles v. Lyons*.[35] Adolph Lyons brought a civil rights action against the city seeking damages, injunctive relief, and declaratory relief stemming from an incident in which a police officer used a "choke hold," allegedly pursuant to city policy, upon stopping Lyons for a traffic violation. The Supreme Court concluded that Lyons did not have standing to challenge the conduct because of the "speculative nature of his claim that he will again experience injury as the result of that practice even if continued."[36] The Supreme Court recognized that there is an exception to the mootness doctrine when a claim "is capable of repetition, yet evades review."[37] However, because Lyons also had an action for monetary relief, the Court ruled that his case did not come under that doctrine. But even if Lyons had not had other remedies, the Court suggested that it would have been hesitant to apply the "capable-of-repetition" doctrine because that "doctrine applies only in exceptional situations, and generally only where the named plaintiff can make a reasonable showing that he will again be subjected to the alleged illegality."[38] Lyons could not make such a demonstration. In so ruling, the Court cited *DeFunis v. Odegaard*,[39] an educational, reverse discrimination case in which the plaintiff was in his final quarter of his last year of law school when the case reached the Court. Although the fact pattern may have been typical of other such cases, the Court declined to exercise jurisdiction, concluding that the issue raised by the plaintiff would likely be reviewable in the future. In two major civil rights cases involving injunctive relief—*Lyons* and *DeFunis*—the Supreme Court therefore declined to apply the "capable-of-repetition" doctrine to maintain jurisdiction over the plaintiff's request for injunctive relief.

The standards for the capable-of-repetition doctrine are stringent, but, in some cases, the Supreme Court has diluted the requirement that an individual must be likely to be affected by a future recurrence of a mooted dispute. The most well known example is *Roe v. Wade*.[40] Observing that the normal gestational period is 266 days, the Court concluded that the case presented "a classic justification for a conclusion of nonmootness"[41] as a dispute capable of repetition yet evading review. The Court made no specific finding that the plaintiff was likely to face another unwanted pregnancy while residing in the state of Texas. Similarly, the Court has been seemingly liberal in accepting jurisdiction in a series of voting cases without any individualized showing that the problem is likely to recur. John Anderson, for example, was permitted to challenge a time-of-filing requirement that would have kept him off the 1980 presidential election ballot in Ohio.[42] The Court heard the case, although the election was over by the time it did, and never asked whether Anderson was likely to seek the presidency again. Thus, the Court refused to acknowledge a public policy exception to the mootness doctrine in *DeFunis v. Odegaard*, but the abortion and election law decisions suggest that the Court is sometimes willing to dilute the mootness requirements when a public policy issue is likely to evade review.

Courts that have applied *Lyons* to ADA Title III cases have applied the doctrine too stringently and have arguably misconstrued the nature of Title III actions. They do not involve extreme situations in which only a plaintiff's criminal conduct could cause future discrimination to occur. Instead, in ADA Title III cases plaintiffs represent a class of litigants who repeatedly face instances of discrimination as a result of their own voluntary and lawful conduct. In *Honig v. Doe*,[43] the Supreme Court distinguished between a situation in which an individual with a disability is likely to face future unlawful actions due to his disability and the *Lyons* situation in which standing would require an expectation of repeated police misconduct:

> Our cases reveal that, for purposes of assessing the likelihood that state authorities will reinflict a given injury, we generally have been unwilling to assume that the party seeking relief will repeat the type of misconduct that would once again place him or her at risk of that injury. . . . No such reluctance, however, is warranted here. It is respondent Smith's very inability to conform his conduct to socially acceptable norms that renders him "handicapped" within the meaning of the [Education for All Handicapped Children Act].[44]

Although Bragdon and other ADA plaintiffs may not be at risk of physical harm as a result of defendants' conduct, they, like the plaintiff in *Honig*, have the ability to put themselves in the position of having to face unlawful conduct in the future. Sidney Abbott could seek medical services from Bragdon in the future. And it is unlikely that Bragdon's refusal to treat patients with HIV infection in his office would change absent a court-ordered injunction, especially because he had taken a strong public position concerning his right not to treat patients with HIV. The choice of service provider belongs to Abbott, and the right to choose is reinforced in the ADA. An injunction would maintain the right to lawful choice. To preserve that right, an injunction is absolutely essential as a remedy.

Although Abbott strategically stated that she would continue to use Bragdon for dental services if she prevailed in the litigation, it really makes no sense to conclude that Congress intended to require Abbott to assert that she would use his services after he had made his private prejudices known—and refused to serve her—in order to have standing to sue. Application of the capable-of-repetition doctrine permits clearly unlawful conduct to be remedied by enjoining such conduct for the benefit of Abbott and other individuals with a disability. In the context of personal services, it is unlikely that anyone would engage the services of a provider again after the provider had engaged in blatant discrimination, because other providers are usually available. In deciding to cover personal service enterprises, and permitting only injunctive relief, Congress must have intended effective relief to be available. By narrowly construing the capable-of-repetition doctrine, the courts have departed from Congress's intentions. None of the courts that considered the *Bragdon* litigation raised the justiciability issue, although they could have raised the issue of their own accord. The Supreme Court's decision in *Bragdon* implicitly reflects its understanding that jurisdiction is appropriate in this category of cases in that the Court had the power to raise the jurisdictional issue itself.

There is a long tradition of the courts ordering "structural injunctions"—injunctions that involve a court actively in the life of a public entity such as a segregated school. Federal courts have invoked this power to take control of prisons, mental institutions, and public housing, and even to raise local property taxes and impose contempt citations and daily fines for failure to comply with judicially mandated spending increases.[45] Although the courts' use of these broad powers is controversial in the area of constitutional litigation, it is far less controversial for Congress to enact legislation explicitly designed to avoid a constitutional problem at the outset. Professor John Yoo, for example, a critic of constitutional structural injunctions, has argued that "Congress can cure constitutional violations before they occur, or it can make constitutional litigation unnecessary by providing clearer, more precise standards and procedures."[46] ADA Title III is an example of such clear and precise standards and procedures. If a court has the power to require affirmative action—which benefits individuals in the future who were not a party to the original litigation—it is hard to see how a court does not have the power to grant injunctive relief to a named plaintiff who theoretically could seek to use the service she was denied in the future. Congress obviously concluded that injunctive relief was necessary to remedy the evils that it made unlawful through passage of ADA Title III. It is wrong to use Article III's standing requirements to undermine Congress's purpose in enacting the ADA.

This kind of problem rarely arose under CRA Title II because plaintiffs in those cases were likely to want to return to the restaurant or hotel in question (or at least could assert they had an interest in returning). Because CRA Title II does not cover personal service situations, it does not cover *Bragdon*-like fact patterns. When enacting the ADA, Congress was repeatedly told that the remedies under ADA Title III were the same as the remedies under CRA Title II. No one focused on whether the remedies would be adequate in the different kinds of fact patterns that exist under ADA Title III.

In addition, it is important to remember the historical rationale for injunctive relief under CRA Title II: a concern about the possibility of prejudiced juries not awarding any relief at all. Although that concern may have been appropriate in the United States in 1964 with regard to race discrimination lawsuits, it has little or no applicability to disability discrimination lawsuits brought after 1990. My own research under ADA Title I (the employment discrimination title; see chapter 3) suggests that plaintiffs may fare better before juries than judges. If compensatory damages were available, the rare plaintiff in an ADA action who feared a prejudiced jury would still have the option of seeking only injunctive relief and thereby avoiding a jury trial.

II. ADA Title III Results

The most significant impact of ADA Title III's limited scope of relief is probably the small number of cases that have been filed under that title. Courts of appeals issued decisions in 475 cases under ADA Title I (the employment title) from June 1992 to July 1998 (see chapter 3). I have been able to locate only 25 ADA Title III appellate decisions for the same time period, 5 percent of the reported appellate cases.

Twenty-five appellate decisions are too few to provide a clear sense of how effective ADA Title III has been in remedying discrimination problems. Hence, I have tried to supplement these results with other kinds of results, verdicts and settlements. Verdict data are reported in part B, below. Settlement data are discussed in part C, below. The verdict and settlement data suggest that Title III may be effective, particularly when supplemental state actions are available. It also may be effective when the federal government brings suit and seeks broad relief. But the verdict and settlement data are reflective of small sample sizes, suggesting that ADA Title III's effectiveness may be largely dependent on voluntary compliance rather than litigation. Attorney General Thornburgh may have been correct to suggest that incentives to pursue litigation would be diminished through a limited remedial scheme, but it is hard to imagine that voluntary enforcement is effective when private parties can calculate that it is highly unlikely that any enforcement action for noncompliance would be brought against them. Twenty-five appellate decisions is quite disproportionate to the 475 cases decided under ADA Title I. Although 475 cases may be considered excessive, 25 appear to be too minimal.

A. Appellate Litigation Results

I was able to find only 25 appellate decisions that were reported on Westlaw. Of those decisions, defendants prevailed through dismissal or summary judgment in 18 (72 percent). After the appellate process was completed, defendants still prevailed in 18 of 25 cases (although the mix of cases changed through 6 reversals). Although this is a prodefendant outcome, it is less prodefendant in orientation than the results I have found under ADA Title I. Under ADA Title I, defendants prevail in 94 percent of the cases from which appeals were taken (448 of 475). After the appeal process was completed, defendants continued to prevail in 82 percent of the cases from which appeals were taken (389 of 475). In the Title I area, the appeals courts appear to have played a modestly corrective role, lessening the defendant-win percentage from 94 percent to 82 percent. Apparently, plaintiffs have a somewhat easier time prevailing under ADA Title III than ADA Title I but are not very inclined even to attempt litigation under ADA Title III.

B. Verdict Data

The verdict data confirm that plaintiffs are unlikely to sue under ADA Title III. Verdicts are rarely reported in published decisions, so they are not a part of the set of cases discussed above in part A. Although not all verdicts are readily available, some verdict services in various regions that report verdict data. Westlaw and Lexis report the results from many of these services.[47]

I used these verdict services to locate ADA cases reported by September 28, 1998. I was able to locate 109 verdicts in ADA cases heard in either state or federal court, among them were only 16 ADA Title III cases (about 16 percent of all ADA verdicts). Seven of these cases were brought in federal court; 9 in state court. Plaintiffs were successful in 4 of 7 federal court actions and in 4 of 9 state court actions, overall in 8 of 16. Title I and III actions were comparable. In Title I actions, plaintiffs were successful in 27 of 51; in Title III actions, in 17 of 39. These figures are consistent with what the judicial expectations model would suggest. Cases are most likely to go to trial when each party estimates that it has about a 50 percent chance of prevailing. Very strong and very weak cases should settle because the probable losing party should calculate that it is not economically wise to take the case to trial.

It is interesting that the discrepancy between cases that go to a jury trial and are not appealed, and cases that are decided by the judge or jury that are appealed. Jury trials rarely occurred in the cases in my appellate sample. Most ended at a pretrial stage through the entry of summary judgment. In the cases that did not go to a jury, plaintiffs had a much lower chance of prevailing than in cases that did go to the jury. In chapter 4, I hypothesized in the Title I context that judges are misusing the summary judgment device to avoid having potentially meritorious cases go to the jury. These Title III statistics, although not as extreme as the Title I statistics, provide further confirmation for this hypothesis.

The Title III data also suggest that we need not be concerned about excessive jury awards if compensatory and punitive damages were available under ADA Title III. All of these ADA Title III cases also included a supplemental state law action in which compensatory or punitive damages were available, such as a negligence theory. The typical plaintiff suffered a serious injury as a result of faulty accessibility standards, and therefore was eligible for damages under a negligence theory for a violation of a substantive standard (ADA) that led to an injury. Such plaintiffs typically received an award of about $10,000, although one plaintiff received an award of $512,000 against a physician and a hospital for the failure to admit him to the hospital in violation of the ADA, the Emergency Medical Treatment and Active Labor Act (EMTALA), and state tort law. These awards reflected compensation for actual physical injury due to a failure to meet ADA Title III standards.

Very few of these cases involved what might be considered stigmatic harm due to a lack of accessibility. The only exception was a case against Sunnyvale Town Center in California for failing to provide crosswalks and parking for individuals with disabilities at its mall. The jury awarded a verdict for the plaintiff of $74,097 in economic damages and $160,000 in noneconomic damages. The case was then settled for $145,000, including costs.

These verdicts suggest that where plaintiffs have only a stigmatic claim of injury due to lack of accessibility but no physical injury, juries will tend to calculate their injury as relatively minor. If the ADA were amended to include a right to relief for compensatory damages, it is reasonable to conclude that this trend would continue.

It is also important to recognize that the jury verdict cases almost always involve situations where the plaintiff suffered a physical injury as a result of the failure to comply with ADA standards. Few of these cases involved solely a lack of access. The purpose of ADA Title III, however, was to remedy the lack of access to places of public accommodation by individuals with disabilities. State tort law already provides relief where an individual becomes injured due to a negligent design feature. With the unavailability of compensatory damages, the pure lack of access cases are not going to juries. They are being decided exclusively by judges. And, unfortunately, the reported decision data suggest that judges are not as sympathetic to ADA Title III cases as are juries.

The lack of availability of compensatory damages therefore has two results: (1) a limited availability of relief, and (2) judge rather than jury decisions. Not only do plaintiffs fail to obtain compensatory damages, they often fail to prevail altogether before an unsympathetic judiciary. When CRA Title II was passed, the thinking about the judge/jury distinction was quite different. Civil rights proponents feared that white southern juries might be unsympathetic to CRA Title II claims, so that the decision to permit only injunctive relief had the additional advantage of having the case not eligible for jury determination. The choice of permitting only injunctive relief under the law of race was considered by some civil rights advocates to be the best choice because of the problem of prejudiced juries. By contrast, injunctive relief was considered to be more effective because "the expenses involved are borne by the government, a trial by a prejudiced jury is never necessary, and the remedy is of continuing effect, permitting punishment for contempt when the injunctive order is violated."[48] Under ADA Title III, however, we usually have reason to come to the opposite conclusion: existing data show that juries are more likely to rule in favor of plaintiffs than are judges in bench trials. The limitation to purely injunctive relief not only precludes plaintiffs from obtaining compensatory damages but also causes them to have their cases heard before judges rather than juries.

C. Settlements

One might argue that reported decision and verdict data offer an incomplete picture of ADA compliance because they do not include settlements. Settlement data are probably the hardest to acquire because settlements are often not made public. Nonetheless, the Department of Justice (DOJ) reports its settlements on its Web site.[49] The Web site indicates that the DOJ has attained settlements in 107 ADA cases as of September 2003.

When the DOJ settles an ADA Title III case, it has leverage that is not available to private plaintiffs: the statutory authority to seek civil damages if it brings suit.[50] Private parties can also intervene in their cases to seek damages under state law. Despite this financial leverage, the DOJ appears to rarely obtain civil fines through settlement. Monetary settlements typically range from $250 to $10,000; some settlements come in the form of gift certificates.

A typical settlement involved claimants with mobility impairments who alleged that an existing facility was not accessible, although accessibility was "readily achievable." Often the case was coupled with a claim that the entity failed to provide an auxiliary aid. Most cases involved the "readily achievable" standard for existing structures; only a few cases involved the more stringent standard for new construction.

The remedies obtained by the DOJ under the readily achievable standard for existing entities were often quite significant. For example, Comfort Inn agreed to remove barriers relating to parking, ramps, and walkways; to replace emergency lights; to create accessible restrooms; to lower restaurant cash registers; to provide a lift to the swimming pools; to create accessible drinking fountains; and to create accessible rooms and doorways at its motels throughout the country. Similarly, Friendly Ice Cream (which was also assessed a $50,000 fine) agreed to remove steps; widen doors; redesign vestibules and dining areas for wheelchairs; provide accessible parking, restrooms, and routes; install curb cuts; relocate telephones; and read menus to people with visual impairments at its stores and restaurants throughout the country. There were also many cases with effective but inexpensive compliance, such as changing policies to permit service animals into an entity or changing policies about use of a driver's license as an exclusive form of identification.

Although the DOJ settlements appear to be effective, they are few in number. One hundred seven settlements in approximately ten years of statutory enforcement reflect less than one settlement a month by an agency charged with national enforcement. Although it may be the case that the DOJ can attain effective enforcement in the cases it prosecutes, it is unrealistic to expect that such efforts will have much impact on the pattern of denial of accommodation that may exist in the larger society. It is hard to believe that the kinds of general problems that the DOJ found— inaccessible hotels and restaurants, improper service-animal policies, and inappropriate photo identification policies—are confined to those 107 entities.

Under the existing statutory scheme, DOJ enforcement is a theoretically important part of statutory compliance because the department is settling the pure access cases that ADA Title III was designed to remedy. With the limited financial incentives to file suit for this kind of violation (when a physical injury has not occurred), it is unrealistic to expect the private bar to take many of these cases. Yet the DOJ has only a few dozen attorneys assigned to national enforcement under ADA Title III. In considering the ineffectiveness of the DOJ's ADA Title III enforcement, it is helpful to make a comparison with the FHA.

Under the FHA, if the secretary of housing determines that reasonable cause exists to believe that a discriminatory housing practice has occurred or is about to occur, he or she is required to issue a charge on behalf of the aggrieved person for further enforcement proceedings by the attorney general. If the aggrieved person elects a judicial remedy, then "the Secretary shall authorize, and not later than 30 days after the election is made the Attorney General shall commence and maintain, a civil action on behalf of the aggrieved person in a United States district court seeking relief under this subsection." From March 12, 1989, to December 6, 1993, the DOJ handled 293 FHA cases, entering a consent decree in 171 of these cases.[51] The FHA enforcement mechanism appears to be more effective than the ADA enforcement mechanism. By contrast, the aggrieved individual has the right to intervene in that lawsuit, thereby pursuing both a public and private cause of action at little expense to the aggrieved individual. Thus, when Congress so desires, it knows how to make enforcement by the DOJ effective for the aggrieved individual. The public enforcement opportunities under ADA Title III, by contrast, are quite limited, in part due to Congress's limited enforcement scheme under ADA Title III.

It is worthwhile to remember that when CRA II was passed, individuals who were familiar with state enforcement efforts under state civil rights statutes noted the importance of an administrative enforcement scheme for civil rights laws to be effective. Congress was not willing in 1964 to develop such an enforcement scheme for CRA II but demonstrated its ability to create such an enforcement scheme for FHA in 1998. It is therefore disappointing to see that Congress backpedaled in 1990 and enacted an administrative enforcement scheme that was obviously inadequate.

III. Filling the Remedial Gap

It is arguable that despite the limited relief under ADA Title III, the ADA might spur states to pass or amend their own antidiscrimination laws to provide effective remedies. Some states do have broader remedial provisions under their racial nondiscrimination laws than Congress provided under CRA Title II, which have served as an impetus for lawsuits such as the case against Denny's. However, even states with a strong commitment to antidiscrimination in the disability arena have not amended their statutes to provide more effective relief than is available under ADA Title III. For example, Maine amended its disability antidiscrimination statute in 1995 to parallel the scope of coverage under the federal ADA. It repealed and replaced the section defining "places of public accommodation" so that its scope of coverage was identical to the coverage under federal law.[52] But it left intact the relief provision already existing under Maine law for cases of discrimination brought against places of public accommodation. This provision caps relief at $10,000 for first-time offenders, $25,000 for second-time offenders, and $50,000 for third-time offenders. Although this relief is more generous than the relief available under the ADA because the civil damages can be awarded directly to the victim of discrimination and are available without the intervention of the state attorney general, it is not a product of a deliberate attempt by the state to fill the enforcement gap under ADA Title III. The relief provisions found in the Maine antidiscrimination statute preceded the enactment of the ADA. Thus, the passage of the ADA had an impact on the substantive law of Maine—the scope of coverage—but no impact on the relief available to victims of discrimination at places of public accommodation.

State disability law on discrimination at places of public accommodation can be divided into three categories: Category One comprises states that do not have a state law banning discrimination at places of public accommodation on the basis of disability; Category Two comprises states that have a statute that prohibits such discrimination but that provides narrow remedies such as purely injunctive relief or a modest fine under the criminal code; and Category Three comprises states that provide broader remedies than the ADA (see table 6.1).

The 5 states in Category One do not generally offer the protections of nondiscrimination at places of public accommodation except to provide the right to use a service animal at a place of public accommodation. The 25 states in Category Two prohibit discrimination at public accommoda-

TABLE 6.1.
State Public Accommodation Statutes Prohibiting Disability Discrimination

Category One (No Enforceable Prohibition)	Category Two (Narrow Remedies)	Category Three (Broad Remedies, Year)
Oklahoma (requires seeing eye dogs admittance)	Alabama + (M)	**Arizona (1992)**
	Alaska ($500 cap)	California (1976)
South Carolina (no apparent enforcement authority)	Arkansas (M)	**Delaware (1996)**
	Colorado + ($10–300) (M)	**Florida + (1992)**
Tennessee (no disability law)	Connecticut ($25–100) (M)	Hawaii (1988)
Texas (general statement of rights; no enforcement)	District of Columbia	**Idaho + (compensatory: 1990, punitive: 1997)**
	Georgia + ($100) (M)	
Washington (no remedy other than for "white cane" law)	Iowa + (M)	Illinois (1989)
	Kansas + ($2000 cap) (M)	Indiana (1978)
	Maryland ($500–2500)	Kentucky (1974)
	Massachusetts + + ($2,500) (M)	Louisiana (1980)
	Mississippi + (M) ($100)	Maine ($10,000–$50,000 in penal damages) (1989)
	Montana +	
	Nebraska + (M)	Michigan (1980)
	New Hampshire (M)	Minnesota (1969)
	New Mexico + (M)	Missouri (1986)
	New York (M) ($100–$500)	Nevada (1965)
	North Carolina	**New Jersey (1990)**
	North Dakota	Ohio (1987)
	Oregon ($1,000 cap)	**South Dakota (1991)**
	Pennsylvania (M) ($500 cap)	Vermont (1987)
	Rhode Island	Virginia (1985)
	Utah + (M)	Wisconsin (1975)
	West Virginia ($5000 cap)	
	Wyoming + (M) ($750 cap)	

+ Definition includes individuals who have visual or auditory impairments or are otherwise physically disabled.

++ Definition includes individuals who are deaf or blind or have any physical or mental disability.

(M) Misdemeanor statute.

tions but provide narrow remedies. The most typical remedy provided in these states is a misdemeanor remedy; 17 of 25 states provide that violating their law against public accommodation is a misdemeanor. The misdemeanor statutes provide virtually no relief at all. As indicated in parentheses after the statutes, the misdemeanor penalties range from $10 to $5,000 (see table 6.1).

Twelve of the 25 states in Category Two have very antiquated statutes that limit their coverage to individuals with visual, hearing, or other physical disabilities (see table 6.1).

The states with the most effective remedies are listed in Category Three. Twenty-one states provide some form of compensatory relief. Twenty-one of 51 states (including the District of Columbia) therefore provide for reasonably effective relief beyond what ADA Title III requires.

To the extent that gap filling exists under state law, however, it does not appear that passage of the ADA has been a major factor. The names of the six states whose statutes were amended after 1990 to include compensatory damages are in boldface type. California has the most generous relief provision; a plaintiff can obtain "up to three times the amount of actual damages but in no case less than one thousand dollars ($1,000) and attorney's fees."[53] Although California has increased the minimum penalty several times, the provision for relief has existed since 1976. Similarly, Vermont enacted its disability discrimination statute in 1987 and provided for injunctive relief and compensatory and punitive damages.[54] States' decisions to offer broader relief than the ADA generally seem to be independent of the passage of the ADA. Although many states amended their statutes after its passage to make their definition of "public accommodation" more consistent with the ADA's, only six of those states broadened the relief available in their state statute at that time. There is, therefore, no current groundswell for state law to serve a "gap-filling" function under the law of public accommodations.

By contrast, significant gap filling at the state level has occurred in the area of racial nondiscrimination statutes since the passage of CRA Title II. Four states have no statute banning race discrimination at places of public accommodation. Fifteen states have statutes that go no further than CRA Title II. Thirty-one states provide at least compensatory relief; of these, eighteen took more than a decade to include compensatory damages (see table 6.2).

The issue of relief, however, has a unique quality in the area of racial nondiscrimination legislation that may not translate into the area of disability nondiscrimination legislation. Permitting only injunctive relief of race discrimination was considered by some civil rights advocates to be the best choice because of the problem of prejudiced juries, as discussed above. Hence, state legislatures may have always been willing to create compensatory damages under their race nondiscrimination statutes; they were not asked to do so until the jury climate became more favorably disposed to claims of race discrimination. There is little or no evidence that state legislatures that enacted legislation forbidding disability-based discrimination but limiting the remedies to injunctive relief were willing to consider compensatory damages at the time of enactment.

Nearly every state has a statute prohibiting disability discrimination at places of public accommodation. The question is whether legislatures can

TABLE 6.2.
*State Statutes Prohibiting Race Discrimination
at Places of Public Accommodation*

Category One (No prohibition against discrimination)	No Compensatory or Punitive Damages (date enforcement scheme established)	Compensatory or Punitive Damages (date compensatory damages adopted)
Alabama	Arizona (1965)	Alaska (1970)
Georgia	Colorado (1979)	**Arkansas (1993)**
Mississippi	Connecticut (1980)	California (1905)
North Carolina	Idaho (1961)	**District of Columbia (1977)**
Texas	Illinois (1989)	Florida (1992)
	Kansas (1961)	**Delaware (1996)**
	Maine (1971)	**Hawaii (1989)**
	Maryland (1963)	**Indiana (1978)**
	Massachusetts (1933)	Iowa (1965)
	Nebraska (1969)	**Kentucky (1974)**
	North Dakota (1983)	Louisiana (1988)
	Rhode Island (1991)	**Michigan (1976)**
	Virginia (1987)	Minnesota (1969)
	West Virginia (1967)	**Missouri (1986)**
	Wyoming (1982)	Montana (1895)
		Nevada (1965)
		New Hampshire (1992)
		New Jersey (1990)
		New Mexico (1969)
		New York (1965)
		Ohio (1987)
		Oklahoma (1968)
		Oregon (1973)
		Pennsylvania (1955)
		South Carolina (1990)
		South Dakota (1991)
		Tennessee (1978)
		Utah (1965)
		Vermont (1987)
		Washington (1973)
		Wisconsin (1980)

be mobilized to conclude that legislative action is necessary to improve the existing statutory law. One rationale for legislative action may be that many states have antiquated disability statutes, such as "white cane laws," which provide for a very limited prohibition against discrimination. If states perceive a need to update these statutes, there is the possibility that they also may be persuaded to improve their remedial scheme more generally.

A final difficulty that may exist for the law of disability discrimination is the public perception that this is now an area that is primarily the subject of federal, not state, regulation. When states have amended disability statutes, they have frequently looked to the federal statutes' and their implementation. In the racial civil rights area, we may have once thought of the states as a laboratory for innovative legal developments; in the disability discrimination area, we may now be expecting the federal government to be the leading laboratory. If so, the only way to spur significant change would be for the federal government to take a significant step rather than to expect the states to do so.

IV. Conclusion

ADA Title III was modeled on CRA Title II, specifically borrowing its limited remedial scheme. Plaintiffs who have litigated under ADA Title III have had a reasonable chance of prevailing, but litigation also appears to be a seldom used tool because of the limited remedies available. Settlements have occurred, and their remedies have been effective, but there is little incentive for private individuals to seek settlements unless the Department of Justice initiates an enforcement proceeding. Voluntary compliance is difficult to measure, but any casual observation of the accessibility of places of public accommodation reveals that there is much work to be done in order to attain compliance.

After a decade of enforcement the effectiveness of the ADA's remedies can be assessed. Nearly all of the ADA Title III verdicts involved cases with a state law claim for compensatory damages under a negligence *per se* theory. Plaintiffs were able to attain verdicts only if they had actual physical injuries from a fall due to negligent construction. The ADA Title III cases that resulted in reported opinions or DOJ settlements did involve pure right-to-access issues—without the requirement of an actual physical injury—but those cases were very few in number. The DOJ's national enforcement authority enhanced the relief available in those cases, but the DOJ is able to bring very few cases despite that authority. Its enforcement authority is much more limited under ADA Title III than it is under the FHA. At a minimum, Congress should enhance the agency's enforcement authority to increase compliance with ADA Title III.

State law is also in serious need of expansion, even though 21 states provide for greater relief than ADA Title III, and 6 of those states have enhanced their remedial scheme since 1990. But in general, not only do states need to enhance the relief available under their state statutes, they need to revisit the scope of protection generally provided under state law in the area of disability discrimination. Many state statutes are woefully behind the times and in serious need of updating.

Revision of state law, however, is not an adequate solution to remedy the problem. The purpose of legislation like the ADA is to provide a uniform and national set of antidiscrimination standards. Yet that is still out of reach. Plaintiffs who suffer physical injuries as a result of inaccessibility may have a viable state law claim for negligence with the possibility of compensatory relief. Plaintiffs in sixteen states can sue to challenge inaccessibility problems and recover more than injunctive relief under state law. And a handful of plaintiffs each year can benefit from the DOJ's enforcement efforts on their behalf. But the remaining victims of discrimination under ADA Title III have little, if any, recourse if their accessibility problems have not caused physical injury. If Congress is serious about providing access to public accommodations for all Americans, such regional differences are unacceptable.

To attain uniform enforcement, we should move toward a compensatory damage scheme under ADA Title III, borrowing from the damages scheme available under the FHA. Experience at the state level suggests that there is little reason to fear runaway juries if damages were to be expanded under ADA Title III. The very fact that we need not fear runaway juries, however, also gives us pause: Should we not be even more ambitious about seeking effective remedies under ADA Title III? By permitting injunctive relief and limited compensatory relief, we still may not be giving businesses sufficient incentives to comply with ADA Title III. Businesses might calculate that it is cheaper not to comply because statutory enforcement is unlikely to be as expensive as compliance from the date of enactment of the ADA. In other words, a business that is sued in the year 2000 for failing to comply with ADA Title III may have benefitted for ten years by saving money on an auxiliary service or device. Prospectively offering that device and paying a modest compensatory award to an individual victim of discrimination as a result of enforcement activity may be cost effective. But if the remedial scheme required a business to pay a fine for all the years in which it did not comply with the ADA, then the failure of the business to comply with the statute may not be cost effective. The DOJ's civil fine authority provides that incentive structure but, given the DOJ's limited enforcement resources, it cannot act as a serious deterrent against unlawful conduct under ADA Title III. The FHA's mandatory enforcement by the attorney general would create a significant improvement in ADA compliance.

ADA Title III was a significant and important step in improving the lives of individuals with disabilities. It is now time to ask whether we can do a better job in creating an effective enforcement scheme to achieve those aspirations. Our experience under the FHA and state disability antidiscrimination law should provide models.

7

Dissing Congress

[The ADA is an example of what happens when a bill's] sponsors are so eager to get something passed that what passes hasn't been as carefully written as a group of law professors might put together.
—Justice Sandra Day O'Connor (March 2002)

[The ADA] was the product of two years of careful research, drafting and negotiation between disability-rights lawyers and business community lawyers. —Professor Chai Feldblum, legislative lawyer who helped draft the ADA (March 2002)

The Supreme Court's disparate decisions in the constitutional law and statutory contexts demonstrate that the problem with ADA enforcement lies with the Supreme Court, not Congress. Justice Sandra Day O'Connor was wrong to blame Congress for rushing through a hastily drafted statute. The problem, unfortunately, lies in the Rehnquist Court's twin decisions to invalidate parts of the ADA on constitutional law grounds (*Garrett*)[1] while also interpreting the statute narrowly in an entirely ahistorical framework (*Sutton*).[2]

By looking closely at the conflicting methodologies employed by the Court in these constitutional law and statutory interpretation cases, we can see the lengths to which the Court has gone to reflect profound disrespect for the work of Congress.[3] In *Garrett*, it has chided Congress for not having used the legislative process to produce enough findings of unconstitutional state conduct to justify its regulation of the states. In *Sutton*, it has told Congress that the Court is entirely uninterested in the record Congress creates while drafting legislation. These conflicting methodological approaches to examining the work of Congress can be understood only as a power grab by the Court at the expense of Congress.

Ultimately, individuals with disabilities are the losers in the separation-of-powers battle.

The conflicting methodologies that reflect this disrespectful posture are the "crystal ball" approach that the Court has used in assessing the constitutionality of Congress's handiwork, and the "ahistorical" approach that it has used in interpreting the statutory language. This chapter will explore the consequences of these conflicting methodologies after providing some background on the context in which the methodologies are employed.

The Supreme Court has been asked to consider two different kinds of questions under the ADA. First, it has been asked to consider whether Congress acted in a constitutional manner when it enacted the ADA. Congress is a branch of government of limited powers, and the Constitution requires that it must act pursuant to a specified constitutional authority in its enactments. When Congress regulates the private sector, it can usually rely on its commerce clause authority because nearly all facets of society affect interstate commerce. When Congress provides a cause of action for individuals to sue the states, it must meet a higher threshold to justify its legislation under the Court's "federalism" jurisprudence. (Providing a cause of action by individuals against the states is called "abrogating state sovereign immunity.") The term "federalism" has come to mean that Congress should act in a respectful manner toward the states and be cautious in imposing private legal liability on them. Modern-day federalists typically argue that Congress has exceeded its constitutional authority when it abrogates state sovereign immunity by creating a cause of action by individuals against the states. They have made that argument repeatedly to invalidate parts of the ADA.[4]

The ADA regulates both the public and private sectors. In general, it provides for enforcement of ADA rules by private individuals who have been victims of discrimination. ADA Title I makes it unlawful for states to engage in employment discrimination against individuals with disabilities. ADA Title II makes it unlawful for states to engage in any kind of discrimination against individuals with disabilities in state-provided programs and activities. The Court has therefore been asked to consider whether the ADA is constitutional when it abrogates state sovereign immunity by giving individuals a cause of action against the states under ADA Titles I and II. As we will see, the answer to this question depends on whether Congress has properly used its authority under Section 5 of the Fourteenth Amendment. Section 5 gives Congress the power to "enforce" the due process and equal protection clauses by enacting prophylatic legislation that helps remedy potentially unconstitutional conduct by the states.[5]

To determine whether Congress has enacted ADA Titles I and II pursuant to proper constitutional authority, the Court must determine whether Congress had a proper basis to conclude that such legislation was necessary to enforce Section 1 of the Fourteenth Amendment.[6] The Court has created a very high threshold for Congress to justify such legislation. The threshold reflects a "crystal ball" approach because the Court has expected Congress to create a set of detailed adjudicatory findings under a legal standard that it could not have foreseen. Unrealistically, the Court expected Congress to establish a detailed legislative record of unconstitutional state conduct to support its use of its Section 5 authority, although constitutional law, when the ADA was enacted, imposed no such requirement.

Second, the Court has been asked to interpret ambiguous statutory terms like the definition of "disability." This is not a constitutional law inquiry. Instead, it is a statutory interpretation question. What could Congress have intended various terms to mean?

To answer questions of statutory interpretation, the Court has to make some basic methodological decisions about how it wishes to proceed. Should it examine the legislative history—hearings, committee reports, and congressional debate—to determine how these terms should be interpreted? Should it defer to administrative agencies that may have promulgated regulations to interpret these ambiguous terms? Or should the Court require that the language of the statute, itself, resolve all ambiguities?

The Rehnquist Court has answered most questions of statutory interpretation under the ADA in disregard of the legislative history and agency regulations. Instead, it has relied heavily on the statutory language itself. In general, this is a poor method for interpreting a statute because it makes it too easy for the Court to substitute its own judgment for that of Congress. It is Congress that is supposed to be responsible for "making law." The Court is supposed to "interpret law."

But even if the ahistorical approach to legislative interpretation made sense as a "good" methodology, it flies in the face of how the Court has treated Congress in the constitutional law context. The Court has chided Congress for not creating *enough* findings to justify the constitutionality of parts of the ADA when exercising its Section 5 authority under the

Fourteenth Amendment. But then, in the statutory interpretation context, the Court disregards Congress's legislative work in its entirety. If the legislative work is so useless that it should be ignored in the statutory interpretation context, then it seems odd to chide Congress for not doing enough legislative work in the constitutional law context. The crystal ball approach in the constitutional law context and the ahistorical approach in the statutory context are convenient ways for the Court to "diss" Congress by invalidating key sections of the ADA and substituting its own view of the meaning of key statutory terms for those of Congress. But "dissing" Congress is not the Court's proper role; its proper role is to treat Congress with the respect of a coequal branch of government.

I. The Crystal Ball Problem: Garrett

Historically, the Supreme Court and the Congress were considered coequal branches of government and the Supreme Court presumed that acts of Congress were constitutional. In a speech in April 2000 at Michigan State University—Detroit College of Law, Justice Antonin Scalia threatened to stop respecting the work of Congress as a coequal branch of government:

> My Court is fond of saying that acts of Congress come to the Court with the presumption of constitutionality. That presumption reflects Congress's status as a coequal branch of government with its own responsibilities to the Constitution. But if Congress is going to take the attitude that it will do anything it can get away with and let the Supreme Court worry about the Constitution . . . then perhaps that presumption is unwarranted.[7]

The Supreme Court's decision in *Board of Trustees v. Garrett*[8] reflects the Court's growing disrespect for Congress. The Court in *Garrett* demanded a depth and breadth of documentation to support the exercise of Section 5 authority under the Fourteenth Amendment that Congress could not possibly have foreseen in 1990 when it enacted the ADA. This is the crystal ball problem.

When Congress enacted the ADA in 1990, the leading case on the scope of its authority was *Pennsylvania v. Union Gas Company*.[9] In that decision, the Court had ruled that Congress had the authority to abrogate state sovereign immunity under its commerce clause power. In other words, Congress could regulate the states directly and provide a cause of action for private individuals by acting under its commerce clause authority when it enacted the ADA. The commerce clause authority had been broadly construed for several decades, so Congress would have had little reason for concern in 1990 when it enacted the ADA. It would not have even envisioned that it needed to justify the legislation under Section 5. Hence, when Attorney General Richard L. Thornburgh testified before Congress concerning the ADA, he was not asked about the statute's constitutionality. In chapter 2's recitation of the ADA's legislative history, I did not discuss concerns about the ADA's constitutionality because none existed in the legislative record.

Beginning in 1995, however, a series of Supreme Court decisions dramatically altered the separation of powers landscape. In 1996, the Court overruled *Union Gas* and concluded that Congress could not use its commerce clause authority to abrogate state sovereign immunity in *Seminole Tribe v. Florida*.[10] In the future, Congress would have to look elsewhere in the Constitution to justify its abrogation of state sovereign immunity.

The most likely place to look for this authority would be Section 5 of the Fourteenth Amendment. Section 5 gives Congress the power to "enforce" Section 1 of the Fourteenth Amendment through "appropriate legislation." Section 1, in turn, prohibits the states from violating the "equal protection of the laws." Hence, the civil rights laws could be justified under Congress's Section 5 authority as enforcing its equal protection authority. Laws banning race discrimination, gender discrimination, age discrimination, and disability discrimination could be justified on that basis because they were seeking to guarantee that each state provide "equal protection" to all its citizens. Until 1997, Congress's authority under Section 5 was understood to be broad and could easily justify ADA abrogation of state sovereign immunity. Accordingly, the ADA seemed relatively safe in its entirety despite the *Seminole Tribe* decision. Even though its coverage of the states could not be justified under the commerce clause, it could be justified under Section 5.

Beginning in 1997, the Court began to cut back on Congress's Section 5 authority. For the first time since 1883, the Supreme Court ruled, in *City of Boerne v. Flores*,[11] that Congress exceeded its Section 5 authority when it enacted the Religious Freedom Restoration Act. In reaching this conclusion, the Court adopted a new framework that imposed a high burden on Congress to prove that its work was constitutional: a legislative record to support the need for remedial legislation to enforce the Fourteenth Amendment. The Court chided Congress for producing an inadequate legislative record even though the legislative history reflected that Congress had given consideration to the problem of religious discrimination before enacting the antidiscrimination legislation at issue.

The threshold created in *Boerne* proved unattainable in *Garrett*. When Congress drafted the ADA, it relied not only on extensive direct testimony and decades of prior legislative experience regulating on this same subject but also on a task force that it had created specifically to assess the need for new national disability discrimination legislation.[12] The Court, however, gave little respect to the handiwork of the task force. When it concluded that Congress did not adequately document the existence of disability discrimination in state employment, the Court questioned the relevance of the evidence compiled from all fifty states by the task force because the evidence of disparate treatment by state officials had been submitted to the task force rather than directly to Congress.[13] In addition, the task force and various congressional committees collected evidence about discrimination by cities and counties as well as states. The Court refused to extrapolate from this evidence of discrimination by units of local government to state government, because principles of sovereign immunity do not apply to these units of local government.[14]

At the time it enacted the ADA, Congress had little reason to foresee any constitutional requirement for detailed record building, given that *Seminole Tribe* and *City of Boerne* were six or more years in the future. But even had it anticipated a need for more extensive evidentiary support, Congress in 1990 could not possibly have foreseen that its historic methods of educating itself outside the formalities of the hearing room, or its reliance on evidence of discrimination engaged in by closely analogous government actors at the local level, would be excluded from consideration when the record was being reviewed.

In *Garrett*, the Rehnquist Court has effectively sought to reshape the lawmaking process by imposing a litigation-based model on Congress. Traditionally, the Court has been attentive to Congress's expertise and judgment in perceiving and reporting the pervasiveness of discrimination. By contrast, the level of precision and detail in the formal legislative record that the Rehnquist Court requires is more akin to the factual predicate needed to support a class action claim for constitutional relief. Even if it were a road map to constitutional validation for future statutes, this approach would raise serious separation of powers concerns. In undervaluing, if not ignoring, essential elements of the legislative enterprise, the Court's approach cannot help but impede Congress's ability to fulfill its distinct responsibilities.

In the end, the Court in *Garrett* demanded that Congress *prove* something to justify its exercise of Section 5 powers against the states, a considerable departure from expectations of Congress under the civil rights cases of the 1960s and 1970s. Indeed, the earlier decisions suggest both that Congress should play a positive role in strengthening the antidiscrimination norms of the Fourteenth Amendment and that Congress's legislative efforts can support the Court's own evolving approach to understanding and enforcing those norms outside the racial setting. The Court in the past decade has largely abandoned this deferential stance, replacing it with a more constrained vision in which congressional fact-finding and support for antidiscrimination laws are subject to searching, skeptical review. Congress's unsurprising inability to keep pace with such a remarkable change in perspective has produced a troubling shift in the balance of power between the branches.

Nonetheless, there is a modest ray of good news from the Supreme Court with respect to Congress's authority under Section 5 of the Fourteenth Amendment. In *Tennessee v. Lane*, 124 S. Ct. 1978 (2004), the Court held in a 5-4 decision that Congress did not exceed its authority when it gave individuals a private right of action under ADA Title II to challenge the inaccessibility of state courthouses. It is a narrow decision and is discussed extensively in chapter 5. For our present purposes, what is most interesting about the *Lane* decision is that the majority opinion cited with approval various sources that the majority opinion had considered unreliable or irrelevant in *Garrett*. For example, the task force, whose work was discredited in *Garrett*, is now cited with approval. In dissent, Chief Justice William H. Rehnquist noted that fact. He stated (with disapproval): "[T]he majority today cites the same congressional task force evidence we rejected in *Garrett*. . . . As in *Garrett*, this 'unexamined, anecdotal' evidence does not suffice."[15] Rehnquist, of course, is correct to note that this evidence did not suffice in *Garrett* but has apparently become probative in *Lane*.

Clearly, the Court has flip-flopped. The rigorous standard that the majority applied in *Garrett*, under which virtually no amount of evidence can suffice to justify a congressional intrusion into states' rights, has seemingly evaporated through the change of one vote, that of Justice O'-Connor. The fate of the "crystal ball" problem appears to lie in her hands. Will she continue to side with the liberals on the Court who have a more permissive attitude about the constitutionality of Congress's handiwork or will she return to siding with the conservatives? If Justice O'Connor remains on the Court, the fate of ADA Title II may lie in her hands.

II. The Ahistorical Approach: Sutton

Key members of the Rehnquist Court have expressed a persistent lack of faith in the reliability of legislative history when construing the meaning of federal statutes. Justice Scalia has disavowed the usefulness of legislative history to the courts when they are confronted with a question of statutory interpretation. He has referred to "the fairyland in which legislative history reflects what was in Congress's mind" and dismissed it as "fiction of Jack-and-the Beanstalk proportions to assume that more than a handful of . . . members . . . were . . . aware of the drafting evolution [of a statute]."[16]

The hostility toward legislative history stems from a belief that such history is at best underrepresentative of the Congress as a whole and at worst susceptible to strategic or insincere manipulation by its drafters. Justices Scalia and Thomas, the leading textualists on the Court, have been especially emphatic in contending that courts should not view committee reports, hearing testimony, or floor debate as informative for members in general, much less as reflective of an institutional understanding as to the basis for particular legislation.

Spurred by these textualist reservations, the Court in the 1990s has become more focused on parsing the literal terms of each statute while minimizing the role of legislative intent. By the mid-1990s, the Court was invoking legislative history in statutory cases far less often than it had a decade earlier. The decline in use persisted through the late 1990s, particularly in opinions authored by justices Scalia and Thomas—the very justices who have identified the importance of the legislative record when reviewing the constitutionality of Congress's work.

The disfavored status of legislative history can be seen in many of the ADA cases decided by the Supreme Court. For example, in *Sutton v. United Air Lines, Inc.*,[17] Justice O'Connor wrote an opinion for the Court in which it had to determine whether Congress intended the term "disability" to include someone's condition *after* he or she had used mitigating or corrective measures. The statute states that the term "disability" means "a physical or mental impairment that substantially limits one or more major life activities." The definition is silent on the question of whether a court should measure the substantiality of an impairment before or after the plaintiff uses mitigating or corrective devices. An inquiry into the legislative history, as discussed in chapter 2, would have revealed that various committees explicitly stated in their reports that they expected the courts to evaluate whether someone was disabled *before* he or she used mitigating or corrective measures. Further, an examination of the legislative history would have revealed that Congress understood the ADA to be covering many conditions that are susceptible to ameliorative treatment, such as epilepsy. In fact, the opponents of the ADA routinely complained that the statutory definition was very broad, and no supporter of the ADA disagreed with this characterization. Yet, in a completely ahistorical example of statutory interpretation, Justice O'Connor concluded that the term "disability" should be understood to cover only individuals who are substantially limited *after* the use of corrective devices.

Justice O'Connor relied on two aspects of the statutory language to reach that conclusion. First, she emphasized that Congress wrote the definition of disability in the *present tense*. In her mind, present tense usage implied that Congress wanted the courts to consider an individual in his or her corrective state. Second, she emphasized that Congress claimed to be covering only 43 million Americans. She argued that more than 43 million Americans would be covered by the statute if the broader definition of disability were employed. (In doing so, she overlooked the rest of that same clause, in which Congress stated that the number of disabled Americans was *growing*. She treated the 43 million figure as if it were a static figure. She also overlooked the legislative history—discussed in chapter 2—which reflected that Congress had deliberately expanded this number as it considered the ADA. Congress understood it to be a floor rather than a ceiling.)

Although Justice O'Connor, unlike Justices Scalia and Thomas, has not been a leading figure in the movement to disavow legislative history, her opinion in *Sutton* does reflect that movement. And her decision in *Sutton* is all the more baffling because she asserted in her speech at Georgetown Law School that the ADA was drafted in a hurried and unthinking atmosphere. Had she engaged herself in the rich legislative history underlying the ADA, she would have discovered that her textual decision in *Sutton* was at odds with that history. Who, one might ask, was hurried and unthinking? Congress or Justice O'Connor?

Law review commentators often discuss the methodological question of whether courts should consider legislative history as a theoretical inquiry about the proper role for Congress and the courts. As *Sutton* reflects, however, this methodological question is far more than a theoretical issue. The consequences of the Court's ahistorical approach are felt daily by individuals with disabilities who now fall outside the statute's protection. The disability community's active and historic engagement with Congress through the drafting process is erased by the Court's ahistorical approach.

Congress learned a great deal about how to deal with individuals with disabilities with dignity and respect as it drafted the ADA. As an institution, Congress became more accessible as sign language interpreters and wheelchairs filled its hallways and chambers. It was not possible for Congress to draft language to reflect all of its newfound knowledge about disability discrimination. It is unfortunate that a Supreme Court that has not bothered to educate itself about that history can interpret the statute so narrowly that the people Congress understood itself to be protecting would fall outside the scope of statutory protection. Individuals with disabilities have become the victims of a methodological dispute between the courts and Congress about how to interpret legislation.

III. Implications

The Supreme Court's confusing line of decisions concerning legislative history places Congress in an inappropriate strategic posture. Rather than perform as neutral gatherers of the facts, congressional committees must become advocates, culling the almost limitless record of state conduct to focus on incidents and practices that have the greatest potential for establishing unconstitutional intent under Section 5. But this is exactly the *opposite* role that Scalia and Rehnquist are supposed to desire for Congress. They assert that they want Congress to move *away* from "false or contrived legislative intent"[18] in the statutory interpretation context while giving Congress more incentives to create such contrived legislative intent in the constitutional law context to justify its work under Section 5!

The *Garrett* and *Sutton* decisions therefore reflect starkly contradictory messages about the role of Congress. In *Garrett*, the Court chides Congress for not doing enough in creating a legislative record, yet, in *Sutton*, the Court tells Congress that it is entirely uninterested in the legislative record.

Unfortunately, the Rehnquist Court is sending exactly the wrong message to Congress. When Congress is drafting legislation, such as the ADA, we want it to hold hearings and engage in careful work within the committee structure. It is far more efficient to craft statutory language within a committee structure than in Congress as a whole. The purpose of the committee structure is to allow individuals with expertise on the subject matter to draft careful language and offer an explanation of that language in the accompanying reports. These reports are made available to members of Congress in advance of major votes. Further, these reports are far more readable than dry statutory language. The legislative record shows repeatedly that members of Congress relied on the reports to understand what the ADA meant. There was no attempt to hide legislative decisions; they were transparent in the reports themselves.

A statute should not be the same as regulations. A statute should provide an outline of the major policy decisions and allow the agencies to fill in the details consistent with Congress's intentions. The ADA is a perfect model of how this process worked well. Congress wrote a careful statute, wrote lengthy committee reports to fill in some of the holes, and expected the agencies to draft regulations consistent with that clearly expressed intention. The agencies fulfilled that role, being faithful to Congress's policy choices. Yet, in *Sutton*, the Court ignored both the legislative history *and* the EEOC's regulations on the definition of disability to arrive at its own unworkable definition of disability that was derived entirely by parsing the statutory language out of context. The consequence is that the lower courts are now struggling with how to fulfill Congress's intentions to cover individuals with epilepsy, hearing impairments, and mental health disorders within the statutory framework. Justice O'Connor has blamed Congress for this confusing set of affairs, and she and the other members of the Court have done little to be faithful to Congress's intentions. An ahistorical approach is not a sound way to interpret a statute.

In the constitutional law context, there is no way we can expect Congress to act as an adjudicator to justify its use of its Section 5 powers. Constitutional law is not a static discipline, so it is impossible for Congress even to anticipate what kinds of facts it must gather. Further, it is does not make sense to expect Congress to create a record of states that have actually violated the Constitution. Why would the states cooperate in the gathering of such facts, given the legal liability that such findings might entail? Further, why in the name of federalism, would we want to put Congress in the position of "dissing" the states by creating a record of their unconstitutional conduct? A combative relationship between Congress and the states is scarcely consistent with the dignity deemed appropriate for state sovereignty and would certainly be destructive to our sense of national unity. Finally, how could Congress reasonably be expected to gather such evidence? Unless Congress wants to get in the business of broadly using its subpoena powers, it has no realistic way of gathering credible evidence of unconstitutional behavior by the states yet the Supreme Court appears to be requiring that kind of fact-gathering.

The repeated abrogation of federal statutes, including ADA Title I, has resulted in a considerable transfer of power to the judiciary. Respect must be earned, and it is easy to ridicule Congress by saying that it has not earned the Rehnquist Court's good opinion. But ours is a system of government in which Congress is expected to engage in broad-based thinking on matters of concern to the nation. States are well able to protect their own interests as participants in this national political process, and it is neither necessary nor prudent for the Court to insist repeatedly on a redistribution of authority at Congress's expense. In doing so, the Rehnquist Court has conveyed the message that Congress is suspect in the powers it exercises and the manner in which it exercises them. That is not a message we should countenance the Court's sending to this or any future Congress.

Justice Robert Jackson once said, "We are not final because we are infallible, but we are infallible only because we are final."[19] The Rehnquist Court's inconsistent and unwise treatment of legislative history in the statutory and constitutional law settings has demonstrated its fallibility. I can only hope that future courts will correct this injustice and resurrect the ADA and other federal civil rights statutes to their rightful respectful position in our society. The majority opinion in *Lane* provides a modest basis for hoping that the Court will return to a more respectful attitude toward Congress. In the meantime, Congress appropriately needs to wonder if it has much authority to protect the rights of individuals with disabilities.

Notes

NOTES TO CHAPTER 1

1. TIME MAGAZINE, August 15, 1988.

2. *Blank Check for the Disabled*, NEW YORK TIMES, September 6, 1989, at A24.

3. There are a few modest exceptions to that principle in the employment context when individuals are asked to take unlawful medical examinations or face associational discrimination. *See* 42 U.S.C. § 12112(d) (medical examinations) and 12112(b)(4) (associational discrimination).

4. TIME MAGAZINE, August 15, 1988.

5. LOS ANGELES TIMES, August 4, 1988.

6. *Id.*

7. TIME MAGAZINE, August 15, 1988.

8. Susan F. Rasky, *How the Disabled Sold Congress on a New Bill of Rights*, NEW YORK TIMES, September 17, 1989.

9. Like so many others who worked tirelessly to pass the ADA, Senator Harkin has a very personal connection to this issue because his brother Frank is deaf.

10. Senator Kennedy also has a personal connection to this issue. His sister Rose is retarded and his son lost a leg to cancer.

11. 136 CONG. REC. 17361 (July 13, 1990).

12. 135 CONG. REC. 19804 (September 7, 1989).

13. For an excellent discussion of the laws of various countries, see DISABILITY, DIVERS-ABILITY AND LEGAL CHANGE (eds. Melinda Jones & Lee Ann Basser Marks 1999).

14. Ruth Shalit, *Defining Disability Down*, NEW REPUBLIC, April 25, 1997, at 16.

15. Trevor Armbrister, *A Good Law Gone Bad*, READER'S DIG., May 1998, at 145, 149.

16. WALTER OLSON, THE EXCUSE FACTORY (1997) (as quoted in John Leo, *Let's Lower the Bar*, U.S. NEWS & WORLD REP., October 5, 1998, at 19).

17. Charles Lane, *O'Connor Criticizes Disabilities Law as Too Vague*, WASH-INGTON POST, March 15, 2002.

18. *See* H. Rept. 101–485, Parts 1, 2, 3, and 4.

19. H. Rept. 101–488.

20. *See* S. Rept. 101–558; S. Rept. 101–596.

21. Cynthia Estlund, *The Supreme Court's Labor and Employment Cases of the 2001–2002 Term*, 18 LAB. LAW. 291 (2002).

22. Estlund, *supra* note 21, at 310.

23. One can actually trace the development of disability laws to the Civil War era. *See* Peter Blanck, *Civil War Pensions and Disability*, 62 OHIO STATE L.J. 109 (2001); Peter Blanck & Chen Song, *"Never Forget What They Did Here": Civil War Pensions for Gettysburg Union Army Veterans and Disability in Nineteenth-Century America*, 44 WM. & MARY L. REV. 1109 (2003).

24. Pub.L. 91-230, Title VI, 602, April 13, 1970, 84 Stat. 175.

25. Rehabilitation Act of 1973, Pub. L. No. 93-112, § 7(6), 87 Stat. 355, 361 (1973).

26. Sen. Rept. No. 93-318, 93rd Cong., 1st Sess.

27. CONG. REC. 35163.

28. *See* EEOC v. Humiston-Keeling, Inc., 227 F.3d 1024 (7th Cir. 2000).

29. *See* Martha Minow, MAKING ALL THE DIFFERENCE 82–84 (1990).

30. *See* 42 U.S.C. § 3604.

31. *See* 42 U.S.C. § 12201(a).

32. *See, e.g.*, Mantolete v. Bolger, 767 F.2d 1416 (9th Cir. 1985) (epilepsy); Scanlon v. Atascadero State Hosp., 677 F.2d 1271 (9th Cir. 1982) (diabetes); Bentivegna v. United States Dep't of Labor, 694 F.2d 619 (9th Cir. 1982) (diabetes); Davis v. United Air Lines, Inc., 662 F.2d 120 (2d Cir. 1981) (epilepsy).

33. *See, e.g.*, EEOC v. Sara Lee Corp., 237 F.3d 349 (4th Cir. 2001) (affirming judgment of district court that plaintiff with epilepsy is not disabled); Runkle v. Postmaster General, 271 F. Supp.2d 951 (E.D. Mich. 2003) (employee's epilepsy/seizure disorder found not to be a disability); Popko v. Pennsylvania State University, 84 F. Supp.2d 589 (M.D. Pa. 2000) (employee's epilepsy, in its mitigated state, found not to be a disability for purposes of the ADA).

34. *See, e.g.*, Doe v. Garrett, 903 F.2d 1455, 1457 (11th Cir. 1990); Ray v. School District of DeSoto County, 666 F. Supp. 1524, 1536 (M.D. Fla. 1987); Thomas v. Atascadero University School Dist., 662 F. Supp. 376, 381 (C.D. Calif. 1986); District 27 Community School Bd. v. Board of Ed. of New York, 130 Misc.2d 398, 413–415 (Supt. Ct. 1986).

35. *See, e.g.*, Cortes v. McDonald's Corp., 955 F. Supp. 541 (E.D. N.C. 1996); Runnebaum v. Nationsbank of Maryland, 123 F.3d 156 (4th Cir. 1997).

36. The question of whether the individual is a member of the protected class under Title VII has risen in the context of discrimination against transgendered individuals. For further discussion of that problem, *see* Ruth Colker, HYBRID: BI-

SEXUALS, MULTIRACIALS, AND OTHER MISFITS UNDER AMERICAN LAW, 103–115 (1996).

37. *See* Peter David Blanck & Mollie Weighner Marti, *Attitudes, Behavior, and the Employment Provisions of the Americans with Disabilities Act*, 42 VILL. L. REV. 345, 377–78 (1997) (reporting that the average cost of a reasonable accommodation was less than $500, with many accommodations costing nothing).

38. *See generally Exploration on Law and Disability in Australia*, 17: 2 LAW IN CONTEXT (2000) (Special Issue) (eds. Melinda Jones & Lee Ann Basser Marks).

39. *See generally* DISABILITY, DIVERS-ABILITY AND LEGAL CHANGE, *supra* note 13.

NOTES TO CHAPTER 2

1. Representative Dan Burton (R-Ind.), 135 CONG. REC. H6440–01 (daily ed. Oct. 2, 1989).

2. Justice Scalia's hostility to the use of legislative history is well documented. *See generally* ANTONIN SCALIA, A MATTER OF INTERPRETATION: FEDERAL COURTS AND THE LAW (1997). Justices Thomas and Kennedy, however, have also rejected the use of legislative history. *See, e.g.*, Thunder Basin Coal Co. v. Reich, 510 U.S. 200, 219 (1994); Negonsott v. Samuels, 507 U.S. 99, 100 n.** (1993); Pub. Citizen v. United States Dept. of Justice, 491 U.S. 440, 470–73 (1989). Justice O'-Connor has sometimes joined opinions that minimize the relevance of legislative history. *See, e.g.*, Gregory v. Ashcroft, 501 U.S. 452, 467 (1991).

3. *See* Sutton v. United Airlines, Inc., 527 U.S. 471 (1999) (refusing to consider the relevance of the legislative history of the ADA when interpreting the meaning of the word "disability"). Justice O'Connor authored this opinion.

4. Doe v. U.S. Postal Serv., Civ. A. No. 84-3296, 1985 WL 9446 (D.D.C. June 12, 1985).

5. Blackwell v. U.S. Dept. of Treasury (Blackwell II), 656 F. Supp. 713 (D.D.C. 1986).

6. Blackwell v. United States Dept. of Treasury, 639 F. Supp. 289 (D. D.C. 1986).

7. 656 F. Supp. at 814.

8. 830 F.2d 1183 (D.C. Cir. 1987).

9. Civil Rights Restoration Act of 1987, Pub. L. No. 100-259, 102 Stat. 28 (1988). The Civil Rights Restoration Act amended Title IX of the Education Amendments of 1972 to define the phrase "program or activity" to mean all of the operations of the entity when an entity received federal financial assistance. It likewise amended the Rehabilitation Act of 1973 to define the phrase "program or activity" to mean all of the activities of the aforementioned entities that received federal financial assistance. Because it expanded the coverage of Section

504, it could potentially lead to more entities being affected by Section 504's nondiscrimination requirements.

10. 134 CONG. REC. S2400–01 (daily ed. March 17, 1988).

11. *Id.* at S2683.

12. *See* Helen Dewar, *Congress Overrides Civil Rights Law Veto*, WASHINGTON POST, March 23, 1988, at A1.

13. U.S. 555 (1984).

14. 134 CONG. REC. S2400 (daily ed. March 14, 1988).

15. 134 CONG. REC. S10520 (daily ed. August 1, 1988).

16. Rollcall Vote No. 279 Leg.

17. 135 CONG. REC. S10776 (daily ed. September 7, 1989).

18. The commission stated:

Comprehensive Federal anti-discrimination legislation, which prohibits discrimination against persons with disabilities in the public and private sectors, including employment, housing, public accommodations and participation in government programs should be enacted. All persons with symptomatic or asymptomatic HIV infection should be clearly included as persons with disabilities who are covered by the anti-discrimination protections of this legislation.

H. Rept. 101–485 (Part 2) at 48 (quoting *Report of the Presidential Commission on the Human Immune Deficiency Epidemic*, June 1988, p. 123).

19. Senator Harkin referenced the HIV Commission's work when he introduced the ADA on May 9, 1989. See 135 CONG. REC. 8506–8507. Harkin mentioned its work again on September 7, 1989, when a new version of the ADA was introduced in the Senate. See 135 CONG. REC. 19801. Senator Kennedy also mentioned its work. *See* 135 CONG. REC. 19807.

20. Before the end of the legislative session, additional cosponsors were Pete Wilson (R-Calif.), John McCain (R-Ariz.), Donald Reigle (D-Mich.), Quentin Burdick (D-N.D.), Daniel Patrick Moynihan (D-N.Y.), David Durenberger (R-Minn.), Timothy Wirth (D-Colo.), Claiborne Pell (D-R.I.), Brock Adams (D-Wash.), Ted Stevens (R-Alaska), Barbara Mikulski (D-Md.), Rudy Boschwitz (R-Minn.), and Carl Levin (D-Mich.).

21. 134 CONG. REC. 9377 (April 28, 1988).

22. S. 2345, sec. 3(1), (2).

23. *Id.* at sec. 3(2).

24. *See* 136 CONG. REC. H. 10856 (May 17, 1990) (remarks by Representative Steny Hoyer (D-Md.) about Tony Coelho (D-Calif.)).

25. 134 CONG. REC. at 9604 (extension of remarks) (April 29, 1988).

26. The term "'reasonable accommodation' means providing or modifying devices, aids, services, or facilities, or changing standards, criteria, practices, or procedures for the purpose of providing to a particular person with a physical or

mental impairment, perceived impairment, or record of impairment the equal opportunity to participate effectively in a particular program, activity, job, or other opportunity." S. 2345, sec. 3 (5).

27. S. 2345, sec. 5(a)(2).

28. S. 2345, sec. 8(h)(3).

29. S. 2345, sec. 9(b).

30. S. 2345, sec. 4(a)(3).

31. 134 CONG. REC. 9386 (1988).

32. *Id.* at 9542.

33. *Id.* at 9543.

34. *Id.* at 11182.

35. *Id.* at 13476.

36. *Id.* at 21425.

37. *Id.* at 22213.

38. 136 CONG. REC. 17369 (July 13, 1990).

39. 135 CONG. REC. 8601 (May 9, 1989).

40. *Id.* at 8712.

41. When Senator Harkin introduced the bill, he stated that it had 32 cosponsors, whom he named. In fact, the bill had 34 cosponsors, including Rudy Boschwitz (R-Minn.) and John Heinz (R-Pa.). Presumably, the last two were added at the last minute and that fact was not communicated to Harkin in a timely manner. Without Boschwitz and Heinz, the bill is somewhat less bipartisan in its support.

42. Senator Hatch had a personal connection to these issues. In the final day of consideration, he paid tribute to his brother-in-law Raymond Hansen who contracted polio and worked up to the day he died despite needing the assistance of an iron lung. 136 CONG. REC. 17375 (July 13, 1990).

43. *See* S. 933, sec. 2(a)(1).

44. S. 933, sec. 3 (2)(a).

45. S. 933, sec. 202(b)(1).

46. Sec. 401(2).

47. The entities included: "auditoriums, convention centers, stadiums, theaters, restaurants, shopping centers, inns, hotels, and motels . . . terminals used for public transportation, passenger vehicle service stations, professional offices of health care providers, office buildings, sales establishments, personal and public service businesses, parks, private schools, and recreation facilities." Sec. 401 (2)(B).

48. Sec. 402 (b)(4)(A).

49. Sec. 402(b)(6).

50. *See* S. 933, sec. 504.

51. *See* S. 933, Title V.

52. The technical assistance provision required the attorney general to develop and implement a plan to assist entities covered under the act to understand their responsibilities. S. 933, sec. 506.

53. 135 CONG. REC. 18647 (1989).

54. 135 CONG. REC. 19811 (1989).

55. S. Rept. 101–116, at 22 (1989).

56. *See infra* chapter 4.

57. *See* S. Rept. 101–116.

58. *See infra* chapter 4.

59. *Id.* at 96.

60. This is an excerpt from the *New York Times* editorial:

With surprisingly narrow public scrutiny, Congress is moving swiftly to extend broad civil rights protection to the nation's 49 million disabled citizens. The sentiment is laudable: to bring the disabled closer to the mainstream of American society. But the legislation is vague; not even its defenders are able to calculate its benefits and costs. Those costs could be monumental. The proposal thus requires patient, unemotional examination.

That won't be easy. The bill was unanimously approved by the Senate Labor and Human Resources Committee last month, and though it still awaits hearings in four separate House committees, it commands strong bipartisan support in both House and Senate and the endorsement of President Bush. As one skeptic put it, "No politician can vote against this bill and survive."

The bill would ban discrimination in employment in all businesses with more than 15 workers. That's caused no controversy. What has is a provision requiring nearly every retail establishment, large or small, old and new—barber shops, banks, restaurants, movie theaters—to be accessible to the disabled. The legislation does not spell out how. But in many cases it would mean building ramps, widening doorways, modifying restrooms. Elevators would be required in all new buildings of more than two stories.

The bill would also require bus companies to include lifts, specially designed restrooms and other facilities on all new buses built five to six years after enactment. The bill calls for a study—after the bill is passed, not before—to determine how much this would cost the companies.

The bus companies are angry. Most businessmen are simply fretful and confused. That's partly because the bill's language is so vague. It says that existing facilities must make only "readily achievable" changes that won't involve "burdensome expense." Yet what do these words mean in practice? Obviously, no bill can give precise instructions to thousands of individual businesses. But several states already have laws on the books that provide business more useful guidance than the Senate bill does. . . .

Predictions about the bill's projected benefits are obviously speculative. Worse, nobody has even tried to speculate about its costs. But it shouldn't be impossible to provide estimates. The Office of Management and Budget has done so before in tough instances, like the costs of air bags.

Congress and the Administration now have a similar responsibility to stand back, to weigh, to calculate. No one wishes to stint on helping the disabled. It requires little legislative skill, however, to write blank checks for worthy causes with other people's money.

Editorial, *Blank Check for the Disabled?* NEW YORK TIMES, September 6, 1989, at A24.

61. 135 CONG. REC. 19803 (1989).

62. *Id.*

63. *Id.* at 19808.

64. *Id.* at 19808–19809.

65. *Id.* at 19808–19809.

66. *Id.* at 19808–19809.

67. *Id.* at 19810 (September 7, 1989).

68. *Id.* at 19812–19813.

69. *Id.* at 19813.

70. *Id.* at 19833.

71. *Id.* at 19833.

72. *Id.* at 19834.

73. *Id.* at 19834.

74. *Id.* at 19835.

75. *Id.* at 19837.

76. *Id.* at 19837.

77. *Id.*

78. *Id.* at 19838.

79. *Id.* at 19840.

80. *Id.*

81. *Id.* at 19840.

82. *Id.* at 19841.

83. *Id.* at 19846.

84. *Id.* at 19848.

85. *Id.* at 19853.

86. *Id.* at 19866.

87. *Id.* at 19867.

88. *See, e.g.,* Cortes v. McDonald's Corp., 955 F. Supp. 541 (E.D. N.C. 1996); Runnebaum v. Nationsbank of Maryland, N.A., 123 F.3d 156 (4th Cir. 1997).

89. 135 CONG. REC. 19871 (1989).

90. *Id.* at 19873.

91. *Id.* at 19875.
92. *Id.* at 19875.
93. *Id.* at 19876.
94. *Id.* at 19881.
95. *Id.* at 19881.
96. *Id.* at 19883.
97. *Id.* at 19884.
98. *Id.* at 19884.
99. *Id.* at 19885.
100. *Id.* at 19858.
101. *Id.* at 19861.
102. *Id.* at 19858.
103. *Id.* at 19860.
104. *Id.* at 19862.
105. *Id.* at 19879.
106. *Id.* at 19881.
107. *Id.* at 19882.
108. *Id.* at 19882.
109. *Id.* at 19882.
110. *Id.* at 19883.
111. *Id.* at 19888–89.
112. The nays included Armstrong, Bond, Garn, Helms, Humphrey, McClure, Symms, and Wallop. Not voting included Adam, Baucus, Bentsen, Breaux, Burns, Glenn, Inouye, Lott, Metzenbaum, Mikulski, Mukowski, Pryor, Roth, Rudman, Sanford, and Sasser. *Id.* at 19903.
113. *See* 136 CONG. REC. 17376 (1990).
114. 135 CONG. REC. 20096 (1989).
115. *Id.* at 20707 (extended remarks) (Sept. 18, 1989) (quoting September 11 editorial from the *Wall Street Journal*).
116. *Id.* at 22734 (quoting Gene Antonio).
117. *Id.* at 28974.
118. *Id.* at 29306 (extended remarks).
119. 136 CONG. REC. 3658 (1990).
120. *Id.* at 3658.
121. *Id.* at 3659.
122. H. Rept. 101–485 (Part 2).
123. *Id.* at 52.
124. *See* Sutton v. United Airlines, Inc., 527 U.S. 471 (1999).
125. *See* H. Rept. 101–485 (Part 2) at 165–67 (1990).
126. *See* H. Rept. 101–485 (Part 3) (1990).
127. *Id.* at 23–24.
128. *Id.* at 88–89.

129. *Id.* at 28–29.

130. H. Rept. 101–485 (Part 4) (1990).

131. *Id.* at 82.

132. 136 CONG. REC. at 9072–73 (1990).

133. *Id.* at 9641.

134. *Id.* at 10419.

135. *Id.* at 10456.

136. *Id.* at 10458.

137. *Id.* at 10459.

138. *Id.* at 10459.

139. *Id.* at 10461.

140. *See, e.g.*, Krocka v. City of Chicago, 203 F.3d 507 (7th Cir. 2000) (lawful to place police officer in the department's "Personnel Concerns Program" merely because he was taking Prozac, even though he had suffered no adverse job performance due to his mental health condition).

141. 136 CONG. REC. 10462 (1990).

142. *See, e.g.*, Runnebaum v. Nationsbank of Maryland, N.A, 123 F. 3d 156 (4th Cir. 1997).

143. 136 CONG. REC. 10463 (1990).

144. *Id.* at 10839.

145. *Id.* at 10840.

146. *Id.* at 10841.

147. *Id.* at 10842.

148. *Id.* at 10851.

149. *Id.* at 10852.

150. *Id.* at 10855.

151. *Id.* at 10856.

152. *Id.* at 10857.

153. *Id.* at 10858–10859.

154. *Id.* at 10899.

155. *Id.* at 10901.

156. *Id.* at 10903.

157. *Id.* at 10903.

158. *Id.* at 10908.

159. *Id.* at 10909.

160. *Id.* at 10911.

161. *Id.* at 10911.

162. *Id.* at 10911.

163. *Id.* at 10912.

164. *Id.* at 10912.

165. *Id.* at 10917.

166. *See* EEOC v. Prevo's Family Market, Inc., 135 F.3d 1089 (6th Cir.1998).

167. *Id.* at 11427.

168. *Id.* at 11432.

169. *See id.* at 11433.

170. *Id.* at 11438.

171. *Id.* at 11440.

172. *See id.* at 11442 (remarks of Representative Don Edwards (D-Calif.)).

173. *Id.* at 11450.

174. *Id.* at 11466.

175. *Id.* at 11466–67.

176. 136 CONG. REC. 13050 (1990).

177. *Id.* at 13057–58.

178. *Id.* at 13062.

179. *Id.* at 13064.

180. *Id.* at 13064.

181. H. Rept. 101–558 (1990).

182. *Id.* at 59.

183. *Id.* at 77.

184. *Id.* at 82.

185. *Id.* at 82.

186. *Id.* at 84.

187. 136 CONG. REC. 16156 (1990).

188. *Id.* at 16250.

189. *Id.*

190. *Id.* at 16727.

191. *Id.* at 16728.

192. *Id.* at 16731.

193. *Id.* at 16740.

194. *Id.* at 16753.

195. *Id.* at 16755.

196. *Id.* at 16755.

197. *Id.* at 16758.

198. *Id.* at 17029.

199. *Id.* at 17030.

200. *Id.* at 17033.

201. *Id.* at 17035.

202. *Id.* at 17036.

203. *Id.* at 17044.

204. *Id.* at 17058.

205. *See* H. Rept. No. 101–596.

206. 136 CONG. REC. 17251–17277 (1990).

207. *Id.* at 17278.

208. *Id.* at 17279.

209. *Id.* at 17279.

210. *Id.* at 17280.

211. *Id.* at 17281.

212. *Id.* at 17284.

213. *Id.* at 17286.

214. *Id.* at 17295.

215. *Id.* at 17360.

216. George Bush, Statement on Signing the Americans with Disabilities Act for 1990 (July 26, 1990).

217. Ann McFeatters, *White House Backs Santorum*, PITTSBURGH POST-GAZETTE, April 6, 2003, at A-1.

NOTES TO CHAPTER 3

1. These statistics were taken from the National Organization on Disability/Harris Survey of Americans with Disabilities, a survey of nearly 1,000 adults with disabilities in May and June 2000.

2. Daron Acaemoglu & Joshua D. Angrist, *Consequences of Employment Protection? The Case of the Americans with Disabilities Act*, 109 J. POLITICAL ECONOMY 915 (2001).

3. Thomas DeLeire, *The Wage and Employment Effects of the Americans with Disabilities Act*, 35 JOURNAL OF HUMAN RESOURCES 693 (2000).

4. Christine Jolls, *Accommodation Mandates*, 53 STANFORD L. REV. 223 (2000).

5. *See* Pamela Loprest & Elaine Maag, *Barriers to and Supports for Work Among Adults with Disabilities: Results from the NHIS-D* (Urban Institute, January 2001).

6. Ruth Shalit, *Defining Disability Down: Why Johnny Can't Read, Write, or Sit Still*, NEW REPUBLIC, August 25, 1997, at 16.

7. *See* Ruth Colker, *The Americans with Disabilities Act—A Windfall for Defendants*, 34 HARV. CIV. RIGHTS-CIV. LIB. L. REV. 99 (1999).

8. *See, e.g.*, Ruth O'Brien, CRIPPLED JUSTICE: THE HISTORY OF MODERN DISABILITY IN THE WORKPLACE 14 (2001).

9. *See* http://eeoc.gov/stats/ada-charges.html.

10. *See* http://eeoc.gov/litigation/study/study.html. This report was issued based on provisional data. The data included in the appendices to this report are not identical with the data currently available on the EEOC's Web site, although the differences do not affect the observations made by the EEOC about the trends.

11. *See* Colker, *supra* note 7.

12. I accessed this data through Theodore Eisenberg's Web site. *See* http://teddy.law.cornell.edu:8090/cgi-binjs/beta7900.

13. *See* Amy L. Allbright, *2001 Employment Decisions under the ADA Title I—Survey Update*, 26 MENTAL AND PHYSICAL DISABILITY LAW REPORTER 394 (2002).

14. Marc A. Franklin, *Winners and Losers and Why: A Study of Defamation Litigation*, 1980 AM. B. FOUND. RES. J. 455, 469–70 (1980).

15. *See* O'Brien, *supra* note 8.

16. A comparison with other areas of the law, however, reflects the limited conclusions that one can draw from appellate data. The mere fact that a type of case is successful or unsuccessful at the appellate level does not necessarily reflect its success rate at the trial court level. This observation is most striking for prisoners' rights litigation. Plaintiffs' success rate at the district court level is only 18 percent in prisoners' rights cases yet is 48 percent when plaintiffs appeal prodefendant judgments. Plaintiffs prevail in 48 percent of prisoners' rights cases on appeal, whereas they prevail in only 38 percent of nonprisoners' constitutional tort cases on appeal. By contrast, at the district court level, nonprisoners' rights claims are successful much more frequently than prisoners' rights claims (50 percent compared to 18 percent). Thus, although the table reflects that ADA cases fare worse at the appellate level than prisoners' rights claims, it would be wrong to conclude that ADA cases necessarily fare worse at the trial court level than prisoners' rights claims.

17. I informally counted the reverse discrimination cases in the Title VII cases. I counted only 3 in a sample of more than 100 cases. Thus, the reverse discrimination cases could not be causing the difference in outcome.

18. Kathryn Moss et al., *Different Paths to Justice: The ADA, Employment, and Administrative Enforcement by the EEOC and FEPAs*, 17 BEHAV. SCI. & L. 29, 43 (1999).

19. A less charitable way to explain this problem would be to say that plaintiff lawyers were not competent in the early years of ADA litigation, so that poor lawyering explains the poor results on appeal. For support of this hypothesis, *see* Jeffrey A. Van Detta & Dan R. Gallipeau, *Judges and Juries: Why Are So Many ADA Plaintiffs Losing Summary Judgment Motions, and Would They Fare Better Before a Jury? A Response to Professor Colker*, 19 REV. LITIG. 505, 574 (2000).("[T]he problem appears to arise largely from lawyering that does not take into account the regulations, interpretation, and guidance in developing the theory of the case, planning and executing discovery, and effectively presenting sufficient probative evidence on key elements of the claim—particularly the existence of a disability—to survive summary judgment.")

If Van Detta and Gallipeau are correct that poor lawyering explains some of these adverse results, one still must wonder why these results have not self-corrected over time. Lawyers who do not prevail under the ADA will rarely receive significant compensation, given the prevalence of contingency fee arrangements in civil rights cases. One would expect that adverse results would have a filtering effect on lawyers' judgments even if it did not improve the quality of their lawyering.

20. The Supreme Court's first major ADA decision in *Bragdon v. Abbott*, 524 U.S. 624 (1998), in which it held that individuals with infectious diseases, like HIV infection, could be considered to be disabled under the ADA, may have actually misled plaintiffs into expecting a liberal interpretation of the ADA from the Court. With the series of conservative decisions from 1999, we may still see a period of miscalculation by plaintiffs in which they lose in the appellate courts as those courts seek to implement the Court's narrow definition of disability.

21. In order to create a data set comparable to the ADA data set, we included only cases decided on the merits, involving issues that could also arise under the ADA. We therefore did not include cases involving statute-of-limitations or attorneys-fees issues (because those kinds of cases had also not been included in the ADA data). We also did not include cases involving jurisdictional or coverage issues, such as whether the defendant received federal financial assistance and was thereby covered under section 504. Because receipt of federal financial assistance is not a requirement for coverage under the ADA, these cases were not parallel to the ADA cases in the database.

22. ADA Title I became effective on July 26, 1992.

23. I used SPSS to enter the data. I conducted the logistic regression analysis that is reported in this article in SPSS. My research assistant also conducted these analyses in Stata Release 6.0. For further discussion of the use of regression analysis in legal scholarship, *see* Deborah Jones Merritt & James J. Brudney, *Stalking Secret Law: What Predicts Publication in the United States Courts of Appeals*, 54 VAND. L. REV. 71, 79–84 (2001).

24. The Fifth Circuit, a circuit with a moderate position on the mitigating measures issue during this time period, served as the reference category for the other eleven circuit court variables. *See* Washington v. HCA Health Serv., Inc., 152 F.3d 464 (5th Cir. 1998).

25. I used the category "white collar" as the reference category for the occupational variables.

26. In the regression analysis, I used the category of prodefendant nonverdict as the reference category for the other lower court outcomes because prodefendant nonverdict was the most common lower court outcome. The variable that is the reference category must be excluded from the regression equation. For the circuits, the excluded circuit for comparison purposes was the Sixth Circuit. I chose this circuit because it is a relatively typical circuit in terms of whether its decisions are proplaintiff. It also has a typical publication practice. The excluded occupational status for comparison purposes is "other white collar." I chose this category because it was one of the largest categories and appeared to have results that were typical for the data set as a whole. For the other variables, it was not

necessary to have an excluded variable because a case could reflect more than one of the results for those variables.

27. Social scientists typically designate results with a p-value of 0.05 or less as "significant." For general discussion of the use of social science techniques as applied to data involving legal issues, see Deborah Jones Merritt, *Research and Teaching on Law Faculties: An Empirical Exploration*, 73 CHI. KENT. L. REV. 765, 780–82 (1998). It is also common for social scientists to discuss a p-value that is greater than 0.05 but less than 0.10 as "approaching significance." *See id.* at 782 n.59. "It is appropriate to note such relationships in exploratory studies like the present one, although such results should be taken as suggestive rather than established." *Id.*

28. Extremities impairments included missing limbs or digits; hand, arm, or shoulder impairments (without paralysis); and arthritis. There was a separate category for back or orthopedic impairments, as well as a separate category for paralysis.

29. *See* Merritt & Brudney, *supra* note 22, at 78 n.70.

NOTES TO CHAPTER 4

1. For further discussion of the antisubordination model, *see* Ruth Colker, *Anti-Subordination Above All: Sex, Race, and Equal Protection*, 61 N.Y.U. L. REV. 1003 (1986).

2. The story of how the courts came to interpret Title VII to prohibit "reverse" discrimination is beyond the scope of this book. In *McDonald v. Santa Fe Trail Transp. Co.*, 427 U.S. 273 (1976), the Supreme Court held that Title VII prohibits racial discrimination against whites as well as African Americans, setting the stage for "reverse" discrimination lawsuits. Although the Court upheld the concept of "voluntary affirmative action" in *United Steelworkers of America v. Weber*, 443 U.S. 193 (1979), it has also found some affirmative action plans to constitute unlawful reverse discrimination. *See, e.g., Sheet Metal Workers v. EEOC*, 478 U.S. 421 (1986).

3. 42 U.S.C. § 12101(a)(4).

4. *Id.* at. § 12101(a)(1).

5. In her concurrence in *Tennessee v. Lane*, 124 S. Ct. 1978, 1995 (2004), Justice Ginsburg implicitly recognized the ADA's antisubordination framework. She described the ADA as a "measure expected to advance equal-citizenship stature for persons with disabilities." Moreover, she noted that this equal citizenship status can occur only with a system of accommodation rather than formal equality. "Including individuals with disabilities among people who count in composing 'We the People,' Congress understood in shaping the ADA, would sometimes require not blindfolded equality, but responsiveness to difference; not indifference, but accommodation."

6. *See generally* Colker, *supra* note 1.

7. They also could narrowly interpret the reasonable accommodation requirement so that it does not provide affirmative protection for individuals with disabilities. The Supreme Court has offered little guidance on the reasonable accommodation principle, so it is too early to know if the case law will go in that direction. The *Tennessee v. Lane* decision reflects the competing views on the reasonable accommodation principle. The majority accepted the principle that an individual might be entitled to reasonable accommodation so that he could enter a state courthouse. The dissent, by contrast, found that Lane had no claim of discrimination when he refused to allow court personnel to carry him up stairs to attend his hearing. *Tennessee v. Lane*, 124 S. Ct. 1978, 2000 n.4 (2004). Chief Justice Rehnquist stated, in dissent, that "[i]n light of these facts, it can hardly be said that the State violated Lane's right to be present at his trial; indeed, it made affirmative attempts to secure that right." *Id.* (His dissenting opinion was joined by Justices Kennedy and Thomas.) Justice Scalia, however, went even further in his dissent. "Requiring access for disabled persons to all public buildings cannot remotely be considered a means of 'enforcing' the Fourteenth Amendment." *Id.* at 2013. Justice Scalia is correct if the Court were to import the Fourteenth Amendment's antidifferentiation model into the ADA.

8. Sutton v. United Airlines, 527 U.S. 471, 487 (1999).

9. 42 U.S.C. § 12102(2).

10. *See* Sutton v. United Airlines, Inc., 527 U.S. 471 (1999).

11. *See* Sutton v. United Airlines, Inc., 1996 WL 588917 (D. Colo. 1996).

12. *See* Sutton v. United Airlines, Inc., 130 F.3d 893 (10th Cir. 1997).

13. *See* Albertson's, Inc. v Kirkingburg, 527 U.S. 555 (1999).

14. The trial court opinion was unpublished. It is not available electronically.

15. *See* Kirkingburg v. Albertson's, Inc., 143 F.3d 1228 (9th Cir. 1998).

16. *See* Murphy v. United Parcel Service, Inc., 527 U.S. 516 (1999).

17. *See* Murphy v. United Parcel Service, Inc., 946 F. Supp. 872 (D. Kan. 1996).

18. *See* Murphy v. United Parcel Service, Inc., 141 F.3d 1185 (10th Cir. 1998) (unpublished opinion) (text available on Westlaw).

19. Martin v. PGA Tour, Inc., 532 U.S. 661 (2001).

20. *See* Richard Sandomir, *Martin Receives Support on Capitol Hill for his PGA Suit*, NEW YORK TIMES, January 29, 1998.

21. *See* 29 CFR § 1630.2(j) (Appendix) ("For example, an individual who had once been able to walk at an extraordinary speed would not be substantially limited in the major life activity of walking if, as a result of a physical impairment, he or she were only able to walk at an average speed, or even at a moderately below average speed. . . . Nor would a professional baseball pitcher who develops a bad elbow and can no longer throw a baseball be considered substantially limited in the major activity of working.").

22. Because the Court of Appeals ruled in favor of Kirkingburg, it had to consider the employer's defenses. Those defenses were also discussed in the Supreme Court opinion.

23. H.R. 4498, § 3(1). For further discussion, *see* chapter 2.

24. *See* Statement on Signing the Americans with Disabilities Act of 1990 (July 26, 1990).

25. *See* Sutton v. United Airlines, 527 U.S. 471 (1999).

26. *See generally* Nick Wenbourne, *Disabled Meanings: A Comparison of the Definition of "Disability" in the British Disability Discrimination Act of 1995 and the Americans with Disability Act of 1990*, 23 HASTINGS INT'L & COMP. L. REV. 149 (1999).

27. *See, e.g.*, Krocka v. City of Chicago, 203 F.3d 507 (7th Cir. 2000) (psychological impairment); McKenzie v. Dovala, 242 F.3d 967 (10th Cir. 2001) (psychological impairment); Matlock v. City of Dallas, 1999 WL 1032601 (N.D. Tex. 1999) (hearing impairment); Todd v. Academy Corp., 57 F. Supp.2d 448 (S.D. Tex. 1999) (epilepsy); Pacella v. Tufts Univ. Sch. of Dental Med., 66 F. Supp.2d 234 (D. Mass. 1999) (monocular vision and severe myopia).

28. *See* Gillen v. Fallon Ambulance Service, 283 F.3d 11 (1st Cir. 2002).

29. *See* Matlock v. City of Dallas, 1999 WL 1032601 (N.D. Tex. 1999).

30. Nonetheless, the court did allow Matlock to proceed on a "regarded as" disability theory. The "regarded as" theory, however, is a poor substitute for the "actually disabled" theory. The city was not acting on the basis of a false belief about Matlock's hearing; it was acting on the basis of his genuine hearing loss. Those actions should be subject to scrutiny under an actually disabled theory of discrimination.

31. Sutton v. United Air Lines, 523 U.S. 471, 512 (1999) (Stevens, J. dissenting).

32. *See generally* chapter 2.

33. H.R 4498, § 3(1).

34. *Id.* at § 3(2).

35. *See* Murphy v. United Parcel Service, 527 U.S. 516 (1999).

36. *See* Sutton v. United Airlines, 527 U.S. 471, 499 (1999) (Stevens, J. dissenting).

37. *See* Colwell v. Suffolk County Police Department, 967 F. Supp. 1419 (E.D. N.Y. 1997).

38. *See* Colwell v. Suffolk County Police Department, 158 F.3d 635 (2nd Cir. 1998).

39. *Id.* at 646.

40. *See* Sorensen v. University of Utah Hosp., F. Supp. 2d 1306 (D. Utah 1998).

41. *See* Sorenson v. University of Utah Hospital, 194 F.3d 1084 (10th Cir. 1999).

42. *Id.* at 1087.

43. *See* Demming v. Housing & Redev. Auth., 66 F.3d 950 (8th Cir. 1995).

44. Taylor v. United States Postal Service, 946 F.2d 1214 (6th Cir. 1991).

45. *See generally* Murphy v. United Parcel Service, Inc., 527 U.S. 516 (1999).

46. 527 U.S. at 525.

47. *Sutton,* 527 U.S. at 491–92.

48. *See* 42 U.S.C. § 12113(b) (listing "defenses," including the direct threat defense).

49. Reeves v. Sanderson Plumbing Products, Inc., 530 U.S. 133, 149 (2000).

50. *Id.* (quoting Anderson v. Liberty Lobby, 477 U.S. 242, 255 (1986)).

51. 53 F.3d 55 (4th Cir. 1995).

52. *Id.* at 57.

53. *Id.*

54. *Id.* at 62.

55. 123 F.3d 156 (4th Cir. 1997) (en banc).

56. 95 F.3d 1285 (4th Cir. 1996).

57. 123 F.3d at 176 (Michael, C.J., dissenting).

58. *Id.* at 172.

59. *Id.* at 172.

60. *Id.* at 162.

61. *Id.* at 163 n.3.

62. *Id.* at 162.

63. *See* EEOC v. Prevo's Family Market, 135 F.3d 1089 (6th Cir. 1998).

64. 135 F.3d at 1091.

65. *See* 42 U.S.C. § 12112(d)(4)(A).

66. 136 CONG. REC. H2471-01, 2478 (daily ed. May 17, 1990).

67. 136 CONG. REC. S7422-03, 7436 (daily ed. June 6, 1990).

68. *See* 42 U.S.C. § 12113(d).

69. 135 F.3d at 1096–97.

70. 135 F.3d at 1104 (Moore, C.J., dissenting).

71. *Id.* at 1104.

72. *See* Centers for Disease Control, U.S. Dep't of Health & Human Services, *Recommendations for Preventing Transmission of Human Immunodeficiency Virus and Hepatitis B Virus to Patients During Exposure-Prone Invasive Procedures,* 40 Morbidity & Mortality Weekly Report, 1, 4 (July 12, 1991).

73. 137 F.3d at 404.

74. *Id.* at 408 (Boggs, C.J., dissenting).

75. *Id.* at 416.

NOTES TO CHAPTER 5

1. *See* L.C. v. Olmstead, 1997 WL148674 (N.D. Ga. 1997).

2. *See* L.C. v. Olmstead, 138 F.3d 893 (11th Cir. 1998).

3. *Id.* at 597.

4. 42 U.S.C. § 12111(9).

5. *Id.* at 12111(10).

6. *See* Kinney v. Yerusalim, 9 F.3d 1067 (3d Cir. 1993).

7. 28 C.F.R. § 35.150(a)(3).

8. 28 C.F.R. § 35.130(d).

9. 28 C.F.R. § 35.130(b)(7).

10. 138 F.3d at 905.

11. H. Rept. No. 101-485, pt. 3 at 50, *reprinted in* 1990 U.S.C.C.A.N. at 473.

12. 527 U.S. at 606.

13. In Brown v. Board of Education, 347 U.S. 483 (1954), the Supreme Court found that separate can never be equal but did not order specific relief. The issue of relief was to be decided on remand. Subsequently, in Brown v. Board of Education, 349 U.S. 294, 301 (1955), the Court ordered the defendants to move with "all deliberate speed" to remedy the unconstitutional discrimination. When school districts around the country failed to comply with this request, the Court ultimately had to move to a more stringent remedy, such as mandatory busing. It is ironic that the Court would once again choose a vague remedial formulation, giving public entities an opportunity to avoid compliance with an integration mandate when that formulation was unsuccessful in *Brown*.

14. In Seminole Tribe v. Florida, 517 U.S. 44 (1996), the Supreme Court held that the commerce clause does not grant Congress the power to abrogate state sovereign immunity. Prior to that decision, it was understood that Congress could regulate the states as part of its authority to regulate interstate commerce. *See* Pennsylvania v. Union Gas, 491 U.S. 1 (1989).

15. *See* Seminole Tribe v. Florida, 517 U.S. 44 (1996).

16. City of Cleburne v. Cleburne Living Center, 473 U.S. 432 (1985).

17. *See* Cleburne Living Center v. City of Cleburne, 726 F.2d 191 (5th Cir. 1984).

18. 473 U.S. at 446.

19. 531 U.S. at 367.

20. The Court actually had several grounds for determining that Congress exceeded its constitutional authority. It also found that Congress did not amass sufficient evidence that states were engaging in unconstitutional employment discrimination against individuals with disabilities and that many of the nondiscrimination rules in ADA Title I went well beyond the kind of invidious discrimination made unconstitutional by the Fourteenth Amendment.

21. *See* Garrett v. Board of Trustees, 989 F. Supp. 1409 (N.D. Ala. 1998).

22. Garrett v. Alabama, 193 F.3d 1214 (1989).

23. 123 S. Ct. at 1982.

24. *Id.*

25. 42 U.S.C. § 2000d.

26. 28 CFR § 42.104(b)(2)(1999).

27. *See* Popovich v. Cuyahoga County Court of Common Pleas, 276 F.3d 808 (6th Cir. 2002).

28. *Garcia v. S.U.N.Y. Health Sci. Ctr. of Brooklyn*, 280 F.3d 98, 111–12 (2d Cir. 2001).

29. *See* Hason v. Medical Board of California, 279 F.3d 1167 (9th Cir. 2002).

30. *See* Thompson v. Colorado, 278 F.3d 1020 (10th Cir. 2001); Reickenbacker v. Foster, 274 F.3d 974 (5th Cir. 2001); Brown v. North Carolina Division of Motor Vehicles, 166 F.3d 698 (4th Cir. 1999).

31. *See* Ex Parte Young, 209 U.S. 123 (1908).

32. *See* Bruggeman ex rel. Bruggeman v. Blagojevich, 324 F.3d 906 (7th Cir. 2003); Carten v. Kent State University, 282 F.3d 391 (6th Cir. 2002); Grey v. Wilburn, 270 F.3d 607 (8th Cir. 2001); Roe No. 2 v. Ogden, 253 F.3d 1225 (10th Cir. 2001); Randolph v. Rodgers, 253 F.3d 342 (8th Cir. 2001); Armstrong v. Wilson, 124 F.3d 1019 (9th Cir. 1997); Koslow v. Pennsylvania, 302 F.3d 161 (3d Cir. 2002).

33. *See* Townsend v. Quasim, 328 F.3d 511 (9th Cir. 2003).

34. *See* 28 C.F.R. § 35.151 (e).

35. *See Ability Center of Greater Toledo v. City of Sandusky*, 181 F. Supp.2d 797 (N.D. Ohio 2001). Two other trial courts have similarly refused to apply *Sandoval* to ADA Title II. *See* Frederick L. v. Department of Public Welfare, 157 F. Supp.2d 509 (E.D. Pa. 2001); Access Living of Metropolitan Chicago v. Chicago Transit Authority, No. 00 C 0770, 2001 WL 492473 (N.D. Ill. May 9, 2001).

36. These facts can be found in the briefs filed in the Supreme Court in *Tennessee v. Lane*. *See* Brief for the Private Respondents, Tennessee v. Lane, No. 02-1667 (filed November 12, 2003), found at 2002 U.S. Briefs 1667 (LexisNexis).

37. Brief for Petitioner at *2, Board. of Trustees v. Garrett, 531 U.S. 356 (2001) (No. 99-1240), *available at* 2000 WL 821035.

38. *Id.* at *4.

39. *Id.* at App. A.

40. *Garrett*, 531 U.S. at 374 n.9.

41. *See* Kinney v. Yerusalim, 9 F.3d 1067 (3d Cir. 1993).

42. OHIO REV. CODE ANN. § 3781.111 (Λ) (West 1998).

43. TENN. CODE ANN. §§ 68–120, 202–1, 120–203 (2001).

44. WIS. STAT. ANN. § 101.13 (21)(a) (West 1997).

45. 911 P. 2d 1319 (Wash. 1996).

46. WASH. REV. CODE ANN. § 49.60.215 (West 1985).

47. *Fell*, 911 P. 2d at 1329.

48. *Id.*

49. David v. Flexman, 109 F. Supp. 2d 776 (S.D. Ohio 1999).

50. OHIO REV. CODE ANN. § 4112.02(6) (West 2001).

51. *Davis*, 109 F. Supp. 2d at 797–98.

52. *See* D.B. v. Bloom, 896 F. Surp. 166 (D. N.J. 1995).

53. CAL. CIV. CODE § 51 (1982).

54. 100 Cal. Rptr. 2d 39, 42 (Cal. Ct. App. 2000).

55. *Id.* at 42 n.4.

56. State of Delaware as a Party to an Equal Accommodation Complaint, Op. Del. Att'y. Gen. No. O0-1B09, at 1 (May 30, 2000), *available at* 2000WL 1092966, at *1.

57. DEL. CODE ANN. tit. 1, § 4504 (1999).

58. DEL. CODE ANN. tit. 1, § 302 (16) (2001).

59. *Testimony on the Americans with Disabilities Act of 1989*, Staff of the House Subcomm. on Select Educ. of the Comm. on Educ. and Labor, 101st Cong. 928 (1990) (Statement of Howard Wolf, Partner, Fulbright C. Jaworski).

60. ALA. CODE § 21-4-7 (1975).

61. *Id.* 636-19-12; *see id.* 36-19-13.

62. ALA. CODE § 21-7-1 (1975).

63. *Id.* § 21-7-2.

64. *Id.* § 21-7-3.

65. *Id.* § 21-7-4.

66. *See* COLO. REV. STAT. ANN. § 24-10-102 (West 2001); N.C. GEN. STAT. § 168A-11 (1999).

67. FLA. STAT. ANN. § 768.28 (West 1994 & Supp. 2000).

68. NEV. REV. STAT. ANN. § 41.031 (1) (Michie 1996).

69. KAN. STAT. ANN. § 44-1005 (2000).

70. S.C. CODE ANN. § 43-33-540 (Law Co-op.1976).

71. 657 N.E. 2d 281 (Ohio Ct. App. 1995).

72. OHIO REV. CODE ANN. § 4112.99 (Baldwin 1995).

73. 347 N.E. 2d 527, 528–29 (Ohio 1976).

74. 657 N.E. 2d. at 282.

75. *Id.* at 283.

76. 421 U.S. 240 (1975).

77. *See* Motorists Mut. Ins. Co. v. Brandenburg, 643 N.E. 2d 488 (Ohio 1995); OHIO REV. CODE ANN. § 2721.16 (Supp. 2001).

78. *Garrett*, 531 U.S. at 374 n.9.

79. *Id.* at 368 n.5.

80. *See* Conn. Gen. Stat. App. §§ 46a-7 (West 1995).

81. *See* Sutherland v. Nationwide Gen. Ins. Co., 657 N.E.2d 281 (Ohio Ct. App. 1995).

82. MICH. COMP. LAWS § 37.1101–37.1601 (1997).

Notes to Chapter 6

1. *See* John Ripley, *Ruling Upheld in HIV Dental Patient Treatment*, BANGOR DAILY NEWS, April 13, 1996.

2. Abbott v. Bragdon, 163 F.3d 87 (1st Cir. 1998).

3. 135 CONG. REC. 19,803 (1989).

4. Fair Housing Act of 1968, 42 U.S.C. § 3602 (h) (1994).

5. *See* 42 U.S.C. § 3610 (g)(2)(A) (1994).

6. *See* Brunnen v. Mission Ranch, 2000 WL 33915634 (N.D. Calif. 2000).

7. H.R. 4498, 100th Cong. § 9 (b) (1988).

8. U.S.C. § 12188 (a) (2) (1994).

9. 134 CONG. REC. 9386 (1988).

10. S. 933, 101st Cong. § 405 (1989).

11. *See generally* Hearings before the Committee on Labor and Human Resources and the Subcommittee of the Handicapped on S. 933, 101st Cong. (May 9, 10, 16, and June 22, 1989).

12. 42 U.S.C. § 12181(a) (1994).

13. 135 CONG. REC. 19,803 (1989).

14. 134 CONG. REC. 9376 (1988).

15. *See* CHARLES WHALEN & BARBARA WHALEN, THE LONGEST DEBATE: A LEGISLATIVE HISTORY OF THE 1964 CIVIL RIGHTS ACT 1 (1985).

16. *See* STAFF OF THE HOUSE OF REPRESENTATIVE COMM. ON THE JUDICIARY, 88TH CONG. H.R. 7152, at 43 (Comm. Print No. 2, 1963).

17. WHALEN & WHALEN, *supra* note 15, at 110.

18. Additional Majority Views of Hon. Robert W. Kastenmeier, House Judiciary Committee Report No. 88-914 (1963).

19. 378 U.S. 226 (1964).

20. *Id.* at 252–53, 254–55.

21. *See* Joseph William Singer, *No Right to Exclude: Public Accommodations and Private Property*, 90 NW. U. L. REV. 1283, 1290 (1996).

22. *See* JACK GREENBERG, RACE RELATIONS AND AMERICAN LAW 15–16 (1959).

23. *See* Arthur Earl Bonfield, *State Civil Rights Statutes. Some Proposals*, 49 IOWA L. REV. 1067, 1114–19 (1964).

24. *See* Dennis L. Wright, Note, *State Legislative Response to the Federal Civil Rights Acts: A Proposal*, 9 UTAH L. REV. 434 (1964–1965).

25. *See* 42 U.S.C. § 2000e-5 (amended 1972).

26. *See* 42 U.S.C. § 1981(b).

27. *See* 42 U.S.C. § 2000a-3 (a).

28. *See* 42 U.S.C. § 1981 (a).

29. *See* 42 U.S.C. § 3612.

30. *See* 42 U.S.C. § 3613.

31. *See* H. Rept. No. 100-711, at 40 (1988).

32. Hearings Before the Comm. on Labor and Human Resources and the Subcomm. of the Handicapped on S. 933, 101st Cong. 209 (1989).

33. *Id.* at 209–210.

34. *See* Betsy Pisik, *Denny's Mails Check to Suit's Black Diners*, WASHINGTON TIMES, December 12,1995, at B10.

35. 461 U.S. 95 (1983).

36. *Id.* at 109.

37. *Id.*

38. *Id.*

39. 416 U.S. 312, 319 (1974).

40. 410 U.S. 1131 (1973).

41. *Id.* at 125.

42. Anderson v. Celibrezze, 460 U.S. 780, 784 n.3 (1983).

43. 484 U.S. 305 (1988).

44. *Id.* at 320.

45. *See generally* John Chuon Yoo, *Who Measures the Chancellor's Foot? The Inherent Remedial Authority of the Federal Courts*, 84 CALIF. L. REV. 1121, 1121–22 (1996).

46. *Id.* at 1168–69.

47. I used cases found in the LEXIS VERDCT Library from 1993 to 1998.

48. *See* Wright, *supra* note 24, at 449.

49. *See* www.usdoj.gov/crt/ada/settlemt.htm (visited on October 1, 2003).

50. *See* 42 U.S.C. § 12188(b)(2)(c)(i)–(ii).

51. *See* UNITED STATES COMMISSION ON CIVIL RIGHTS, THE FAIR HOUSING AMENDMENTS ACT OF 1988: THE ENFORCEMENT REPORT 212, table 11.4 (1994).

52. See ME. REV. STAT. ANN., tit. 5 § 4553(8).

53. CAL CIV. CODE § 54.3 (West Supp. 1999).

54. VT. STAT. ANN. Tit. 9 § 4506 (1993).

NOTES TO CHAPTER 7

1. Board of Trustees v. Garrett, 121 S. Ct. 955 (2001).

2. Sutton v. United Air Lines, Inc., 527 U.S. 471 (1999).

3. For fuller discussion of this thesis, *see* Ruth Colker & James J. Brudney, *Dissing Congress* 100 MICH. L. REV. 80 (2001).

4. It is important to understand that sovereign immunity principles apply only when private individuals are given the power to sue the states for monetary damages. Those principles do *not* apply when individuals sue the private sector or branches of local government. They also do *not* apply when the federal government brings an enforcement action. They also do not generally apply when private individuals seek injunctive relief against the state. Thus, the Supreme Court's recent sovereign immunity jurisprudence has not been able to undercut

all enforcement of the ADA—only enforcement of the ADA by private individuals seeking monetary relief from the states.

5. Section Five states: "The Congress shall have power to enforce, by appropriate legislation, the provisions of this article." AMENDMENT XIV (1868).

6. Section One states that no state shall "deprive any person of life, liberty, or property, without due process of law; nor deny to any person within its jurisdiction the equal protection of the laws." AMENDMENT XIV (1868).

7. Antonin Scalia, Associate Justice, U.S. Supreme Court, Speaking at the Telecommunications Law and Policy Symposium (April 18, 2000).

8. 121 S. Ct. 955 (2001).

9. 491 U.S. 1 (1989).

10. *See* Seminole Tribe v. Florida, 517 U.S. 44 (1996).

11. 521 U.S. 507 (1997).

12. *See Garrett*, 121 S. Ct. at 976–993 (Appendices A, B, and C) (Breyer, J., dissenting).

13. *Id.* at 966.

14. *Id.* at 965.

15. *Lane*, 124 S. Ct. at 1999–2000.

16. Bank One Chi. v. Midwest Bank & Trust Co., 516 U.S. 264, 279–81 (Scalia, J., concurring).

17. 527 U.S. 471 (1999).

18. ANTONIN SCALIA, A MATTER OF INTERPRETATION: FEDERAL COURTS AND THE LAW 32 (1997).

19. Brown v. Allen, 344 U.S. 443, 540 (1952) (Jackson, J., dissenting).

Index

About the Author

Ruth Colker is the Heck-Faust Memorial Chair in Constitutional Law at the Michael E. Moritz College of Law, Ohio State University. She is a nationally acclaimed expert on the law of disability discrimination. Her work has been cited by the United States Supreme Court and she is a frequent commentator for the national media.